BROONLAND

BROONLAND

The Last Days of Gordon Brown

Christopher Harvie

VERSO

London • New York

First published by Verso 2010
© Christopher Harvie 2010

All rights reserved

The moral rights of the author have been asserted

1 3 5 7 9 10 8 6 4 2

Verso
UK: 6 Meard Street, London W1F 0EG
US: 20 Jay Street, Suite 1010, Brooklyn, NY 11201
www.versobooks.com

Verso is the imprint of New Left Books

ISBN-13: 978-1-84467-439-8

British Library Cataloguing in Publication Data
A catalogue record for this book is available from the British Library

Library of Congress Cataloging-in-Publication Data
A catalog record for this book is available from the Library of Congress

Typeset by Hewer Text UK Ltd, Edinburgh
Printed in the UK by Bell & Bain

To the family: my parents, Isobel and George Harvie, in their 92nd year, my sister Dr Jane George, my brother Stephen, and my daughter Alison

Contents

Preface		ix
1	Through the Whole Island	1
2	Gordon's Kingdom, 1295–2009	38
3	Where There Was Industry, 2005–6	52
4	Light Touch	80
5	Annus Horribilis, 2006–7	110
6	A Handful of Dust, 2007–9	137
7	Walking with the Others	174

Preface

'National Discretion, the End of Decline, and the International Economy' was Helen Thompson of Cambridge signing off on the massive *Oxford Handbook of British Politics* in August 2009. Hers was by then an improbable chapter title to add to the anthology.

I found distinct advantages in securing a last-minute revision to my contribution on 'Scotland and Wales'. Such prudence stemmed from doubts about a renascent British economy, generated in a project on modern British politics by my students at the University of Tuebingen during the 2001 general election. The result was précised three years later as a *Guardian* article, and early 'teaching' versions of *Broonland* appeared on my website (recently revamped as chrisharvie.co.uk) from 2005 until 4 May 2007, when I was elected as SNP list member of the Scottish Parliament for Mid-Scotland and Fife, based in Gordon Brown's home base of Kirkcaldy. In late 2008 Tom Penn at Verso found the online version of *Broonland* and presto!

Much of *Broonland* was developed at Tuebingen and on the *Guardian*'s 'Comment is Free', to which I contributed after October 2005. Meanwhile, I acclimatised to the Scottish Parliament and my time became increasingly concentrated on the Economics, Energy and Tourism Committee, Political Liaison Officer work for the first minister and Mike Russell, Culture, Europe and Constitution Minister. Fife business meant coping with the Kingdom in a steepening depression on various panels within the SNP and with local communities, the Council, Chamber of Commerce and NHS.

The Nationalist minority government in Edinburgh was an explicit challenge to London. Scotland and England both suffered under a British politics which was showing signs of terminal cultural and institutional failure. Bodies which had traditionally balanced the system – the BBC, academia, publishing – were being sucked into a market maelstrom, in crisis by mid-2008.

In the equally unpredictable climate of Victorian Scotland, the geologist and journalist Hugh Miller wrote *My Schools and Schoolmasters* (1852), trying to make biographical sense of the tensions of industry, religion and mass-culture. In *Broonland* I have tried to abstract myself more than Miller did, but I could never escape the personal because at one stage I had known my subject himself. Only in the above sense is this a biography of Gordon Brown. It uses the genre to analyse the forces bearing down on the UK and its leadership, and the changes in the self-analysis and capability of its nervous politics: Westminster, international and Scottish.

I tackle Brown's biography and environment in Chapters 1 and 2. The problems of a de-industrialised and irregular economy occupy Chapter 3, and internationality and 'light touch' regulation Chapter 4. Chapter 5 begins the chronology of crisis in 2006-7, and Chapter 6 sees the great black crow of the slump descend. Chapter 7 attempts to sum up, though not to reassure:

> And worse than present jeopardy
> May our forlorn tomorrow be.

My students of history, English, politics and international economics at Tuebingen were fascinated by the UK economy during the Thatcher and Major, Blair and Brown period, and puzzled. Here was an economy which earned the praise of theorists for adherence to market principles, and grew, yet which failed to do many of the things which economies were supposed to do. Infrastructure and education were poor, manufacturing shrank; the UK's nations drifted further apart, while London seemed to wilfully detach itself from Europe.

By summer 2009 much of their indoctrination in the Chicago-school pabulum of mathematical economics had been eroded

– something evident in the 'insider' treatments of the crisis by Augar, Mason and Tett, which ended up as intellectual history, anthropology or criminology. Yet Adam Smith remained relevant. He had started as a teacher of 'belles lettres'; he remained absorbed in the unquantifiable factors which coalesced to create the 'nation' in which his self-acting order worked. Impressions, rather than facts, led to his generalisations about success or failure. 'Wealth' in *The Wealth of Nations* seemed to refer to manufacturing industry, though it turned up in only a small section of the book. This reminded me of North Sea oil, which I covered in my *Fool's Gold* (1993). To some the oil was important and immediate; to others (notably most politicians) it rapidly became only one of several economic and electoral factors.

Concerned to see how such developments interlinked with a reality that ran wider than economics, I focused in particular on a phenomenon that paralleled Brown's career. I have called it 'illegalism', which is the shadowland between 'robust business practice' and outright crime. Here, I was influenced by Richard Cobb through my friend Professor Clive Emsley, and Cobb's notion that the incision of crime opened up an unparalleled range of social evidence. My wife Virginia pointed me, via Alfred Hitchcock, in the direction of Eric Ambler (she always preferred the gifted technicians – both were trained electricians – to those with more elaborate agendas: the Conrads and Greenes). Ambler led to John Mack and Hans-Juergen Kerner and their *Crime Industry*, commissioned by the Scottish Home Department in 1975, the year of Brown's *Red Paper*. A 2009 Arte TV interview suggested that the successful German economics minister Peer Steinbrück had gone through a similar learning process.

Were these dark corners in fact native to that post-Calvinist theoretical playground which was the Anglo-Scottish union-empire? The captains and kings had long departed, but the inequalities, the rule of force, the ethos of 'never apologise, never explain' remained – if anything intensified, as the centre sought to maintain its command over the peripheries. The problem was to trace the way this was now exercised. What emerged was at one level unexpected – the rubric 'crime' was quite alien to orthodox political studies – but at another it seemed inevitable. My study in political fiction *The Centre of Things* (1991) had shown that the 'good behaviour' conventions of the UK constitution were already crumbling by the 1950s, and what they left behind was first division, and then a politics based on money as a digitalising instrument. Marx had surmised something of the sort in the 1860s, only to be confronted by the resilience of the old order. Now our researches in tax avoidance and microstates showed how that order ensured its own survival, without any moral or territorial embarrassments.

Finally there was the spatial change. In *Floating Commonwealth* (Oxford, 2008) I argued that the pre-1914 UK didn't break down into nationalities but *between* a western Atlantic-oriented arc and a London-centric core. The latter reasserted itself through the weakness of the post-1920 British 'rustbelt', but the latter's decline would paralyse both. For someone as concerned as Brown with Britain-outside-London, one is struck by a contemporary alienation: a deeper division exists between the conflicting *polises* than at any previous time: a lack of interest on the side of a fragile metropolis, successors to Noel Annan's *Our Age*, in what the provinces (defined as anywhere north of Watford Gap) think and say. To borrow from Jane Austen and Anthony Powell, Brown's intellectual allies have proved to be Crawfords, not Knightleys; or maybe near-relatives of Widmerpool. Quite easy to better their instruction; more difficult to tell a reliable tale.

Altogether elsewhere, the German seminar system let students loose on some complex problems and honed their new media skills. In particular I am indebted to Alex Boehm, Helmut Zaiser, Stefan Buettner, Adrienne Wiener, Wolfgang Altvater and Scott Stelle in the course of the central inquiry into fiction, crime and economics. This also benefited much from conversations with and the expertise of other Tuebingen colleagues, notably Gerhard Stilz, the late Horst Trossbach, Roland Sturm, Norbert Hofmann, Hans-Juergen Kerner and Rudolf Hrbek. I would like to thank, in Fife, my assistants David Torrance, Carol Lindsay, Elisabeth Roeber; Councillor Ian and Di Chisholm for hospitality and talk; David MacHutchon of the Midnight Oil bookshop; and Pat Kane, Rob Brown, Chris Smout, Bronwen McSween, Kishor Dangol, Tom Hubbard, Bob Purdie, Tom Nairn, the late Duncan Glen, Helaine and Brian Scott.

In Edinburgh and Glasgow there live to be thanked Paul Addison, John Brown, Ralph Jessop, Lindsay Paterson, Paddy Bort, Henry Cowper, Michael Fry, Owen Dudley Edwards, Christine Frasch, Bill Jamieson, Iain MacWhirter, Joy Hendry, the other David Torrance, Robbie Dinwoodie, Alan Cochrane, David Maddox, Campbell Gunn, George Kerevan, Gerry Hassan, Harry Reid, Derek Rodger, Allan Massie, Ian Fraser, George Rosie, Alan Taylor; and the EET team – Katy Orr, Janet Anderson, Gail Grant, Jim Dewar and Steven Imrie.

In London the flat is quiet: no more rows, but no more making-up, no more kindness and wit – save in the books and pictures Virginia brought and the gift for hospitality she left my daughter Alison. She and my friends Sue Bennett and Douglas Lowndes, Bill and Doris Fishman, David Walker and Polly Toynbee, Neal Ascherson, David Hayes, Tony Peake and the late, much-mourned Kate Jones, Simon Coates of the BBC, Boyd Tonkin, Pat Thane have contradicted my sceptical generalisations about London. Iain McLean, Geoffrey Best and Michael Brock have welcomed at Oxford, and Eugenio Biagini and Andrew Gamble at Cambridge – while at the Open University, Bernard Waites, Clive Emsley, Bill Purdue, Cicely Havely, Anne Laurence and the late Arthur Marwick and the late John Golby have shown me the real strengths of the place at its fortieth birthday; and Jane Aaron, John Koch, Jean and Geraint James, Serena and Barry Pugh, Kenneth O. Morgan, Marion Loeffler, John Osmond, Richard Wyn Jones, Dai Smith,

Ieuan and Alun Gwynedd Jones and Gwyn Jenkins, John Barnie and Helle Michelsen, Dafydd Wigley and the late Phil Williams have made Wales and Aberystwyth a delight to return to.

What my utility to Scottish politics has been, history will judge if she has a mind to do so. The collegiality of MSPs has been welcome, and I have particular praise for Brian Adam and Bruce Crawford: party managers whom I have given many a *mauvais quart d'heure* but who have borne up well.

Politics had intervened at a critical moment in late 2005 when I was seemingly between careers. Alex Salmond, leader of the Scottish National Party, phoned up my Tuebingen flat and asked me to stand in the looming Scottish election. His shrewd appeal ended with the words of the Marquess of Montrose:

> He either fears his fate too much,
> Or his deserts are small,
> Who dares not put it to the touch,
> To win or lose it all.

A politician who quoted poetry! By the time I found out that he quoted Montrose to everyone he was persuading to stand, the First Minister had quoted much more. The conclusion to his opening campaign speech – 'The present's theirs, but the past and future's oors!' – was from Hugh MacDiarmid, and that's enough epigraph to be getting on with.

Holyrood – Aberystwyth – Tuebingen
January 2010

1 Through the Whole Island

> Mull was astern, Rum on the port,
> Eigg on the starboard bow.
> Glory of youth glowed in his soul.
> Where is that glory now?
>
> *Robert Louis Stevenson*

I An Epiphany

Late February, 1979. Strikes and social unrest – the Winter of Discontent – gripped the campaign for an Assembly which would end Callaghan's Labour government and a torrid decade in Scottish politics. Gordon Brown, chair of Labour's Assembly campaign, and I were rushing for an Edinburgh train at Glasgow Queen Street Station, Gordon clutching a decayed briefcase under his arm, packed and surrounded by masses of political and academic papers. Then, under the great arch of the roof, the whole lot burst free and poured across the platform, to be retrieved by a head-shaking squad of porters and guards. An epiphany of sorts: symbolising the sheer uncontainability of the man's information and ambition – 'an' him no' yet thirty!'

The Brown of 1978–83 was an idealist, generous and anarchic, continually pouring out new ideas (far too many, in fact, which meant that Tam Dalyell, harping on anti-devolution, got further). The pamphlet that Brown and I wrote together, *The Scottish Assembly and Why You Must Vote for It*, wagged a finger at Scotland's nascent civic nationalism but left it neither stirred nor shaken. In 1975 Brown's socialism was explicit and robust: 'It is the erosion of the power of the market – and of the multinationals who now manipulate the market

– to determine social priorities that is the forging-ground for socialist progress.'[1] Far removed from the Labour 'revisionists' who had followed Hugh Gaitskell such as Tony Crosland and John Mackintosh, dead only months before, he was more like D. H. Lawrence (mining background, scholarship, idealism, aristocratic German girlfriend) in his consciousness of class, work and love.

In January 2010, Prime Minister Brown had by the skin of his teeth survived financial meltdown, economic slump, appalling polls and Labour Party rebellions. His government had stabilised, and after Michael Martin's resignation as Speaker – the first to have been forced out of office since the seventeenth century – Labour held his Glasgow seat against the Scottish Nationalists. The direct pressure seemed to be off, in the sense that systemic failure now went far beyond the Labour Cabinet, clawing at David Cameron's bland Tory front bench. The Commons' reputation had fallen to an all-time low after a campaign against MPs' expenses by the *Daily Telegraph*, run by ex-soldiers appalled by the mismanaged Afghan war. Centred on house 'flipping', it involved politicians at all levels in both main parties. The MPs and their blog-based accusers seemed in the same boat. Behind the criticism was the real fear of a Middle England – assailed by Europe on one side and renascent Celtic nationalism on the other – that was losing not just jobs, houses and savings, but its very identity.

Brown had become 'a prince of the latter days'. His downfall was epochal: the 'Bard of Britishness', as Tom Nairn called him, pursued to the cliff-edge by his tormentors. Was he expected to hurl himself off, while his bonus-crowned masters watched from the tax-haven Islands of the Blest? Was he, fervent believer in Britain – the one constant throughout his Westminster life, it seems – responsible for the eclipse of Britishness? Despite new citizenship tests and statements of loyalty, a centralised media working hard to preserve it – from the 'bonnet films' of Jane Austen to grand infotainments like 'Coast', or Simon Schama's histories – the magic had gone. In its place was a London media whose banal yardsticks (profit and personal ambition in Anglophone business culture) waned with City finance. It was under simultaneous pressure from the former industrial provinces – as with Scotland – and the ambitious international elite whose interests dovetailed with those of the media. Brown's political troubles, fighting alongside and against a fading political class, left him trailing behind Obama, Merkel and even Sarkozy. The 2009 European and local elections on 4 June had been a crushing defeat for him, though Cameron hardly did well either.

The international standing of the British elite was low. France had its *énarques,* or grand administrators, of SNCF, EDF or Airbus. Germany had the *Länderfürsten* of Düsseldorf, Westphalia and Baden-Württemberg, the bosses of Daimler-Benz and Siemens. Britain's commercial bosses had cashed in and left, while the politicians were in their forties, reared under the *sauve-qui-peut* materialism of Thatcher, juggling average salaries and expenses to keep up with the matadors of the City. Brown tried to get rectitude from the first and remorse from the second. He failed, and the result discredited British politics.

The situation in mid-2006 (when I started this study, Downing Street was almost in his grasp) was more promising but still enigmatic. Was the United Kingdom the frontrunner among the major European nations, as the government continually claimed and at least some of the numbers seemed to bear out? Economic growth was higher than in France and Germany, real wages rising faster, unemployment lower. London was unquestionably the European capital of finance, and, perhaps, of culture. Had Britain transcended the curses of Labour – 'stop-go' economic policies, endemic labour unrest, mediocre products – and captured new, if unorthodox, positions in a global marketplace which Europe scarcely acknowledged? Or was the whole thing smoke and mirrors?

The UK was a *financial* powerhouse that carried on shopkeeping but lacked popular consensus or contentment. Poverty persisted at about double the German level in a society where inequalities went far beyond anything Margaret Thatcher had provoked. Drug addiction was widespread and insoluble, trapping thousands in emptied country towns and old industrial areas. British youth established European records for drunkenness, teenage pregnancy, and educational underachievement. In late 2006, as Lord Stern and others added up the data on climate change, other achievements such as the dominance of UK transport by plane and car were put in question.

If the economic situation in 2007 was positive, who should take credit? Tony Blair's once glamorous career had ended in eclipse, and the Labour Party was set on elevating the Chancellor of the Exchequer: the dour architect of Britain's sound finances, the redistributionist heart of the New Labour project. John Rentoul, writing on the 2004 budget debate, reflected a fairly common opinion: 'Brown's record as Chancellor is genuinely outstanding, bearing comparison with David Lloyd George, whose record for sound economic management combined with social reform was unrivalled for 82 years.'[2]

Finding out had a personal urgency: I had been selected as a Scottish Parliament candidate in Kirkcaldy, Brown's local fiefdom. Various questions now became relevant, even while the man's reputation held. Brown was unobtrusive in Kirkcaldy: the guarded civilities of public life weren't in evidence. But did personality matter in an age of markets and bureaucrats? Or had Westminster personality politics crowded out debate on economics, citizenship and participation? Britain was in an unstable state – helter-skelter social and communications changes demanded such dialogue, interrogating the links between politics, region and society. Was Westminster's agenda practical, because elites prioritise what they're good at? Or did it hold only in London's drive-to-work area?

This added up to a two-pronged inquiry. How had Brown evolved from socialist credulity to market credulity? What led to the disorder which was to throw his career into chaos? And did the first affect the second?

II 'Mean-Eyed Boats'

> I got the first hint in an inn on the Achensee in Tyrol. That set me inquiring, and I collected my other clues in a fur-shop in the Galician quarter of Buda, in a Strangers' Club in Vienna, and in a little bookshop off the Rachnitzstrasse in Leipsic. I completed my evidence ten days ago in Paris . . .
>
> *John Buchan*

In 2007 the hour that Brown and his allies had been waiting for approached, yet his non-presence in Scottish political life was a mystery. And a complicated and increasingly impenetrable financial drama threatened to drive British economic politics, and indeed Britain, off the road. If it looked like a political thriller this was because it involved systems of control which the voter and indeed the politician didn't know about: what the City called 'asymmetrical information' – something bad guys knew but weren't telling. Franklin Scudder's travels, at the beginning of John Buchan's *The Thirty-Nine Steps* (1915), hinted at the sort of evidence that came to hand: paranoid stuff but somehow relevant. Why was I making a TV programme about Buchan, also the son of a Kirkcaldy manse, in autumn 2006 (nearly all his books were still in print) while solid political novelists like C. P. Snow, who promised insight into the world of government in the 1960s and 1970s, had vanished from the shelves? Was this a nostalgic fascination with tweed-and-mahogany antiquity? Or were readers drawn to the sense of crisis – 'some big subterranean business going on' – which Buchan shared with his successors: Graham Greene, Eric Ambler and John Le Carré?[3] Peer Steinbrück, the German finance minister, cited these four in an Arte TV interview in March 2009 as providing more clues to the international finance disorder than conventional economists.

A lot had been claimed for New Labour, principally in terms of economic management: this was the 'Goldilocks economy'

– not too much, not too little, but just right. Writing abounded on the ruling dyarchy of Blair and Brown: the individuals and their courts; manoeuvres, insults, plots. But important subjects that didn't fit securely into the character of one or the other simply vanished into the cracks. Observers as celebrities instead *became* their own subject. Robert Peston, BBC TV's economics correspondent, wrote two elegant and exciting books, *Brown's Britain* (2005) and *Who Runs Britain?* (2008). The first flattered Brown, but scarcely mentioned industry or Europe, beyond the euro issue. The second, on private equity, was optimistic about the tsunami of debt bearing down on the banks:

> Citigroup, UBS, J P Morgan Chase, Barclays and Royal Bank of Scotland . . . will suffer billions of dollars in losses, probably somewhere between $10 billion and $20 billion in aggregate (my estimate is that they will lose around £13 billion).[4]

Peston was out by a factor of thirty-seven. He was like a medieval mapmaker whose maps show monsters at the margins next to a vertical drop. In March 2009 the losses of the Royal Bank *alone* reached £24 billion, and Citigroup shares were wiped out. By summer 2009 French banks had clocked up €20 billion in losses, German €35 billion, UK €180 billion and US €350 billion: a total of €585 billion or about £480 billion.[5]

The hit on the USA was €13,000 per capita, compared with €30,000 in the UK. In *The Accidental American*, James Naughtie, another broadcaster, concentrated on Blair and his personal stand-off with Brown but didn't analyse where the common Americophilia of both men broke down. Tom Bower arraigned the chancellor's character alongside confederates like Geoffrey Robinson MP, cheerleading for Brown at the *New Statesman*, but neglected the ubiquity of wealth around Blair–Brown and its socio-economic distortion. Dave Osler in *Labour Party PLC* (2002) had no doubts: 'New

Labour is institutionally corrupt, in the same sense that the Metropolitan Police is institutionally racist . . . not an easy or comforting thing to say.'[6] But he made no attempt to locate this within a study of the country's economic evolution. Most academic accounts were clotted with jargon, destined for the Research Assessment Exercise, and outside that for tiny readerships. Ways of analysing *and influencing* British society meant involvement with one camp or the other. Yet from the standpoint of a continental media which had traditionally indulged its 'Britishness' – there are ten times more European correspondents in London than British correspondents in Europe – such accounts made for unease. Bower's Brown as modern Iago lacked nuance and historical distancing. Edward Pearce's comment, 'The man's half an inch deep', summed up Blair. But Brown, even when portrayed by Bill Keegan, Bower, Routledge or Naughtie, remained opaque.

If he was good, why was he chancellor for £180,000 a year, which wouldn't get a Wall Street banker out of bed?[7] As political patron, he was not impressive – see the brief career of his protégé Henry McLeish as Scottish first minister – though he had the freedom that Scots MPs enjoy to build a power elite at Westminster. (Members of the Scottish Parliament (MSPs) take care of constituency business.) Was cash replaced by Calvinism? Like Buchan, John Reith and Rupert Murdoch, he reflected the 'Disruption' of 1843, when the Presbyterian Kirk split. The Free Kirk mind, businesslike and 'gifted', was detached from a sinful – and thus by definition London-centric – world, and low on self-criticism. Was he British or Scottish? Broon's attempts to invoke Britishness in his 2004 British Council lecture were facile;[8] his high-mindedness had been screwed by Murdoch. But he was different from Blair's 'I'm a regular guy/It's a fair cop, guv' alternations: more honourable, more disciplined, and ultimately – if wrong – more menacing.

To Rupert Murdoch's King David, he was Absalom, the beloved son.[9] In 2005 Blair looked compromised, yet the chancellor escaped this. The mantra 'Gordon will see us right' fed Labour loyalism. But what *was* his record? How did it appear on the ground? Or compare with other nations?

After 2007 the question changed. Brown's multiplying crit-ics saw him as a political version of Bernard Madoff, whose fraud took thirty years to unravel. Other finance ministers had failed as premiers: notably Ludwig Erhard, the creator of the German 'economic miracle' under Adenauer, 1949–63, who as chancellor, 1963–6, presided over a severe slump. Lloyd George beat the kaiser, but ruined much of industrial Britain in the process. The Brown of 2009 had left the UK's finances devastated, the economy down by over 6 per cent, with many honest citizens poor and some incompetent or crooked finan-ciers very rich.

Narratives need a setting, and behind sequences and statistics are people and places. A little colour can bring statistics and ideas to life. In spring 2005 I was in Lymington, near where Nelson's three-deckers were built. Yachts were moored everywhere but though it was an ideal sailing day, only a handful were out. Lymington River seemed a colossal wardrobe for the rich. In 1985 the critic Jonathan Raban, circumnavigating Thatcher's Britain in a motor-boat, wrote of the place: 'Behind each mean-eyed boat there lay the rich pickings of the property business, the money markets, North Sea oil, silicon chippery or the legerdemain of tax accountancy.'[10] Brown's Britain in 2006 was Thatcher's Britain, only more so. One of Britain's last booming manufactures was the building of luxury yachts; the coast to the west was a littoral for millionaires.

On 3 March 2004 a helicopter carrying Stephen Curtis, a lawyer, crashed in flames at Bournemouth. Curtis was head of the vast Russian Menatep holding company, the tax-dodging creation of Mikhail Khodorkovsky and Boris Berezovsky, both Russian oligarchs. Walled up in Pennsylvania Castle on the Isle of Portland, Curtis, a forty-six-year-old graduate of Aberystwyth

University, was anything but a recluse. He threw parties for hundreds of well-heeled locals, many Lymington yacht owners among them. Thousands of miles away, the cash once belonging to the Russian people was extracted from polluted nickel-mining towns in Siberia, in sub-zero temperatures and darkness for most of the year; desperate places where poisoned women gave birth to deformed children. A prime mover in this was Roman Abramovich, who sold his gas business back to Putin and became Britain's richest man (£13 billion net worth) and a tabloid hero by buying the all-conquering Chelsea Football Club. Brown welcomed such wealth, but its illegalism spread a culture of oligarchic ruthlessness, which led ultimately to the poisoning of Aleksandr Litvinenko in November 2006. For all the chancellor's personal austerity, his 'redistribution by stealth' reputation and the moans of business about over-taxation, the distance between the rich and the rest of society had never, even under Thatcher, been so great. A FTSE 100 CEO earned seventy-five times more than the average employee, more than trebling the 1988 gap. Much of this wealth, particularly if it settled in London, was novel, exotic; ethically dubious if not politically destabilising.[11]

In 2008, such facts didn't leap out of conventional economic and social science accounts. The UK no longer benefited from Anthony Sampson's synoptic flair, displayed in his six *Anatomies of Britain* (1962–2004). The Labour government was encircled behind the walls of the City. Brown talked about redistribution, like 'Britain', in the abstract, only fitfully aware of this other side of the coin.

To see how things connected up, you had to read what the people read, to walk the walk and remember it. Bearing in mind Daniel Defoe's *Tour through the Whole Island of Great Britain* (1724–7) and the 1707 Union he helped bring about, Winchester and Hampshire were appropriate departure-points. It had been from near there that William Cobbett, farmer and radical, had set out on his 'rural rides' 175 years earlier.

Cobbett was an educator, grammar teacher and publicist; he made English working-class radicals into articulate contestants of print-capitalism. John Ruskin was another, more consistent critic, whose epiphany came on the Belvedere at Schaffhausen, watching the distant Alps in the sunset turn from ivory to amber. When Ruskin assaulted laissez-faire in *Unto this Last* in 1861 he would scandalise the Victorian middle class with his proto-green thinking. His words from *The Stones of Venice* (1851) seemed appropriate to place and time:

> Since first the dominion of men was asserted over the ocean, three thrones, of mark beyond all others, have been set upon its sands: the thrones of Tyre, Venice and England. Of the First of these great powers only the memory remains; of the Second, the ruins; the Third, which inherits their great-ness, if it forget their example, may be led through prouder eminence to less pitied destruction.[12]

These themes had been raised by Raymond Williams in *Culture and Society* (1961), basic reading matter to Brown's generation. Where were they now?

III *Red Paper* to Granita

'New Labour has no objection to entrepreneurs becoming disgustingly wealthy!' So said Peter Mandelson in 1997, less Prince of Darkness than grandson of another leftie of Scots descent turned Westminster manipulator. Herbert Morrison was famous for his robust definition of socialism: 'Socialism is what the policy of the Labour Party is.' The rich of 2006 weren't just different. Like Curtis of Portland, they were elusive. As well as the yachts, big new houses attested to unparalleled luxury, but this didn't show up in the tax statistics. To find them you had to read the *Sunday Times Rich List*, flagship of the Murdoch press. Murdoch was worth about £3.7 billion in 2006, thanks to NewsCorp and his near-monopoly of UK satellite TV. He paid about 7 per cent tax in the USA, and none at all in Britain; nonetheless, he conferred regularly with Blair and Brown. When Irwin Stelzer, his nuncio in London, edited a book titled *Neo-Conservatism*, Brown helpfully found it 'thought-provoking and controversial'.

The Murdoch press was synonymous with Downing Street, but how did Gordon Brown get involved? In the mid-1970s, while student rector of Edinburgh University (a scandal to a stuffy establishment) and a rising man in Scottish Labour, he worked for Scottish Television and aided the abortive *Scottish Daily News* in Glasgow, a cooperative set up to run the old *Scottish Daily Express* after it had been wolfed down and spat out by Labour's favourite tycoon, Robert Maxwell.

Brown started university in 1967, at the time of a sharp if belated switch by the Scottish intelligentsia from religion to politics. Robin Cook, matriculating in 1964, had wanted to be a minister of the Kirk; three years later he was an atheist. Commitment shifted (though Ibsen mattered more than Marcuse): he was ambitious but also imaginatively limited. An eccentric counter-current also made its way from Edinburgh. In 1967 Malcolm Muggeridge was elected rector: he got religion in John Knox's pulpit at St Giles. Ranting against contraceptive machines in the student union, he roused God, who blew the roofs off much of southern Scotland. The 'tabloid Voltaire' and serial adulterer went on to beatify Mother Teresa and encourage the Catholic counter-revolution that would help end the Soviet system in which he had once believed.

I first met Gordon in 1976 when we were both Open University teachers. I saw him more or less daily when helping to run the Lothian Labour Yes Committee during the 1978–9 referendum campaign, trying to get the Scots to endorse Callaghan's Assembly. Gordon was glamorous, his lovely Hohenzollern girlfriend Margarita prompting the occasional Buchanesque fantasy that he might end up King or at least Consort of Romania. Otherwise he was self-deprecating and chaotic – a combination of dynamism and poor sight left a trail of jumbled papers, hieroglyphic scrawls and wrecked type-writers. He was not all-conquering; in fact he filled the vacuum left by another protégé of the politics lecturer and Labour Party magus Henry Drucker. Colin Lindsay had been the driving force of 1968 in Edinburgh and the originator of a series of *Red Papers* attacking the right-wing *Black Papers*.

Lindsay left in 1970. Gordon inherited activism, but he was honest and reliable: an important link-man in a fissured party. He kept the Lothian Assembly campaign going, and only just managed to beat Cook, who was shamelessly anti-devolution: 'Some people call Robin Machiavellian, but at least you knew where you were with Machiavelli.' Cook tried to force a recount to ensure a 'No' victory in the region, in near-suicidal dissidence – hadn't Denis Healey said that whoever won in 1979 would be kept in power by North Sea oil for a genera-tion? – and the SNP gave the *coup de grâce* with a motion of no confidence in Callaghan, which passed on 1 April by a single vote. Gordon fought South Edinburgh in the General Election in May. It snowed. We lost. And Thatcher went to work.[13] That was the limit of my cooperation with GB. During the 1980s, teaching in federal Germany, my own views on nationalism changed and I left Labour for the SNP in 1989.

Gordon's PhD on 'Scottish Labour 1906–29' (1976) was pessimistic about Labour's resistance to economic depression. His political writings – besides *The Red Paper*, *The Politics of Nationalism and Devolution* (1980, written with Drucker), a disap-pointingly bald historical account; *Scotland: The Real Divide* (1982) on social deprivation (which caused another, worse break with Cook, his co-editor); and *Where There Is Greed* (1989) – were soft left arguments for redistribution, welfare extension and industrial modernisation. Their background was Tribunite left: Michael Frayn's 'herbivores' reared by debating or council work, which rapidly separated politicians and posturers. Not the sort of 'five nights a week' Trotskyite activist who wore Gordon down in 1979–83. Out of this period came the new generation which he and a repentant Cook after 1992 marshalled behind the amiable and un-dogmatic John Smith. Smith was from the debating world of the Scots universities: an eccentric but competitive milieu – alumni included Smith himself, Donald Dewar, Malcolm Rifkind and Neil MacCormick – and quite collegiate. Cook was a social gadfly: friends on the Tory side, time for literature, horses and a complicated private life.

Twenty-five years on, some Trots, notably Alistair Darling (then an Edinburgh councillor) had become New Labourites – the same five-nights-a-week methods, but this time promoting a neoliberal 'project' with 'Labour-friendly' millionaires. I had endured Robert Maxwell in Buckingham Labour Party between 1970 and 1974. He was every bit as toxic, and I never thought that manipulators and millionaires would click. But then I never knew the graduate-driven Westminster world of think tanks, spads and policy wonks, its expense and its need for external funding.

Brown followed the 1968 generation in their long march through the institutions, using such ideology as came to hand: in Brown's case, the unions and the Scottish Labour Party. This came to fruition when on John Smith's untimely death in 1994 Brown and Blair thrashed out a deal in Granita, an Islington restaurant. This compact gave Blair an unopposed run at the Labour Party leadership and, if electorally successful, two terms in office; Brown, in return, was guaranteed oversight of finance, training, transport and trade policy, and the reversion of power. After May 1997 this brought an extraordinary accession to the power of the Treasury, and effectively ended Cabinet government. Had Brown learned from Mrs Thatcher's clever appointment of her 'wets' to the spending ministries, calculating rightly that they would compete to claw lumps out of each other and keep her 'dries' in control? The outcome went well beyond the personal melodramas of Downing Street record. It was a foreign sort of compromise, effectively an *Ausgleich*,[14] a division of powers, which could only be ended with the over-throw *from within his group* of either Blair or Brown.

Blair and Brown weren't ideologically at odds: they needed each other. As Peter Hennessy put it, 'Tony survives by consol-ing the people Gordon offends': this worked parallel to New Labour's abandonment of broad-based campaigning in favour of smooching focus groups and picking off swing seats. The risk was an absence of overview, a narrowing of vision, and a dangerous reliance on wealthy donors and a right-wing press sited in tax havens.

Was there consistency? This question will irrupt throughout the story. Brown took decisive actions – over the leadership in 1994, over the independence of the Bank of England in 1997, over the Lloyds merger in 2008. But he wasn't preoccupied with himself. There was no *Kim*-like 'I am Broon. Who is Broon?' What happened were deliberation, decision, and then a crashing gear-change. This involved how he saw himself: how this view altered; who he consulted. In 2004–5 Brown talked a great deal about British history and identity. Socialism figured little and the 'social-critical' tradition reprised by Raymond Williams even less. Cultural capitalism didn't mean the diffusion of Matthew Arnold's 'one thing needful' but its transformation into a profit-driven community with a sideline in social responsibility.

Brown knew his history and it was discouraging: witness the taming of Scottish Labour. Maybe he hoped to pluck some-thing out of his diagnosis, probably thinking of himself even in 2008 as a fusion of Baldwin and Ramsay MacDonald in 1931, winning a victory *although the bankers were largely to blame* while remaining Labour's prime minister. By 1997, he had seen off Will Hutton's 'stakeholding' challenge *The State We're In* (1994) – and borrowed a few feel-good terms. If Broonism had an intellectual paternity it lay with *Marxism Today*'s 'New Times' scenario by Martin Jacques, Charlie Leadbeater and Geoff Mulgan, and some Fabians who evolved the notion in the 1980s that, if developed enough, the capacity embodied in the modern family unit (house, car, electronics, etc.) was enough to make it work as social base plus economic input. After 1992, with the increasing influence of Ed Balls, this may also have reflected the experience of his Open University days: cutting edge innovation piggybacking on existing universities, schools and, not least, housebound graduate mums.[15] Brown borrowed extensively from Bill Clinton's Treasury and its boss Larry Summers, Balls's Harvard teacher. If the US could generate economic potential from its exurban expansion – Greater Chicago, Phoenix, Silicon Valley – why not Britain?

In this vision, Britain could survive in a specialised interpretive steering role, which downgraded manufacturing (avoiding carbon-spewing furnaces, factories and so forth) and instead used computers to tweak family investment, switch welfare into work, and enhance individual choice. Coupled with Chinese expansion after unity with Hong Kong in 1997, this would be an oriental-American injection into *étatiste* Europe. It also appears in the writings of Brown's Scottish protégés Douglas and Wendy Alexander: 'Forget town centres and public transport, they're for losers', the Scots were advised by Harvard's urban expert Ed Glaeser. 'Sprawl is good for you!'[16]

These components were not new: they had figured in the Left's reaction to early Thatcher. 'Servitor capitalism' (what Ken Livingstone did with the GLC) thought it could square Mammon with social welfare and satisfy a number of notionally hostile and vocal groups: metro-literati, migrants, home workers and job-sharers, devolutionists, motorists, the educated classes, cyberfolk (much of whose hardware was imported), the trade unions (by now largely in the public sector), charity and third-sector NGOs. Some forces were beneficial (Bob Geldof's 1984 African crusade was still in the memory), some propelled by the international rich who since the mid-1980s had increasingly given the United Kingdom of London (UKL: coined by Larry Elliott of the *Guardian*) its tone. Don't try to compete with core Europe, but offer services (law, accountancy, PR, entertainment, auctions, sport) and promote the elaborate structures built up to cosset and titillate that the Anglophone rich can't refuse. To ignore this chance, the Balls line ran, would be crazy.

Another much more alien factor – perhaps thanks to the influence of Hillary Clinton and Alan Greenspan – may have been Ayn Rand. The 'Objectivist', almost unknown in Britain but as present among Ivy League graduates and on Wall Street as Milton Friedman, had created a strong silent hero with the strong Scottish name of John Galt. A market-forces Lenin, in whom the belief in free enterprise was combined with the *Führerprinzip*, in *Atlas Shrugged* (1957) Galt brings down a decadent democracy by going on strike with his brainy/wealthy associates. Paul Mason fingers Rand as an influence on banking megalomania;[17] she also featured in 'The Simpsons', which is recognition of a sort.[18]

Consider Brown in action in Whitehall and Downing Street, isolated from his old Edinburgh social-democrat colleagues. Remove Old Labour from his background; remove the solid predictability of cabinet government and the precedents to be culled from Walter Bagehot, Dick Crossman, Nigel Lawson, etc.; insert turbo-capitalism Greenspan-style. You will probably get something Rand-like. Brown's religion was sublimated into the secular power that lurked in his black armour, held in check by the contest with Blair.

Moreover, this came at the same time as 'Airstrip One', when the US was shifting New Labour policy not just from manufacture to financial services but towards soldiering and arms dealing. This was never publicly discussed; it got under way *sotto voce*. Why? Underneath the reverence, Brown had lapsed from 'John Smith Labour'. The years 1978–83 had made him sceptical of militancy (a spasm in the public-sector unions and higher education) and of Henry Drucker's 'open-party ethos' in the Labour Party, with its implications of devolution, PR, and coalitions. Nor did the civic element in Gramsci's socialism (*commune* in Europe means locality as well as collective) appeal, with its link through Piero Sraffa – Italian Communist turned Cambridge don – to left Keynesianism. Under the languors of Kinnock, 1983–92, 'pessimism of the intellect' was unredeemed by much 'optimism of the will'.

Matters weren't helped by the tombstone work of writing *Maxton* (1988). Had Brown written about other Scottish socialists – Tom Johnston, John Wheatley, the Fabian R. B. Haldane – he would have grasped the making and deploying of institutions; and in Wheatley, the Irish nationalist's case, the *weakness* of 'Britishness'. Or he could have read Hugh MacDiarmid on Lenin and the 'fire and iron' of cultural ideology, which, unlike his chaotic politics, MacDiarmid did well. Maxton, the Kinnock of the thirties, was charming, kindly, principled, but lazy and disorganised: he killed the Independent Labour Party.

Elements of millenarianism hung about as the brothers from the unions departed. One Member One Vote seemed at the time to free the constituency idealists but Brown answered these by *force majeure*, not political dialectic. No one surrendered more abjectly to the neoliberal triumphalism of 1989–90, the burial of social democracy by the likes of Ralf Dahrendorf and Tim Garton Ash, and the takeover by wildly optimistic market models that ignored both the corruption of the new order in the ex-Soviet sphere and the enormous productive power of Chinese Stalinist capitalism. Brown could have contributed a socialist analysis of the practical progress made in 'transformational' organisations – think of Google or Wikipedia or countless mutualities connected by print or computer, activating and inspiring their ordinary members. He did not. This wasn't so much Douglas Jay's 'the man in Whitehall knows best' as 'the professional knows best', because the political science generation had taken over – competent but without adaptive skills, and pricey to run. The pragmatic (and highly professional) business of selling Neil

Kinnock ran into trouble when the Tories shot his fox, Mrs Thatcher: this was educational, but not inspiring.

Harold Wilson's line against the Labour right – 'What would a member of the Salvation Army say if you told them there is no salvation?' – didn't survive, so Brown compromised after the velvet revolutions of 1989–90, Balls and Summers focusing him on the US paradigm. Granita supervened. Effective Cabinet government vanished and, leaving personalities out of it, what remained was the controlled competition between Team Blair and Team Brown.

Blair had few cards, and even fewer which favoured organised Labour, but he played them expertly. Focus groups replaced the Maxtonian / *Red Paper* belief that disadvantage was educative. The Ulster peace process which produced the Good Friday agreement in 1998, a deserved solo triumph for Blair, removed a nagging threat of the IRA blitzing the City of London. It also presented the USA with experienced troops freed up from Northern Ireland for its 'sole superpower' role – first in the Balkans, later in the Middle East. Against this, Brown found that the sophisticated manufacturing investment of *Where There Is Greed* took too long. Ditching this for his New Deal meant instant job creation which was labour intensive and cheap (the MGt call-centre at Kirkcaldy required only about £6,000 capital investment per job): an effective short-term manoeuvre, but nothing more.

IV Interpretations I: The Uses of Regionalism

This history did not show up in the literature; neither in the high-investment court gossip from Downing Street, nor on the coral reef of abstract academic discourse. Studying it from Germany was different. Thatcherism and then New Labour became a concern of my regional studies seminars for economics students, which otherwise followed extremely orthodox – and narrow – mathematical theory. This brought challenges, since orthodox economics was inadequate for three reasons:

One: neoclassicalal orthodoxy was stubbornly based on the miniature *polis* of the firm, no longer relevant in the vast, trackless, labour-intensive jungle of the 'service industries' which was ignored by finance-oriented economics.

Two: neoclassic pro-business theory also ignored troublesome associated costs. The glowing accounts of Chinese industrialisation which underlay much of the pro-globalisation hype neglected environmental catastrophe and repression. They managed to celebrate twenty-five years of Solidarnosc at the Gdansk Shipyard *and* demand free entry for textiles from the Chinese industrial gulags, without noting that the 21,000 Gdansk workers of 1980 had dwindled to 3,000 in 2005.

Three: business economists, analysts and consultants didn't explore the disreputable elements of commercialism: Adam Smith and Adam Ferguson's 'luxury and corruption'. Fraud, pornography, tax evasion, money laundering and old-fashioned villainy were immense economic sectors estimated at \$1.3 trillion by *Die Zeit*, and these powerfully influenced 'legitimate' economics.[19]

Brown's *Red Paper*, often cited, was little read. Few of its authors were still alive; fewer remained Labour. Vincent Cable had become a formidable Liberal finance spokesman. Mention of Adam Smith was absent from the *Red Paper*; after 2000, without any explanation of the change of course, he was continually present. But Adam Smith and Karl Marx were master storytellers as well as analysts. Smith had his magic pin factory in which the division of labour multiplied the efficiency of production, and the most readable part of *Capital* (1867) was 'The Working Day', in which Marx distinguished between the 'subjective' and 'objective' ordering of industrial processes (the first around people, the second around machines). But Marx's objective ordering, his obsession with quantification, was not the only way forward. Technology conditioned economic choice and change, and the wealthy could live by, and buy, sheer lack of scruple. Economies naturally evolved *away* from manufacturing towards distribution, and hence to a more 'subjective' world of specialised producers and consumers, alive to the seductions of technology and leisure. There was also the other side of scientific materialism: the romance as well as the statistics of intrigue, hype, and sheer mischief in the magical world of false consciousness found in sport, crime, politics, education and business organisations. Levitt and Dubner's *Freakonomics* (2005) would tell me this and more, but I had got there already.

Services and shopkeeping were Smith's 'social union'. In Broonland, the 'clone town' megamalls provided cheap food for motorists, despite the collapse of social norms they helped accelerate. Urban decay had been written about by Tory commentators such as Ferdinand Mount in *Mind the Gap* (2004), and by Nick Davies in his exhaustive reports in the *Guardian* on educational inequality, child abuse and drug addiction, but the impact of illegalism could be calculated quite precisely in places such as the chancellor's own Scotland. The surface was unpleasant enough: the drink and drugs of 'yoof' in cities and provincial towns, often inebriated by loss-leading booze from the local mall. What mattered to Brown was cheapness. Below this slurped a tough and resilient criminal culture, which the police were often incapable of restraining. This drew particular sustenance from one of New Labour's 'successes', post-Good Friday diversification in the ghettos of Belfast: from bar-room guerrilla to career criminal.[20]

Replacing civil society, for the insecure middle class, was retail therapy. In a late but alas typical happy-go-lucky piece Will Hutton celebrated a spree among the fake shops of Hong Kong. The moralist of the 1990s seemed to give up and beat the tambourine for shopping as salvation, with its cultural outliers *Sex and the City* or 'shopping and fucking'. This in turn led back to the consumption-based economics of New Labour, where the last thing wanted was a personal politics of rational decision-making in the style of Adam Smith's citizenry. Dumbing-down had its place, and a very important one, in the 'real foundations' of New Labour.[21] Compare the chancellor's archaic complacency in his British Council address with the generous anger of the novelist Nina Bawden in her polemic *Dear Austen*. Typical of the herbivore intelligentsia that had for a century kept continuity in the Labour party, Bawden saw her husband Austen Kark killed before her eyes in the Potters' Bar collision of 10 May 2002. To blame was the shambolic system of 'control' through commercial contract, the continuation of which on the railways was aided by both chancellor and transport minister.[22]

V Interpretations II: Flannelled Fools, Muddied Oafs, and Geld

How to transmit collectivity? Tony's team effort, the Millennium Dome, was an embarrassment. Sport, however, was something Brits did well, and Blair and Brown were seldom far from it. At a conference in Swansea in 1998, American historian Randy Roberts highlighted how presidents, from Nixon on, had obsessed about sports. An attempt to identify with a vanished blue-collar world? Piggybacking on the existing mass media? Brown had been its victim, almost blinded by a rugby injury. By 2000 football mania was de rigueur for politicians and businessmen, even intellectuals. It marked Britain off from the continent, except Berlusconi's Italy.

Was this evidence of social health? Politicians seemed to think it was. I couldn't remember Gordon taking any interest in football in the 1970s: like most of us I supposed he regarded the Tartan Army as the comic supporters of Scotland's comic football team, whose early exit from the 1978 World Cup helped wreck devolution; yet in 2005 he would emerge as the saviour of Raith Rovers, Kirkcaldy's flagging eleven, through a community buyout. Was this workers' control? Then why was it invisible elsewhere?

There was a respectable parallel between this and Ancient Greece. The fixers from the little states kept some sort of confederation together by meeting at places combining healing, sport, drama and politics: Olympia, Delphi and Epidaurus. Something of this survived the twentieth century, perhaps in fact thrived as sexual orthodoxy decreased – the Blair government was the first with openly gay ministers – and handsome athletes could be admired.

Despite the romps of the Tartan Army (always back before their postcards), football was less salient in Scotland. Rangers and Celtic were sectarian-toxic, and golf had long been the main institution of middle-class socialisation. But 2006 was World Cup year and Britain's role in it was worrying. The Scots won Germany the tournament. Charlie Dempsey, the ageing delegate of the Orwellian-sounding Oceanic Football Association (a non-institution, since no one played soccer in Australasia) was schmoozed by Kaiser Franz Beckenbauer to vote against his own delegation and carry the decision against South Africa, a country which could have done with the cash. The qualifiers provoked tensions between the home nations, and would in particular sour and damage the prospects of Brown, vacillating uncomfortably between Scotland and England.

Back in 2000 the tabloids discovered a Chinese cult of David Beckham. In fact the workers concerned were churning out Manchester United strips to be sold at enormous mark-ups in Britain: ultra-big business for a nation on the brink of industrial bonanza. If anything typified English gurning about national dysfunction, football was it. In Newcastle in 2007 thousands of black-striped 'Toon' supporters milled about the gigantic St James stadium, decked out in the local bank's 'Rock Solid' strip. Lively local patriotism? North-East England had rejected any form of self-government in November 2004. Curtains to political revival? Newcastle still seemed to have a regional rather than English identity, despite the weakness of its print media and the 2004 merger of Tyne-Tees Television with ITV. 'English' consciousness seemed to come from the football stadia, the new Colosseums of the provinces, and the local patriotism of town-centre prestige developments: the Baltic Mills, the Gateshead Sage.

Sport in the industrial age had been a mixture of working-class self-organisation and commercial entertainment. But by 2006 football was a classic example of dysfunctional social capital. It absorbed around £11 billion per annum directly; with merchandising, TV, travel and gambling it made up to 3 per cent of Britain's total GDP, about the same as crime. Footballers, along with lottery winners, made up about half of the country's million-a-year earners. The amateur game, meanwhile, was evaporating from such sports grounds as had not been sold off. The teams were gladiators bought in from East Europe or South America; owners were from all over the place (Abramovich at Chelsea, Glazer at Manchester United, Romanov at Heart of Midlothian). Only the middle classes could afford their season tickets of £600–£1,000; the others paid £250 odd annually to Rupert Murdoch in TV fees. Pubs only survived by paying him over £10,000 per plasma set. Warned off a bid for Manchester United by Peter Mandelson in 1999 (he never forgot), Murdoch controlled its television outlet until November 2005 when Brussels intervened, against the protests of No. 10 *and* No. 11 Downing Street.

The results were ambiguous. Did football hold together a vestigial blokeish Englishness? Or was it as evanescent as various random rugby or cricket manias? What was certain was sport's highly capitalised nature and its close interlinking with marketing – of computers, or phones, or booze, and latterly online gambling and dodgy mortgages – by an advertising and PR industry whose self-belief was absolute, particularly when directed at parting the quasi-socialised from large sums of money. It wasn't just overpriced shirts for the kids. British *quality* papers devoted a third of their space to it; *Le Monde* or the *Süddeutsche Zeitung* did not. Not a profile of a business tycoon or civil servant was published without him being labelled a 'fanatical fan' of some team or other, something that would warn share-holders off any such German businessman. The modest talents of many metro-lit authors and journalists, the Nick Hornbys and Tony Parsonses, seemed to be based on it. Was this a tech-nical reaction to the Internet's takeover of main-line news and business stories, or was English sport assuming the consolatory quality that football had in non-self-governing Scotland?

Sport provided two things which polished the economy while sapping society. It boosted the rest and recreation area, a rapidly growing import-driven part of GDP equal to food or motoring; second, it diverted from 'real' politics. Confected rivalries (for local talent had long vamoosed from the pitch) provided a diversion from the civic 'business of good govern-ment', from tracking ill-doing to its roots in the political dealing at the centre. Something of the sort, morphing into politics, had happened with Silvio Berlusconi and his Forza Italia ('Go for it, Italy!') compound of party, media, Fininvest and Inter Milan, only just dislodged from power in April 2006, and soon to return.

VI Interpretations III: Crime

Special sorts of conditions must exist for the creation of the special sort of criminal that he typified. I have tried to define these conditions – but unsuccessfully. All I do know is that while might is right, while chaos and anarchy masquerade as order and enlightenment, these conditions will obtain.

Eric Ambler

Gordon Brown's Free Kirk view of the world found no room for chaos and anarchy, nor did Maxton's Independent Labour Party. But the psychopath and fraudster Robert Maxwell (also one of the first celeb football magnates) in Buckingham Labour Party was for me an apt introduction to the economics of huge transnational flows of capital, seldom analysed or even quantified.

Out of it came an interest in the pathology of economic and social theory in the 'ideal types' of political discourse which underlay crime fiction, Eric Ambler's in particular. Another book had been published in Scotland in 1975, when two academics, John A. Mack of Glasgow University and Hans-Jürgen Kerner of Tübingen, wrote *The Crime Industry* for the Council of Europe. Their research had originally been under-taken for the Scottish Home Department, which had, even in the early 1970s, grounds for worry about links between white-collar crime, 'Mr Bigs', and so on. The Kray Brothers had been moving in on gambling and politics; the Scottish Co-operative Wholesale Society was scammed to death in the fringe bank-ing binge of 1973–4. 'Gorgeous George' Pottinger, head of the Scottish Development Department, went to prison over the multi-million pound bribes which made Yorkshireman John Poulson Britain's biggest architect. Brown's *Red Paper* was the idealistic response to this, but Ambler would gut *The Crime Industry* for his last great thriller, *Send No More Roses* (1977). In it, academic researchers move in on the 'able criminal' Paul Firman, who prospers by robbing crooks Madoff-style and, if threatened, shopping them to his friends in the police. An interview between Scott Stelle and Kerner, now Tübingen's Professor of Criminology, endorsed *The Crime Industry*'s line that little separated sophisticated villainy from sharp business practice. The division was becoming even more blurred with computers, tax havens and multinational capitalism.

If matters were menacing in 1975, what about 2005? After the demolition of an organised working class, a 'populist' black economy, propelled by criminal activity, was growing from the bottom up. In Europe in 1999, 1.5 million out of 375 million citizens, or 0.4 per cent, were problem drug users. The equiva-lent figure in Scotland was 60,000 out of 5 million or 1.2 per cent: three times that level. If the UK economy was doing well, why had this happened, and why the 'generally worrying level of hard drinking and unprotected sex' among British teenagers that the World Health Organisation survey found in 2004? Why was the per capita level of gambling *at least* twenty times that of Germany? The money laundering that Nick Kochan found in *The Washing Machine* (2005), particularly acute in Britain at City level, was in the provinces the end-product of a dense network of illegalism, ranging from the old components of prostitution and gambling to minicabs and tanning studios. In Scotland such transactions had a turnover which came to over £5 billion annually or about 3.7 per cent of GDP. This was happening under the chancellor's nose: two-thirds of Scotland's biggest villains lived in Speaker Martin's Glasgow constituency.

Had the 'economic crime' situation got worse? I had covered the oil issue through the crisis of 1973–4 and there was illegality then – but not on the scale of 2006. Read the headlines in a typical edition of the *Financial Times*:

Page 2	Tory MEP must repay expenses
Page 4	BA executives bailed
Page 4	FSA lowers customer fairness bar
Page 7	US abandons plan to buy toxic assets
Page 8	Mafia cashes in on Italian downturn
Page 12	India grapples with poisonous legacy
Page 15	Coldly efficient predators of the loan market
Page 19	UBS executive indicted[23]

After this lot there was no need for the editorial: 'Finding a Way to Regain Trust in a Battered Financial System'. By mid-December, when the Madoff fraud was uncovered, the question was purely rhetorical. Studies of the Brits and their press forecast worse to come.[24] Hard news had once been about manufacturing or strikes; now it was war (no shortage under Blair), crime, sex, telly, football and racing, bankrolled by houses and cars. As the last two fell off a cliff, froth increased in the drive to survive.

This had already buried the provision of information: editorial was swamped by 60–80 per cent of advertising, PR plants or celebrity flim-flam. This analysis isn't by me, but that old Westminster hand – and sound historian – Andrew Marr, in *My Trade* (2004).

This suggested dumbing down as a *purposive* element of government and media: its object to deliver a responsive, knee-jerk market for consumption/demand management basic to the economics of the housing-retail driver. The German government had tried to get people to spend instead of penny-pinching, only to be met with the cry 'Geiz ist geil!' ('Stinginess is fun!'), but Brits had been determined to shop until they dropped. Result: 45 per cent of British food was binned; Chinese-made clothes worn only once ended up on eBay; 'street-gear' was de rigueur for kids in deprived neighbourhoods, where wearing the wrong trainers meant ostracism or worse; and billions of toxic batteries ended in general rubbish.[25]

VII Occlusion and Convergence

The *Anatomy of Britain* died with Anthony Sampson, the twentieth-century Defoe, in 2004. Revising it would be difficult as so many sovereign decisions are taken overseas – but an excursion into the 'back-self' of civil society is necessary. The political component came from my own research. *A Floating Commonwealth*, published in 2008, studied the impact of technology on the mentality of the Atlantic arc of west coast Britain during the steam age, from 1860 or the eve of Civil War to 1930, after the Wall Street crash. It looks at the ever-changing effect of technical change and migration, but also the discipline coming from technology itself and, in part concordant with it and in part opposed to it, the democratic 'dream of beauty dernin' yet' of peace and justice endured among the poets: in Burns, in Whitman, in MacDiarmid and MacNeice.

This animated links across the disciplines which asocial

economics had neglected. In the 1990s some of my own effort
was diverted into *Fool's Gold* (1994) and North Sea oil. Both
fields involved intellectual and cultural assumptions which
either validated or rejected patterns of economic development.
The littoral had won World War I for Britain, but David Lloyd
George, a politician of genius, was unable either to save the
Clyde from economic collapse in the early 1920s, or to retain
Ireland within the Union. UK political history had provided no
links between the two. North Sea oil dropped out of the 1970s
political picture. It figured nowhere in the three long biographies (by Ben Pimlott, Austen Morgan and Philip Ziegler)
of Harold Wilson, Prime Minister at its most decisive point,
1974–5, and got only a few lines in the memoirs of Margaret
Thatcher, whom it bankrolled.[26]

Reverting to Brown, did the business of integrating finance
and technology with labour relations and market create an overspecialised mind-set for politicians as much as businessmen? Did
it pare their agenda down to what could be integrated into the
dominant system, ignoring other approaches? In Britain there
was a case for a cosmopolitan regional politics, a new *Floating
Commonwealth* whose tendencies were broadly European, while
Atlanticism, once powerful and democratic, was now pluto-
cratic and manipulative. Yet Granita, weakening the Cabinet to
boost two careers, had been followed by devolution to Scotland,
Northern Ireland and Wales. The ensuing Blair–Brown soap
destroyed debate within government, and the literature about
it camouflaged a restrictive agenda of economic manipulation,
patronage, politicised finance and metropolitan preference.

Such bestseller politics elbowed aside and ignored the
culture of a living, breathing non-London-centric Britain.
Under the Tweedledum–Tweedledee dealings in Downing
Street, Britain's flexible constitution – which combined the
conventions of Cabinet government and parliamentary debate
with an enticing literary culture of 'good behaviour' – lost
its totemism and dynamism. What replaced it? In mainland

Europe governmental requirements and obligations were written down, even if the constitutions lacked glamour, and powers were shared with Brussels. 'Read Europe' and be choked by the acronym-peppered patois, the unrelenting boredom of Eurospeak.[27] In 1993 I suggested in *The Rise of Regional Europe* (1993) that the British tradition of convention and corporate responsibility, conveyed in the classic accounts of Walter Bagehot, John Stuart Mill and James Bryce, might provide bureaucratic Europe with much needed cultural flexibility. What had actually happened?

Another form of integration in London and Brussels was the power and coordination of the big firm, its bosses, their PR and marketing outfits. Multinationals could provide the efficient part of European unity, its conventions and permissible short-cuts. Given the sclerotic EU bureaucracy and the private sector's efficiency . . . maybe. But what if the firms themselves were atrophying, ICI as much as IBM? This was Edward Luttwak's 'turbo-capitalism': shareholder value and concentration on profit centres; senior executives pursuing their own wealth; bonuses evicting corporate wellbeing. Such action could be concealed under the conflicting jurisdictions of EU, national state, region and microstate.[28]

The abandonment of corporate responsibility led among City dealers and bankers to excesses of vulgarity and greed which paralleled young footballers or chance celebrities on the qui vive. The rapid turnover of 'masters of the universe' suggested that they were cashing in and pissing off. This wasn't peculiarly British. France and Germany had their mega-rich, muses, mistresses and fixers tagging along, who were followed by the scandal sheets of the 'rainbow press'. America had Enron and its supermarket shockers. Italy was *run* by its Murdoch. But Britain concentrated this in a metropolis that ignored the rest of the country. Studying the City required anthropology, not economic analysis, in which microcommunities – of analysts, dealers and computer geeks – ignored their economic context, the workings of neighbouring disciplines, and any sense of humanist civics.[29]

Behind this was the importation of behaviour typical of privileged elites in poor countries and post-industrial anomie: of nepotists, oligarchies and mafias. Mack-Kerner would say it fostered 'able criminality'. Wealth *wasn't* trickling down: it was taking off to tax havens, while something toxic seeped upwards from the wastelands of social dislocation. Writers of a hitherto liberalish tone such as John le Carré and Harold Pinter became obsessed with this, and linked its political malignity to giant firms and the neo-conservatism of the USA. Brown, as much as Blair, was regarded as complicit.

VIII A Walk Round the Policies[30]

Broonland's chapters are chronological, but they are also governed by Patrick Geddes's triad of 'work, place and folk'. These examine 'the matter of Britain' through urbanism, manufacturing, provincial culture, Scotland and Europe, transport, culture and the metropolitan mindset. Two areas of technical contention emerge: one of quantification and description, the other of perception and communication. The UK's gross national product came to an estimated $2,674 billion in 2008; that of Scotland to about $216 billion (8 per cent). Crude figures in every sense, they had to be divided into primary production, manufacturing, construction and services. Most economists stopped there. But services, at about 70 per cent of output, notoriously ranged from hamburger-flipping to computer software. Growth and employment, the politicians' virility symbols, were no more than aggregates of turnover and in this sense socially neutral. Assessing Brown meant judging the UK against continental comparisons, and analysing the positives and negatives within economic growth.

Conventional economists weren't concerned with enabling citizens to multiply life-chances and collective resources.

National income accounting dated only from World War II and the work of James Meade. 'Social capital' was only now being stressed by the American political scientist Robert Putnam in his influential *Bowling Alone: the Collapse and Revival of American Community* (2000). The complex mathematical modelling in Chicago School economics had aided 'more perfect markets' and securitisation, following the 'Black–Scholes' equation which enabled the level of risk in loans to be calculated and 'provided the basis for the explosion of derivatives trading'.[31] MBA graduates might flock to it like iron filings to a magnet, but social economists found that within aggregate statistics of growth were negativities which *diminished* it.

To analyse key grey areas within the UK's service sector-dominated economy meant separating positive and negative elements: measuring the inflation of property values and the rise of retailing, sport and recreation against the reach of the black economy and the evasion of environmental responsibility. Even before 2006 the cumulative impact did not tell an upbeat story.

Within the student estate and its teachers, the 'Class of '68' was leaving, accepting early retirement offers they couldn't refuse. The survivors no longer sneered at European colleges and universities, where technical education supplied a work-force skilled in innovation. German students paid only nominal fees, but (usually after an interval of social service) worked hard and used their own initiative, sometimes running their own faculties (much to the relief of the staff) and living pretty frugally. There was little drinking or drug-taking but enough book buying to make bookshops the largest single category of town-centre shops. In Britain graduates would pile up an average of £5,000 in debt in 1999, rising to at least £7,000 in 2005; this was *before* top-up fees kicked in.

In education, economics and ecology, comparisons were worrying. The PISA study of European educational perform-ance in 2000 put Britain seventh in reading, eighth in maths and fourth in science: quite respectable. But examples were skewed towards highly performing schools and pupils; problem kids bunked off. On a properly comparable basis, the results would have been eleventh in reading, eighteenth in maths and twelfth in science. In Germany all parents must be registered with local authorities, and truancy is rare. But this meant that the outcomes inevitably included problem kids and non-native speakers, who dragged the average down.

Brown claimed to have cured 'stop-go' economics and the statistics seemed to support him. In the former manufacturing economy, 'go' (boosting demand) implied tooling up factories to produce new consumer goods, and time spent on this inevitably delayed any upswing until the balance of payments flashed red lights. If you don't manufacture much, you don't have this problem. But you don't have much technology or the trained manpower that enables high value-added services by combining computers with metal-bashing. By 2009 this was evident in British transport, power generation and computer networks.

The ground rules of market economics didn't help by ignoring ecological costs. A. C. Pigou founded 'welfare economics', under which only immediate economic benefit could be accepted as criteria for evaluating an economic transaction. This invalidated any environmental economics, which were necessarily long term. In *Unto This Last* (1861), a book that had fascinated J. A. Hobson (and through him Lenin), Gandhi, Tolstoy and Geddes, John Ruskin's concept of housekeeping derived from the 'invisible' world of Victorian women, and assessed long-term impact on the 'life-chances' of those involved. It was a world away from the billions sloshing through the City.

Economics was limited by its conventions: it had to extend into civic order, manufacturing technology, and non-quantifiable 'goods', and showed no inclination to do so. To examine the milieu in which Brown's policies had (or hadn't) taken effect, a broader view of civic economy was required, which consistently included not just 'unquantifiables' but the black economy itself. This involved: i) an extension into social pathology, crime in particular; ii) management theory; iii) the nature of economic thought.[32]

Management theory was housed within MBA culture (which often seemed closer to evangelical religion than social science). Did it have to be there? There was, even within the market system, an alternative. In 1920s Chicago, Walter A. Shewhart evolved theories about what 'knowledge-based economy' and 'process management' in fact meant. Shewhart was a product of the American 'pragmatic philosophy' of Charles Sanders Pierce, William James and John Dewey, in many respects derived from the Scottish common sense school of Thomas Reid and Sir William Hamilton, which linked theory to practical systems analysis and problem solving, and on which the ideas of Carlyle and Ruskin were based. In the 1920s, faced with an inefficient telephone works, Shewhart stressed that in diagnosing production difficulties one had to estimate the capability of the system, distinguishing between 'noise' (customary irregularities in measurement) and 'signals', in which problematic elements in the process indicated the need either to modify or, if significant enough, to restructure completely.[33]

If applied to contemporary Britain, 'noise' was represented by inefficient production and social misbehaviour: worrying enough, with a higher education system churning out 'rental' skills for the law/public service/big-firm bureaucracies, rather than continually refined technical competence. Dysfunction ought to mean that noise is replaced by signals which, in a technologically capable society, demand action and repairs. But could this diagnosis be made without adequate trained manpower, cooperation and high morale? Without it, would politicians misinterpret noise and signals and – to show initiative and capture publicity – impose quite arbitrary targets which were impossible to meet in an unaltered system?

Evident in the turbulent history of the Blair–Brown bureaucracy were near-automatic announcements of 'targets', oblivious of actual performance, which threatened to turn processes into

chaos. Think of the replacement of education by testing and
the accompanying mental stress and imaginative aridity, or the
unending succession of computer crises – mega-schemes that
didn't work – in the public service. Or of cognate catastrophes
in the non-computer area: in railways or helicopters or military
equipment for Iraq. We were supposed to be good at software:
if we failed there, could the rest be any better?

An investigation of the economy through systems theory,
pragmatism and common sense led back to the birth of economics in the Scottish enlightenment: to practical assessment and a
distrust of self-interested rhetoric, and strangely to two of my
own places: the Tübingen of Sir James Steuart and the Kirkcaldy
of Adam Smith. If we asked questions about the mixed economy,
and whether it had the people with the technical competence,
social information and *sociability* to steer it, we came back to
Steuart's 'political economy' and Adam Smith's 'conspiracies of
merchants' with a near-vested interest in dysfunction. In North
Sea oil in the 1970s, the oil companies simply bought over
the civil servants who were supposed to be regulating them.
(State salaries never could match the private sector.) Others
made a packet out of the unregulated 'wild capitalism' phase of
Thatcherite privatisation, sold out and cleared off.[34]

Blair–Brown emphasised market and management – but were
the two compatible? The supply of competent technically trained
management in a mixed economy was, like education or transport, an element of infrastructure that ought to be available
cheaply (i.e. by state subsidy/control) for the industrial market to
function efficiently. Under the turbo-capitalist order, management overstated its competence in order to increase demand,
and hence payment. Regulation – what the eighteenth-century
savants would have called 'police' – was where the state should
intervene to patrol the market and ensure that it wasn't being
distorted by 'sinister interests' such as Adam Smith's Conspiracies of
Merchants and those resilient old rotters, Luxury and Corruption.
Bearing Ambler, Mack and Kerner in mind, if police was thinned

down too much, or directed at the wrong targets, the result would be not efficiency and enterprise but exploitation and criminality.

The Department for Work and Pensions estimated that the government lost £900 million in 'benefit theft' by the poor in 2005 but HM Revenue and Customs were silent on tax losses to the rich. In June 2006 leaked Treasury papers revealed that the government 'estimates a staggering annual loss of between £97 billion and £157 billion to tax theft, representing an appalling 8 per cent to 12 per cent of the nation's GDP'.[35]

Collapses – especially national ones – are not monocausal. It's more often the case that a determined agenda, in its own terms successful, underestimates the cumulative complexity of the situation – fails, in Shewhart's terms, to separate noise from signals – and prescribes remedies which make a bad situation irredeemable. On the other hand, disruption could create new patterns and options. There was no substitute for seeing how things would pan out on the ground.

IX Audit the Accounts

In 1997 the Ruskin College historian Raphael Samuel, chronicler of ordinary people and wizard of the 1970s History Workshops (which applied the corrective 'socialist and feminist history' to the above), was buried at Highgate Cemetery within sight of the huge bust of Marx. Alun Howkins read the coda to Louis MacNeice's 'Autumn Journal':

> Sleep to the sound of running water,
> Tomorrow to be crossed, however deep.
> This is no river of the dead or Lethe.
> Tonight we sleep
> On the banks of the Rubicon – the die is cast;
> There will be time to audit
> The accounts later, there will be sunlight later
> And the equation will come out at last.

John Prescott, the new deputy prime minister, was there in a heavy politician's coat, with chauffeur and detective. As a Samuel protégé he paid a warm tribute in the *Guardian*, in which he remembered Ralph racing through the Oxford streets, trying to stop him from fleeing the place. The sense that we could at last trust our leaders seemed at that moment quite close.

Below the level of the national institutions there ought to have been a British antidote: something that in 1943 the decent democratic leftie MacNeice, an Irishman at the BBC, called 'The Kingdom', a civil society where people did things for one another, pursued enthusiasms, looked out into a world of mutuality:

> Go wherever you choose, among tidy villas or terrible
> Docks, dumps and pitheads, or through the spangled moors
> Or along the vibrant narrow intestines of great ships
> Or into those countries of which we know very little –
> Everywhere you will discover the men of the Kingdom:
> Loyal by institution, born to attack, and innocent.[36]

This worked for people running local publishers or preserved railways or community markets; in the feedback system of the Open University in which part-time staff sorted out the academics' treasured theories; in information technology, where students who knew far more than their teachers were endlessly generous with advice and repairs. The 1970s, a decade habitually trashed by Blairites and Thatcherites, was rich in this, not least through feminism, which by 2000 had completely changed the personnel of Scots, Welsh and German politics.

Did Brown's imaginative – rather than conceptual – failure to grasp this mean that a hopeful spontaneity was dissipated? For metropolitan media-capitalism, whose business was culture, such questions were awkward impediments. What sold was politics as soap, not politics as analysis. Given this, could metropolis talk to region? Scotland's agenda was dictated by an unravelling Union, which Brown could no longer direct. Celebs like Jeremy Paxman moaned about a 'Scottish Raj' in London, but we weren't the only movers and shakers there who would fail the Cricket Test. Arguments about the economics of separation were dwarfed by the British machine, its commerce undermined by primitive technology, its personnel ineffectual, sometimes corrupt. Opulent but chronically indebted, it was out of control.

2 Gordon's Kingdom, 1295–2009

The Kingdom of Fife: a beggar's mantle fringed with gold.

King James VI of Scotland

I The Master of Ravenscraig

The castle of Ravenscraig lours down on the Firth of Forth just where Kirkcaldy – once Brown's home town, now his constituency – abuts the smaller burgh of Dysart. A dark, drum-like mass, almost out of Hitler's Atlantic Wall, it was built in 1460 on the same principle: to deploy and defend itself against artillery. Perhaps the earliest of its kind in Europe, it was commissioned by King James II only seven years after the fall of Christian Constantinople to the cannon-rich Turks. Properly deployed, its bombards, the first 'weapons of mass destruction', could sink a ship two miles off the Fife coast. In the words of Thomas Carlyle – in 1820 master at Kirkcaldy High School (later Brown's alma mater), then Victorian sage, prophet of the modern, and inspirer of Marx's *Communist Manifesto* – 'Gunpowder, Protestantism and Printing' changed the world of the Renaissance and in due course the economy of Scotland. Gunpowder had its risks. On 3 August 1460, besieging Roxburgh Castle, one of James's bombards exploded and killed him.

Politicians gain by cultivating the local: Lloyd George foregrounded his home town of Criccieth, Aneurin Bevan had Ebbw Vale, Thatcher (at a safe distance) Grantham. One of Blair's weaknesses was his bland London persona. Brown by contrast looked *of* the provinces, where people made things and values were rooted in tradition. Blair had to have a house in Sedgefield, his Durham constituency, but Brown lived in Dramcarling, his Fife eyrie at North Queensferry with a remarkable view over the busy Firth of Forth from Arroll's great railway bridge to North Berwick Law and the Bass Rock, until he moved into 11 Downing Street in 2004.

Yet perhaps because of his clouded sight, Brown was not a man for the symbolic. He didn't seem to notice his environs much or convey their nature, and was loaded with London personality politics. Kirkcaldy figures in the standard biographies – Tom Bower is probably the worst offender – as a grim, run-down working town straight out of Zola's *Germinal* that provided lessons in social deprivation and one social prophet, made much of by the chancellor: Adam Smith. In fact, the 'Lang Toun' was only one of three capitals of the Kingdom of Fife; four if you count the royal hunting-lodge of Falkland. Dunfermline was the old royal seat, burial place of Robert Bruce and birthplace of Andrew Carnegie, the first and most ambiguous of the ultra-rich. The other, St Andrews, wasn't just the home of Scotland's first university (established in 1411); from the 1850s it became the 'home of golf' (perhaps the most important thing for Western businessmen apart from cash) and – fatefully for Brown – the starting-point of the Adam Smith Institute and the Free Market revival in the 1970s.

Kirkcaldy was as 'progressive' in the late nineteenth century, its most prosperous era, as contemporary Cardiff. The district dominated by the Rev. John Ebenezer Brown's gothic, cathedral-size St Bryce's Kirk was a smaller version of Cardiff's grand Cathays Park, with museum, college and town house (neo-classical), concert hall and police headquarters (baroque), sheriff court (Scots baronial) and hotel (art nouveau). A typical product of the town's bourgeoisie was Michael Portillo, whose mother's family, the Blyths, owned a linen works and donated much fine modern Scots art to the gallery built by the Nairn family. The latter had radical kinsfolk too, notably Professor Tom Nairn: intellectual historian, disturber of the Scottish peace and Brown's protégé in *Red Paper* days, now turned the fiercest of his critics.

Kirkcaldy encapsulated Scotland's relation to world history even without Adam Smith, born there in 1723 and connected to it by a sinecure customs post until his death in 1790. Brown would convert the place into a sort of secular shrine, in 2005 schlepping then chairman of the Federal Reserve and neoliberal economics guru Alan Greenspan round its sadly run-down High Street, where a plaque indicates the site of Smith's birthplace. Only after things had fallen apart would Brown (and Greenspan) recognise how gravely both had sinned against the savant's advice:

> People of the same trade seldom meet together, even for merriment and diversion, but the conversation ends in a conspiracy against the public, or in some contrivance to raise prices.[1]

This quotation neatly sums up the 'light-touch regulation' of Brown's Financial Services Authority. Smith's dictum was doubtless drawn from observations of Langtonian shopkeepers and skippers on the links, or as 'drouthy neebors' in their taverns, so vividly described by his disciple Robert Burns on a visit in 1787:

> Up wi' the carls o' Dysart,
> And the lads o' Buckhiven,
> And the kimmers o' Largo,
> An' the lasses o' Leven.
>
> Hey ca' thro', ca' thro'
> For we hae mickle a do. (repeat)
>
> We hae tales to tell,
> An we hae sangs to sing:
> We hae pennies to spend,
> And we hae pints to bring.

The 'Master' of a place was in Scots gentry-speak its heir. But Brown, though he talked a lot about history, failed to make it interesting – even though the real materials of power and psychology lay on his own doorstep. Oddly, Robert Louis Stevenson had anticipated Brown's political career in a grim novel, *The Master of Ballantrae* (1889), with its intestinal conflict between the brothers Durie: James, the charming, amoral Jacobite, and Henry, the dull, conscientious Hanoverian. Both would be destroyed by their mutual hatred. Jabbing into the skyline across the Forth was the spire of Fettes College, alma mater of Brown's doppelgänger Tony Blair.

II Annals of the Parish

The Kingdom's history was always insistent. Alexander III of Scotland broke his neck at Kinghorn in 1285, precipitating the succession crisis, the French alliance and Edward I's invasion, which would drive Scotland and England apart for the following 275 years. In 1601, in the severe new Calvinist Kirk at Burntisland, James VI of Scotland, with his southern inheritance in view, commissioned the English translation of the Bible that would bring them together culturally: the central text of the Union. Balgonie Castle was the seat of Alexander Leslie, Earl of Leven, field marshal in the armies of Gustavus Adolphus of Sweden, which devastated Germany in the Thirty Years War with lasting consequences for national psychology. Leven plotted the military moves that would end the dictatorship of King Charles I in 1641.

Mary Shelley, daughter of anarchist William Godwin and feminist Mary Wollstonecraft, holidayed nearby with the Baxter and Stuart families, and Kirkcaldy is twinned with Bavarian Ingolstadt, where her doomed Dr Frankenstein studied. Largo produced the castaway Alexander Selkirk, the thrawn sailor made over by Daniel Defoe as Robinson Crusoe, prototype economic man. Kellie Castle, a few miles inward, housed

Professor James Lorimer, creator of the formal 'democratic intellect' of the Scottish universities and their elected rectors, who also advanced the first scheme for European federation in 1884. And along the waters off that low coast the tugs of Frank Guelph Cox, a gifted hydraulic engineer, dragged the hulks of the Kaiser's High Seas Fleet from their graves off the Orkneys to be broken up at Rosyth.

Economics, artillery, science fiction, European federalism, survival: all moulded the character of the place, different from Edinburgh over the water. An acute observer might have grasped that Kirkcaldy's prosperity was based on a post-railway generation of payoff consumer-goods industries: wool, canvas, steam-milled flour, distilleries, Wemyss pottery with its famous floral cats and pigs. Most notably its folk made linoleum from jute, cork and linseed oil, the 'queer-like smell' of which still wafts from the one surviving works.

John Galt, the Scots pioneer of the novel of capitalism and politics, studied Scotland's evolving urban republics through the *Statistical Accounts* of the 1790s and dismissed the rituals of Westminster as so much blether. Another local minister's son was more attuned to the ramifying connections of capitalist imperialism. Ravenscraig figures twice in the novels of John Buchan, whose father had the charge of Dysart Free Kirk. On the beach below it John Laputa danced before his African gods at the opening of *Prester John* (1908): by the end of the book, the 'Black General' would prefigure Nelson Mandela. Ravenscraig's owner, the Earl of Dysart and *Huntingtower* (1923), christened another Buchan adventure, which introduced the Gorbals Diehards, sworn foes of meliorism, along with an argument that there were things worse than communism; such as the sheer illegality released by the utopianism of the Bolsheviks. Buchan put this in the words of Princess Saskia, oddly prefiguring Brown's involvement with the pretender to the Romanian throne and the tides of Russian oligarch-extorted wealth that would tear through London after the events of 1989–91. 'Wild capitalism' would ironically enough be observed by another Fife ex-leftie, John Lloyd of the *Financial Times*, in 1990s Russia.

Eastwards, new high-priced houses cluttered on the water's edge where Seafield pit had once stood, like wealthy passengers on a sinking liner. Sir Michael Snyder of Kingston Smith, Finance and Resources boss for the City of London until 2007, owned one such house, convenient for golf at St Andrews – and for chats with the chancellor? Big money held out in landward Fife in greater style, in classical mansions and converted tower houses, yet its spirit was captured by the transatlantic bestseller art of the miner's son Jack Vettriano. Like Edward Hopper, but on the wing: hotels and beaches, girls staring into cocktails, men staring at girls. Everywhere mobility, desire, discontent, to be assuaged by sex, cars or cash.

Westminster had been here before. Sometime in the 1890s four young Liberal MPs climbed Raith Hill, behind the town. 'What a grateful thought,' said Augustine Birrell to H. H. Asquith, R. B. Haldane and Ronald Munro-Ferguson, laird of Raith, 'that there is not an acre in this vast and varied landscape that is not represented at Westminster by a London barrister.' Haldane reorganised the British Army for a war-service competence unsuspected by Germany. Asquith broke the power of the Lords. Birrell ignored the furious Irish rebels who would begin wrecking the British Empire in 1916. Thanks to the Forth Bridge seven miles west, you could step on the midnight sleeping car at Kirkcaldy or Inverkeithing and wake up in London, then as now. The industrial/post-industrial preoccupations of Scotland meant that this Anglo-Scottish tradition continued until Brown's own childhood.[2]

But by the 1990s Kirkcaldy and Dysart, Kinghorn and Burntisland had long lost their civic independence. After 1974 the whole Kingdom was controlled from Glenrothes, five miles inland. A New Town intended to serve a huge, badly surveyed and calamitous coal mine, it became the seat of Fife Council, a capital for a curiously self-regarding state, referred to with heavy irony as 'The People's Republic'. By 2007 the great employers of Fife were no longer coalmines or shipyards or railways, linoleum factories or paper mills or even computer manufacturers. The Silicon Glen clearances had been running for a decade, leaving behind the eerie bulk of an unopened Toshiba factory. The twin monoliths of the Council (22,000 employees) and the Fife NHS (almost 10,000), together made up 20 per cent of jobs.

Unemployment was nominally at 6 per cent in 2006 – add in the incapacitated and round it up to 15 per cent. Manufacture was somewhat over the Scottish average: BiFab at Burntisland and Methil was doing well in offshore wind power; at Cameron Bridge, Diageo had the UK's biggest distillery, producing Smirnoff Vodka and Gordon's Gin, the latter in stills shipped up from Clerkenwell and dating from William 'Gin Lane' Hogarth's day. The other big growth was in commuting, mainly by car, to Edinburgh's commercial exurbia, sprawling west of the city and dominated by the Royal Bank of Scotland's new campus at Gogar. Otherwise

> We hae cold calls to make,
> An' we hae shelves to stack,
> We hae burgers tae flip
> An' we hae wars tae fight!

might sum things up. Plenty of young Langtonians could only get a respected job by enlisting in the Black Watch. In 2004 the playwright Gregory Burke interviewed local boys from the regiment and crafted a drama documentary for the new National Theatre of Scotland, in which the scene shifted from local pubs to Camp Dogwood, south-east of Baghdad, where they had to provide cover for a US redeployment. Critics found 'a relentless energy . . . a potent reminder of the prime of life, so quickly transformed into death, severe physical or mental injury . . . (and of) . . . the great distance between the British population and the wars fought in its name.'

There had been nothing like this since Peter Watkins's film *Culloden*, forty years before, when the brutality of 'the last battle fought on British soil' was harrowingly conveyed by a gifted director and a handful of local people. At the real Culloden, Stevenson's fictive James Durie would have been one of the fine Jacobite gentlemen who clustered around the Young Pretender. In 2003 he was Tony Blair, calling for the 'blood price' to be paid in Iraq. Two years after the invasion, on 6 February 2005, Brown heard his ally Alan Greenspan give the Adam Smith Lecture at St Bryce's Kirk, and in 2006 made him adviser to the UK Treasury.

But what would Adam Smith himself, that kindly, pacific soul, have made of it all: of the rejection of war back home; the Black Watch 'tribe' suffering, losing friends and even its identity as it was merged into a Scottish 'super-regiment'? And where, the *Guardian* wondered, did the Iraqis fit into all this? Had industry and post-industry left the Fifers wiser than Defoe's Robinson Crusoe? 'When asked about their interactions with the population a soldier reacts with surprise: "Whit the fuck hiv the Iraqis got tae fuckin dae wi anythin'?"'

III People's Republic

Jennie Lee, wife of Aneurin Bevan – he created the NHS, she the Open University – came from the 'Little Moscows': Lumphinnans, Kelty, Lochgelly, Lochore; mining villages with their libraries, municipal Lenins, once grand co-op stores (whose business had been vacuumed up by the Big Four supermarkets) and even co-op pubs, the famous Goths.[3] From 1935 to 1951 they returned the UK's one Communist MP, Willie Gallacher. But with the collapse of the mines, starting in the 1960s and ending with the miners' strike of 1984–5, the apparatchiks took over. From then until February 2006, Fife was (apart from the rural north-east) solid Labour at Westminster.

The blending of socialism and Scottish nationalism was seldom put across more eloquently than in the person and writings of

Lawrence Daly, a Communist until 1956 and between 1968 and 1982 the General Secretary of the National Union of Mineworkers, whose Fife Socialist League had backed Home Rule early on. But sometime in the 1990s, Daly – shattered by a car accident which killed his closest relatives, disliking London, drinking heavily – simply leaked out of history. The centenary *History of Labour in Fife* (2006) correctly described him as still alive: he died after ten years of Alzheimer's in a Luton nursing home just as the first draft of this book was completed. 'A lovely man', Daly must have acted as a warning to Brown: dual loyalties would weaken and kill. What remained after the Little Moscows was attenuated: the trade unions as a defensive structure for public service workers, and the historical legacy of the first-past-the-post electoral system.

On 3 May 2007 the political landscape changed abruptly. That morning, in the Mid Scotland and Fife district, Labour held six out of eight seats in the Scottish Parliament: Stirling, Ochil, Dunfermline West, Dunfermline East, Central Fife and Kirkcaldy. A day later it held only two: Dunfermline East and Kirkcaldy. In Fife Council (now elected under single transferable vote) its seats dropped from over half to a third, and an SNP–Liberal coalition took power.

Fife's now vestigial People's Republic would sustain Brown in the Glenrothes by-election in early November 2008, at a point where he seemed on the edge of destruction. But it would be at a cost. Scottish local authorities were huge and only fitfully answerable to democratic control; with a population of 350,000 Fife was one of Scotland's biggest. Brown's protégé and former councillor Henry McLeish was driven from office by a Tory probe into the use of his constituency offices in Glenrothes by a private legal firm, which paid the rent into Labour party funds. On the radio show 'Any Questions', McLeish, an intelligent man caught in Scots Labour's east–western divide, reacted like a rabbit in car headlights: 'a muddle, not a fiddle' was as close as he got to extenuating circumstances. This was the new Scottish Parliament's lowest point.

McLeish was roughly what, in Brown's cosmology, a Member of the Scottish Parliament (MSP) or Welsh Assembly Member (AM) was supposed to be. Not a projection of nationalism or a competitor with Westminster, but rather more comparable to a J. K. Rowling 'house-elf'. By busying themselves with local affairs – rents, pensions, crime and so on – the MSPs left Scottish Westminster MPs much greater freedom of manoeuvre. There might be fewer MPs (by 2005 numbers had fallen from seventy-three to fifty-nine) but they would have more clout. And indeed they did. Compared with British Cabinets of the 1960s and 1970s, the number of Scots members had doubled to around four out of sixteen, but beneath ministerial rank the level of talent was woeful, in tune with the reduced services demanded of Scottish MPs. The Westminster Scots became a rerun of Bagehot's Tory backbenchers, 'the best brute vote in creation', or, put more pithily of a Scots Labour MP, 'He's no' a household name, no' even in his ain household'. There was only a single Scots Tory MP left. Those who looked closely at the UK political landscape (at this early stage, we can leave out the frantic bloggers) saw that Scotland was now markedly different from England, and that the incidentals of the devolution settlement had progressively contributed to this.

IV The Keys of the Kingdom

How to hold on to power? This was where that 1968 ideal of Brown and his contemporaries, and their long march through the institutions, became topical politics. This outcropped both at local and central levels. Its results bore some resemblance to Thatcherite regulatory quangos; but these had usually been forced to obey edicts from Downing Street. What appeared under Blair and later Brown was a strange dualism: on one hand there was devolution and Holyrood's edgy relations with UK and local government; on the other, the competitive enlargement of overlapping empires. Initially these appeared to be part

of that anti-political notion of consumer democracy marketed
in the 1980s by the first of the think tanks; later, they seem to
have ramified to sustain competing teams in the government,
fuelled by complex attempts to realise Adam Smith's 'invisible
hand' and square the market with his other goals of equality
and civic responsibility. Ofcom, Ofgem, FSA, Ofsted, ORR
... Periodically, officials of such bodies would turn up before
committees at Holyrood. The language of such encounters was
permeated by the jargon of a neoliberalism run out of control:
denseness visible. *Private Eye* suggested an overall supervisory
Office of the United Kingdom: OFFUK.

The Health Service was even further into bureaucracy. In
Fife its almost 10,000 employees were theoretically part of a
collective. In practice managers predominated and proliferated.
The real politics were not those of the Council and its public
health committees but compact, well-organised deals between
line-management in adjacent institutions and complicit union
salariats. In this Brown was an accessory before, during and
after the fact. His 1997 'New Deal' meant that managerial
jobs expanded to lance the boil of unemployment. Backs were
covered, dissenters dispatched. Even so, discontent proliferated.
The main hospital had been at Kirkcaldy. In 1995 it was shifted
to Dunfermline, where Brown was MP, and a new medical
campus, Queen Margaret, rose east of the town. In 2005 he
switched to Kirkcaldy, and, as if bidden like a sheepdog, the
infirmary followed him.

Remote from much oversight until 1999, a complicated
oligarchy had evolved which saw itself on equal terms with local
capitalism, with rewards to suit. Councillors with a few thousand in annual expenses were up against departmental heads on
more-than-ministerial salaries, usually gained with the support
of the unions (during this period dissolving into bodies with
'iconic', 'positive' but meaningless names: who *were* Unison,
Unite, Amicus, Community, and what did they actually do?).
The whole was oiled with access to Scotland's proliferating

quangos. Of industrial and technical competence – the doctorates of German or Swiss bureaucracy, the university teaching hospitals, the *préfet* sent down from Paris – there were only fitful signs. This cosy, self-regarding world was like that of John Galt. It had as its symbolic centre the Royal and Ancient Golf Cub fifteen miles north at St Andrews, which has yet to admit a female member but which hosted many of Washington's leading Republican Congressmen bought by the lobbyist Jack Abramoff. It didn't regard itself as likely to be remotely disturbed by the advent of the Scottish Parliament in 1999.

But Broonite economics were disturbing Fife's built environment, at both ends of the scale. In 2007 Halifax Estate Agents, the property wing of HBOS, nominated Lochgelly as 'the number one property investment location in the UK'. The grim ex-mining community (famous for 'Lochgelly Specials', leather belts with which Scots teachers would strike the palms of their pupils) was the last town with average house prices under £100,000. Now they reached £119,000, a rise of 36 per cent.[4] Had the property boom conquered poverty, or had speculation in risky mortgages passed rational limits? Within fifteen months the truth was all too apparent.

Ten miles to the north Melville House presented a far different spectacle. A neo-classical Palladian villa (albeit equipped with gunslits), it had been built in 1697 by Scotland's first classical architect, Sir William Bruce, for the Earl of Melville, William III's Scottish Secretary. After a sad decline into school use it was speculatively restored in 2000 for over £2 million. On the market at £4.5 million in 2006, it figured as 'repossession of the year' in 2009, but the price had gone down to £2.5 million. 'Facts on (the case) and the circumstances surrounding the repossession are difficult to come by', wrote Marcus Binney.[5]

One factor remained from Fife's coercive past: a return to Ravenscraig Castle and its guns. Before 1914 the Admiralty constructed the Naval Dockyard of Rosyth to house Winston

Churchill's giant Dreadnoughts. In 1993 it should have become the refitting base for Britain's Trident ballistic missile submarines 'Vanguard' (1993), 'Victorious' (1995), 'Vigilant' (1996) and 'Vengeance' (2000), the Dreadnought's logical successors, but this contract was given to the privatised Devonport Dockyard in South-West England for political reasons.

1997 was surely a suitable year for Britain to desist from its nuclear role, but Trident was another New Labour reversal, heartily endorsed by Brown as local MP. Defence was, of course, one of 'Tony's things', but Scotland was heavily involved as a site for bases, and Gordon wrote the cheques. Out of this came the decision in 2006 to proceed to a second Trident generation, followed in July 2008 by contracts to build two 65,000-ton aircraft carriers, the *Queen Elizabeth* and the *Prince of Wales*, at an estimated cost of £4 billion (by mid-2009 this had become £5 billion). The components were to be constructed in Portsmouth and Barrow and on the Clyde, but would be welded together in Rosyth. Why did the leadership persist with such vast projects, which in Trident's case might cost £65 billion over thirty years, given a defence budget that made it difficult to sustain troops in Iraq or Afghanistan? The ethical dimension in Robin Cook's foreign policy had long since vanished. The major driver in both projects was BAe, representing power-politics at its least restrained, which did not stint either its expenditure or its influence on Whitehall.

This lucrative trade would return to haunt Brown in the difficult months of early 2009. His old rival George Robertson had left the Ministry of Defence for NATO ten years previously (the Americans loved him); on retiring in 2004 Lord Robertson became director of many companies, including defence contractors. He was followed at Defence by Dr Lewis Moonie MP, a former Fife Labour Councillor who was kicked upstairs in 2005 to make way for Brown in Kirkcaldy and Cowdenbeath. On 25 January 2009 Lord Moonie, now director and consultant of several defence firms, offered to 'make friends and influence people' for an undercover *Sunday Times* reporter. He was later found to have claimed expenses of £150,000 over three years, and to be charging £30,000 and over for consultancy work. Asked to comment, Alex Rowley, Brown's agent, said that Moonie was 'no longer active' in the local Labour Party. Scarcely had this retreated to the inside pages when City misbehaviour and Scots gullibility snuffed out the Dunfermline Building Society, Scotland's biggest, on 29 March 2009.

In politics the 'one thing needful' always stands in danger of crowding out the other parts of the agenda. A point is reached at which either the party structures that converted people into political activists atrophy or the public bodies themselves don't work. Against this, the constituency was supposed to represent enduring loyalty, manoeuvrability and broad agendas. Viewing the man in his Kingdom, was this true of the *ci-devant* devolutionist Brown in the years after 1997? Or did there blow from it an air that killed?

3 Where There Was Industry, 2005–6

The law will gaol the man or woman
Who steals the goose from off the common,
But lets the greater villain loose
Who steals the common from the goose.

Anonymous radical, c. 1820

Services, while important to growth, have not filled the trade gap left by the decline of manufacturing exports . . . it is through manufacturing that we will succeed or fail, and at the moment by any objective criteria we are failing.

Gordon Brown

I Industrial Archaeology

Gordon Brown wrote in manufacturing mode in 1989. In 2006, as he closed in on No. 10, he published an article in the *Scotsman* lauding the 1707 Union. Industry got a couple of lines. In *Moving Britain Forward*, a collection of speeches framed by star-studded introductions, it didn't appear at all: Brown leaped from monetary policy to conquering unemployment. We have met the theory. Now for the impact.[1]

Slaithwaite, south of Huddersfield, is the parish of the social-ist historian Paul Salveson, founder of the 'community railway', one of the hopeful signs of New Labour. In 2005, when I visited, a big four-storey worsted mill was still working, the once universal clack–clack–clack of the shuttles echoing across the valley. It was in profit, with a full order-book. By year-end it would be closed for conversion into yuppie flats. Perhaps, seeing the writing on the Great Wall of China, its owners showed good foresight. But that wasn't New Labour's message in the mid-1990s. The Brown line was that manufacture led to greater profits and productivity, and stimulated training and technical innovation. It also safeguarded the skills to repair and update a high value-added service economy, otherwise neglected by more spaced-out propagandists. As the Scottish journalist George Rosie wrote, reviewing Charles Leadbeater's *Living on Thin Air* (2000), 'Who's going to service and repair all the machines this levitation requires? Magic elves?'

In the 1970s British manufacturing was in crisis. Provoked by the demands of North Sea oil, which sucked in about a third of the money needed for all manufacturing investment, this inspired what was seen as Old Labour's most rash and irresponsible campaign of nationalisation – of steel, cars, aircraft and oil – as well as some experimental cooperatives which Tony Benn, then trade minister, tried to sustain. These measures had logic: without state ownership many firms would have gone bust. As it was, North Sea oil produced some technical triumphs – chiefly 'positioning', which kept an oil rig stationary within a radius of a few centimetres through a combination of satellite signals, computers and electric thruster motors – only to be disremembered by Thatcherite right as well as Blairite left. Thatcher's prentice efforts at monetarism – cutting the money supply by hiking up interest rates – coincided with the Iran–Iraq War and the $30 barrel of oil, with the result that sterling rose to nearly 5 Deutschmarks, export markets dried up and manufacturing fell by about 20 per cent.[2] Some of the casualties were artificial growths undertaken for political reasons, such as the Invergordon aluminium smelter or British Leyland Bathgate. But others were prestige firms, branded British, made to last, training up manpower, sustaining design and research, marketing with sophistication. Many of their products would be in use long after the factories that made them had vanished.

Brown's *Where There Is Greed* was largely devoted to manufacture and its wounding by Thatcher. But once he gained
office, there was a yet steeper decline: manufacturing fell from
21 per cent of GDP in 1997 to 15 per cent in 2003, whereas in
2004 Germany's manufacturing stood at 24 per cent. Numbers
of metalworkers fell by 30 per cent between 1997 and 2005;
even gross manufacturing output rose by only 1 per cent. Brown
claimed that handing over the fixing of interest rates to the Bank
of England, which he did on taking office, was a form of devolution akin to the creation of the Scottish Parliament. In fact it
meant centralisation, as high interest rates favoured speculation
and trade and penalised industry – particularly when low interest rates for industrial investment could be accessed by other
member-countries of the European Union.

The *Financial Times* greeted the millennium with two arti-
cles. The first was an upbeat encomium to 'Britain Inc.' and
its new technology breakthroughs by the *FT*'s grand old
man, Sir Geoffrey Owen: 'Welcome to a sceptred isle burst-
ing with entrepreneurial spirit'. Of the businesses quoted by
Sir Geoffrey, the technology company ARM Holdings of
Cambridge is still British in 2009; British Telecom jogs along;
and Vodafone seems in endemic crisis. But where are Psion,
Marconi, Celltech and Powderjet? Shrunk, sold off. The second
article was a jokey piece by Owen's successor Richard Lambert
about financial villains, from the Victorian fraudster Whittaker
Wright to Robert Maxwell. By the summer of 2006, when City
bonuses were pushing £21 billion, Lambert was chief executive
of the Confederation of British Industry. Just over a year later,
as the credit crisis impacted and the horror of securitisation cut
Maxwell's villainy down to size, he would become a vehement
critic of Brown's regulatory failures.[3]

Brown had gone with the financial flow: away from 'widgets'
and 'metal-bashing'. In the light of Chinese industrialisation,
he denounced attempts to defend European manufacturing as
conservative and protectionist. By 2005, after two terms, the

industrial moderniser had disappeared as completely as the Gramscian Marxist, leaving a curious dualism; a neo-Carlylean worshipper of work who spoke in tones sterner than Thatcher's about Victorian values: 'a belief in the work–ethic and opening enterprise to all'.

A younger Scottish radical, the sociologist, rock singer and University Rector Pat Kane, thought this perverse, given the horizons of a more imaginative existence and community being opened up by new technology.[4] But what were people supposed to work *at*, given the disappearance of craftsmanship along with manufacture? Could the work ethic thrive on cold-calling, the leisure industries and shelf-stacking? Or was a more sinister synergy emerging, in which social capital and Brown's ethical simplicities would be sapped by exfoliating economic activities described euphemistically as 'not transparent' and more brutally linked by Jeremy Rifkin to the 'fourth' – or criminal – 'sector'?

II 'A tax on all the fools in creation'

In his 2004 British Council address, Brown praised the selfless-ness of British civil society, citing 'mutuality, cooperation, civic associations and social responsibility' as the heritage of the left, though the thoughtful Tory Douglas Hurd had earlier chalked these up to the 'particularly English' right. The Charities Aid Foundation, however, noted that 'social responsibility' in the form of donations had fallen 25 per cent since the mid-1990s to £1.70 per household per week. These same households could nevertheless afford £30.50 on eating out, £5.40 on tobacco and £5.90 on additional alcohol, from a 'leisure expenditure' which had doubled since 1982 to 14 per cent of outgoings, roughly equal to the cost of motoring.[56] Affluence there appeared to be, but was it real and had it strengthened civil society?

Take gambling, Adam Smith's 'tax on all the fools in creation'. In May 2005 newspaper reports put the industry's turnover at

£76 billion. This implied that up to 40 per cent of UK growth over that period wasn't coming from productivity gains or a flexible labour market, the things 10 and 11 Downing Street praised. Instead Brits were throwing cash at actual or virtual casinos. The Manchester United footballer Wayne Rooney, whose foot injury weeks before the 2006 World Cup convulsed English blokedom, had just blown £700,000 in a week. The German weekly *Focus* claimed a UK spend of $626 per capita on gambling, collectively $32.5 billion a year, or 2.5 per cent of GDP. That turned out to be well short of the mark. Polly Toynbee and David Walker had guesstimated around £50 billion in 2004; by the end of 2005 the average Briton gambled an astonishing £1,266 a year, or a collective £76 billion, an increase of 300 per cent in four years.[7] Touch-screen gambling at betting shops, something that had evaded regulation, clocked up at least £290 million a week.

In 2001 UK GDP in terms of consumption was £872 billion; by 2005 it had risen to £983 billion, an increase of £111 billion. Much of this growth was due to a surge in online sports betting and casinos. The USA didn't approve, and in summer 2006 jailed various incoming British gaming executives, suspecting that the sector was likely to harbour dubious characters. The former Labour Deputy Prime Minister John Prescott was guest on the ranch of one American gambling tycoon, Philip Anschutz (whose other enthusiasm was Jesus Christ: in America such combinations were not rare). Prescott was trying to get him to settle his fruit machines in the Millennium Dome, New Labour's Thameside folly that had stood vacant since its opening. By 2007 the spirit if not the climate of Las Vegas had arrived, with Premier League teams kitted out in online gambling companies' logos, and provincial cities going head to head in bids for their own supercasinos.

Gambling already supported 90,000 jobs; new casinos were likely to double that number. The chancellor took in £6 billion in taxes. The National Lottery, on which many social and cultural projects relied, paid out £1 billion a year. It would underwrite the 2012 London Olympics – at the cost of many smaller organisations, whose funding was cut if not stopped. Despite Brown's sneers about European economic sloth, the gambling bonanza somehow squared with the shabbiness of British society and infrastructure. Unemployment might be low, but British child poverty was still over 20 per cent. Germany's was 10 per cent. If the Germans were to hit the green baize tables, actual and virtual, with British enthusiasm, they would inject $196 billion (or 6 per cent growth) into their economy. Whether they would benefit from it was another matter.[8][9]

Worries about gambling echoed Robert Putnam's best-selling *Bowling Alone* (2000), which stressed the importance of 'social capital'; infrastructure and institutions, from shops and societies to parks and public transport, which increased citizens' collective life-chances. If economics differentiated between such 'good' growth and 'anti-social capital', or activities whose ill effects had to be remedied by public expenditure, then the alcohol market was reckoned to be 'worth' £30 billion but its social costs were, according to a 2003 Cabinet Office study, £18–20 billion.[10]

Did Brown ever address the huge contribution of booze and gambling to the British numbers? Yes, and affirmatively, given New Labour's 2006 Gambling and Licensing acts, which aimed to encourage both in the interest of urban regeneration and job creation. Brown lauded Adam Smith, who would have accused him of backing an increase in an anti-social activity not encoun-tered on this scale elsewhere in Europe. This emphasised that the shift from factories to services (which were often rooted in culture, law and habit) made societies *less* like one another. Gambling generated service sector jobs in the USA, notably by making every Native American reservation a would-be Vegas. Gambling *may* have boosted British GDP but it also inflated domestic debt and its consequences: financial collapse, family neglect, loan sharks, associated addictions and crime. Brown's own Scotland had 10,000 jobs in gambling, 35,000 'problem gamblers', and an 'illegal' economy (mainly drug-driven, but gambling was an important part) which approached 5 per cent of GDP.[11]

III Is It Globalisation Time Again?

Confronted with pure casino capitalism, Brown embraced it, though without Blair's enthusiasm – one of his early decisions as premier axed Manchester's promised supercasino. He still banked the taxes, though. The loser wasn't just the principle of state control, but the civic, Adam Smithian goal of mutuality. Late 2005 saw the death of Peter F. Drucker, the father of modern management studies, who had come to Britain from Austria in the 1930s as a socialist exile. Drucker later argued that many of the goals of social democracy could be achieved by responsible, mutualised capitalism as 'pension-fund socialism'. Not a lot separates this from 'revisionist' Tony Crosland's version of the mixed economy.

But by 2005 the pension funds were under threat, as a result of Brown's abolition of tax breaks on firms' contributions in July 1997, a blow which in turn struck at the integrity of the traditional firm.[12] Luke Johnson, chairman of Channel Four television and by 2007 owner of Borders Books, quit the consensus of troubled mutualists to praise the development of hyper-individualism and vast wealth such as that of the Murdoch family, the Barclay brothers, or the flamboyant retailer Philip Green. Powerful individuals, euphemised as 'private equity', could survive the stock market decline which menaced the pension funds, many of which first closed their membership to new entrants, then proceeded to dismantle final salary pension schemes. Even Robert Peston's optimism deserted him here: 'This is a less conspicuous but hugely important example of how the wealth of the many is being eroded, while that of the super-rich has soared.'[13]

Was there anything new in this? Between 1880 and 1914

the robber barons of railroad, steel and oil concerns had energetically advertised themselves as world-changers, backed up by
such ideologues as Henry Ward Beecher, the New York cleric,
and Herbert Spencer, apostle of the 'new' discipline of sociology
and unlimited individualism. They welded together the giant
firm or 'trust', technological and communications advances,
and political intrigue. The resulting millionaires – William
Randolph Hearst, Andrew Carnegie, John James Rockefeller,
Lord Pirrie, Alfred Krupp, Cecil Rhodes, and so on – presented
themselves through Social Darwinism as victors in the struggle
for existence.

After 1914 this tide turned. War brought the nation and
the demand for welfare back into politics, imposing a strain
which politics itself could not actually master and which
plunged Europe into the imbroglio of the 1930s. America got
out through Franklin Delano Roosevelt's New Deal of 1933:
not just an economic programme but a somewhat paradoxical
mixture of centralisation and a reassertion of faith in cooperation
and democratic culture – from bankers like Hans Morgenthau
via the young economist John Kenneth Galbraith to Woody
Guthrie, his guitar, and 'This land is your land'. It was in no way
consistent, but it generated enthusiasm and dynamism, some of
which (like the great Galbraith himself) lasted into the new
millennium.

Little of this, however, impinged on Blair and Brown's New
Deal, which used windfall taxes on utility companies to bankroll
retraining for the service industries, not least for a London dominated by multinational wealth. By January 2006, doubts were
growing about Brown's division of economic control between
the Bank of England, Treasury and Financial Services Agency,
and the *Observer* registered 'growing unease at the extent to
which Britain benefits from allowing foreign-based companies
to use our markets. Foreign investors now hold more shares in
UK-listed groups than Britain's own pensions funds do – an
indication of how many companies are really based abroad.'[14]

If there was a strategy for globalisation – either taking advantage of it or controlling it – were British MPs and ministers in charge of it, or was it those whom FDR's uncle Teddy Roosevelt had dubbed 'the malefactors of great wealth'? A survey in the *Sunday Times* based on its 2006 Rich List found that out of the £200 billion stashed in London by the 'non-resident domiciled' billionaires, only about £15 *million* was paid in tax.[15] This did not, however, inhibit their welcome by the chancellor, or their eagerness to influence British politics. Even the *FT*, in the shape of its senior commentator Martin Wolf, warned: 'If we take the principle that successful people are too important and too mobile to pay tax to its logical conclusion, political community will collapse.'

IV Shopping Power

In 2005 Brown saw his eight years as chancellor as proof of the wisdom of the deregulated UK and of the folly of statist 'Old Europe'. His claims were grounded on growth (up to 2004 about three times greater than Germany's) and unemployment (on paper about half). Yet to go from Baden-Württemberg with its hi-tech innovation (Mercedes A-Class cars, midget Smarts, new and ultra-sophisticated trains, trams and buses, environmental engineering from biotech to photo-voltaic) to post-industrial Britain (dereliction in the West Midlands, rail delays up fourfold, air toxicity in Edinburgh four times that of Stuttgart) was always hallucinatory. Brown's miracle-working rhetoric made the feeling more extreme. Think about gambling . . . or think about cars. New Labour was committed to sustainable development, but road traffic *increased* its rate of growth. In Scotland alone, it rose by 18 per cent between 1993 and 2002, and the Forth Road Bridge, carrying twice its designed level of traffic, began to fall apart. Britain's poor and expensive public transport resulted both from Brown's unwillingness to increase public borrowing and from car-buying as a vital part of the consumer boom.

Behind this was the remortgaging of housing stock. Prices were driven up by an expansion in households four times that of Europe, rising numbers of students, and the wholesale property speculation which replaced systematic pensions provision. Get-rich-quick flurries such as 'buy to let' were spectacular but did little for industrial investment or regional planning. Brown deliberately encouraged these, also failing to plan for a high-speed rail alternative to clogged motorways and polluting airports. GNER, the East Coast mainline operator, effectively went bankrupt in 2007, the year in which Deutsche Bahn, still state-owned, took over English, Welsh and Scottish Railways, changing its name to DB Schenker. In July 2008 National Express too would give up on the East Coast line, forcing Brown to take it over. A high-speed line to Scotland remains about seventeen years away.

Like Mrs Thatcher, Brown owed much to chance. Think about Britain's early mobile phone boom, a recurrent theme during his chancellorship. Between early 1999 and the summer of 2000, Britain had a true mania: 24.7 million people bought phones, paid connection charges, and ran up bills. Assume £500 per phone per year and you get an input of £12.35 billion. Set this against total GDP for 2000 of £891 billion, and you get a boost to growth of 1.4 per cent, a third of 2.9 per cent growth if you knock off the 0.4 per cent to trim the phone-growth period to a year. And this was perhaps Brown's most successful year.[16]

More – much more – can be said about phones, under carousel fraud, but they enabled Brown, far from holding hands with Prudence, to have uninhibited sex with the City. Borrowing an Institute of Economic Affairs scheme – suggested but never much used in North Sea oil – he auctioned off 'third-generation' licences (for Blackberry-type mobiles) at the top of the dot-com boom in March–April 2000, banking over £20 billion for facilities worth perhaps £3 billion. This didn't improve the profits of phone companies such as BT and Vodafone, but Brown let loose British 'new technology' (the hardware was almost exclusively imported) on Rhenish capitalism when Vodafone took over the German firm Mannesmann in 2001.

This was part of London's drive to become Europe's banker. A new breed of young financier had quit Germany for London's more profitable pastures and bribed Mannesman's board to betray its 'social partners' by accepting big bonuses and share options to close the deal. The *Land* of North Rhine-Westphalia put board and bankers on trial in 2003. They were let off, but with severe judicial observations, so the *Land* appealed to the Constitutional Court in Karlsruhe. In November 2006 the Judges of Highest Instance fined Josef Ackermann €3 million. He paid up. Having the CEO of the Deutsche Bank stitching mailbags would have been too much for business morale. 80 per cent of German voters disagreed, though this slap made Deutsche Bank prudent, and probably saved it in 2008.

'What people don't realise', a Brown aide said over drinks, 'is how blind Gordon is.' Hieroglyphs and mangled typewriters showed an energetic compensation: he mastered computers, even if he didn't drive. But this meant that much information came over via television and trusted associates. Some of the latter, like Alastair Moffat (director of the Edinburgh Festival Fringe) or Wilf Stevenson (director of the British Film Institute, and later of the John Smith Foundation), dated back to Brown's student days, but his own appraisal of real environments, city streets, collective emotions was thin. He was not the sort to walk through some new shiny-happy town mall and notice the lack of local names on the shops, the 'for sale' notices in adjoining streets.

The Brownite mix of cabal and ideology accords with a Scottish practice, noted by Emanuel Todd, the French social anthropologist. The gifted individual gets surrounded by a protective extended family. But Brown's posse altered with the move south. The London figures surrounding the chancellor

– Ed Balls, Douglas Alexander, Shriti Vadera and, at least initially, the spectacular Charlie Whelan and Geoffrey Robinson – were far from the Scots planning tradition, or the Edinburgh social democrat historians like Paul Addison, John Brown and Robert Anderson who taught him.[17]

The *Red Paper* had called for devolution, but in government Brown did the opposite. The Bank of England, put under Treasury control by the Tory Andrew Bonar Law in 1917 to aid war production on Clydeside and elsewhere, was handed to the City in 1997. The result was compared to the Bundesbank, but 'The Bank of the German Lands' always had a strong regional/industrial responsibility. In Brown's economic fulcrum no Scots, Welsh or northern English Members served on the new Monetary Policy Committee.

For Brown, American enterprise culture displaced a European experience which in 1979 amounted to a school trip to Sweden. During his holidays on Cape Cod, tutored by the Faustian figure of Clinton's former Treasury chief Larry Summers – when he was not convulsing Harvard – Brown absorbed the 'intervention-lite' and 'welfare into work' ethos of the Clinton era. He remained oddly oblivious of US urban collectivism and big-government bruisers: the military-industrial complex and the agricultural lobby. The US productivity increases he applauded were largely down to drastic rationalisation of retail – Wal-Mart's megamalls devouring local 'Mom and Pop' malls – and the computer-driven 'securitisation' of Wall Street.

In terms of post-Granita manoeuvre Brown's Americanism was a way of balancing the Blair paradox: his European ambitions *and* deal with Rupert Murdoch. Peter Hennessy shrewdly inferred that Blair won space as 'the nicer alternative': the trendy vicar rather than the Tesco boss, but Murdoch, regarding Blair as a pliable instrument, revered Brown as much as he suspected him.[18] Brown redux accelerated the galloping de-technologisation of a British economy that had been

saved by technology – the forgotten oil platforms of the North
Sea – in the 1970s. The refinancing of industry, training and
infrastructure promised in 1989 gave way to 'Broon jobbies' –
coordinators, enablers and outreachers – and the quick fixes of
the supermarket, call-centre and virtual casino.

Back to Europe, where after the 1970s redistribution
and conservation mattered more than 'crude rises in GDP'.
Manufacturing persisted along with greenish politics, but its
successes did little for the growth rate, while hi-tech industry produced ingenious machines which eliminated jobs. Still,
European technology seemed more manageable in the long
term. Brown wrote in 1989: 'Today our roads and railways
are congested, our airports and airways uncomfortably and
sometimes dangerously crowded, road and rail maintenance
in disarray and safety now a major issue in the public mind'.[19]
Twenty years on, no change.

V Whatever Happened to Stakeholder Capitalism?

Manufacturing featured prominently in the 1992 Labour
manifesto under John Smith, Kinnock's shadow chancellor.
The unexpected Conservative victory in the general election – mainly down to Labour's failure to win votes in the
south-east of England – did not immediately change policy.
'Stakeholder capitalism' captured the imagination of the liberal
left as John Major's government sank into a swamp of sleaze.
A vague formulation which *maybe* implied mutual ownership
and worker's control, it seemed to be happening in the John
Lewis/Waitrose Partnership and the revival of the Cooperative
in retailing. In fact, Brown dropped it as soon as New Labour
signed up its service sector and finance millionaires – though
this didn't check the rise of the idea's originator, Will Hutton.[20]

In Strasbourg, space-age trams glide through the streets. Built
in York Railway Works in 1994, they were its last products.
Major's rail privatisation dried up orders and the works closed

down. Hutton got the finance story more or less right: the £500 million blown on rail privatisation was wasted. Local Sparkassen and Volksbanken funding networks of technology and training catered for German industry. London-centric high-street banks, in hyper-centralised Britain, wasted time and money. Hutton said the right things but had little practical grounding in technology, just as Brown ticked the regulatory boxes with his Financial Services Authority without funding enough regulators. Individual projects were encouraged – the Dome in London, software around Cambridge, Scotland's silicon glen – but the 'cluster effect' (a 'synergic' interchange of investment, research and skills between neighbouring enterprises) rarely occurred. It *could* happen – around London and the big airports, or offshore on the oilfields – but the overheads, especially housing costs, were so huge that they deterred investment, and in the provinces isolated specialist factories had little chance of generating their own technology-breeding milieu.

There was a bigger imponderable, not mentioned in any of the biographies. In 1997 the UK would hand over Hong Kong, its last major colony, to the People's Republic of China. In the 1990s China was carefully moving into mass-manufacture, taking advantage of the chaos of Eastern Europe (which under communism had been a reliable producer of cheap consumer goods), low interest rates, and speculation by British banks. It was rewarded by a 25 per cent annual growth in exports after 2000.[21] From 1999 to 2001 Marks and Spencer ditched its 'buy British' policy, and by 2007 was sourcing 45 per cent from the Far East.[22] The pioneer historian of this wasn't in a university, or even in finance. He was the boss of glitz publishers Condé Nast. Nicholas Coleridge's book *The Fashion Conspiracy* (1989) showed how cash and prestige could be generated by PR, sex, celebrity and other sorts of mystique to sell expensive garments made for peanuts by old ladies in India or Sri Lanka. On reflection, the mystery is the time taken for this profit-making technique to hit the high street. How did it work?

Fully alert to this was Rupert Murdoch after his marriage in June 1999 to Wendi Deng, daughter of a regional factory boss. China had been the bogeyman of organised labour in Australia since Charles Pearson's advertisement of the yellow peril in *National Life and Character* (1893). Now it offered the chance of drastically reducing the UK cost of living, albeit at the cost of manufacturing capability and community. So what? Murdoch could handle or suppress the story, and could magic even more remarkable triumphs.

Take Formula 1, the remarkable organisation with which Blair first sinned in autumn 1997 when he ditched a ban on TV cigarette advertising after a donation from its boss Bernie Ecclestone. The revenues of Ecclestone's 'Formula 1 Promotions and Administration' went from £7.6 million in 1990 to £837 million in 1995, of which £54.9 million went to Ecclestone himself. Its operations were essentially aimed at TV rights: cars and drivers were almost a distraction. In 1997 he bought the rights to F1 for £6 million a year and grew the operation to £900 million in annual revenues, banking £2.5 billion between 1997 and 2007. In 2000 the diminutive Ecclestone and his lawyer Max Mosley sold 50 per cent of the rights to the merchant banks Hellman and Friedman and Deutsche Morgan Greenfell for £600 million, and in 2001 another 25 per cent went to Leo Kirch for £680 million. Most of the rest went to the private equity firm CVC, its boss Nick Cloud borrowing £1.6 billion to pay for it. Ecclestone retained £270 million. As Formula 1 soared into prominence it towed with it Porsche, Ferrari and BMW, while Rolls Royce and Bentley were sold off to foreign firms. In July 2009 Ecclestone was praising Hitler for 'getting things done'. Ignorance couldn't be pleaded. Mosley, his closest associate, was the son of Hitler's most prominent British admirer.[23]

Likewise, a triangulation of capital, media and expertise marked the 'culture industries'. Holiday firms based in London marketed posh resorts, hotels and cruise liners to the cash-rich and time-poor. Wines such as Bordeaux *en primeur* were transformed into market speculations. Fine dining produced trades on high-grade restaurants: the plonk and cassoulets of Elizabeth David's Islington or Chelsea gave way to the televised grotesqueries of Gordon Ramsay and other *men*. In terms of art, the cash rewards of Young British Artists, boosted by the Saatchi brothers, were far more notable than the talents of Damien Hirst or Tracy Emin. Still, they registered in Sotheby's, Christie's and Google art sales, and were quick to threaten emigration when Brown planned to raise income tax on the wealthy to 50 per cent in 2009.

Brown had earlier welcomed the froth, but he conducted no consistent campaign to unite this 'cultural' advantage with the UK's need for advanced hybrid computer-assistance systems. In other words, he made no concerted attempts to feed information technology with sophisticated manufacturing. As a result Silicon Glen in his own Fife rapidly lost the screwdriver plants persuaded to settle there (software, a longer-term business ignored by the Scots, migrated to Ireland) when a new generation of chip technologies had to be accommodated.[24] Brown's strategic failings were responsible for the seizure by the Chinese of a traditional development cluster which, over time, had shown itself remarkably resilient.

The Rover car plant at Longbridge, south-west of Birmingham, was unlovely and inefficient. After a few years trying to run it, BMW was convinced that it had no future. But the plant did not exist in isolation: it was the centre of a complex of small metal-parts industries, originally clustered round the canals and warehouses of Birmingham, which could churn out the components that the assembly line required. BMW concentrated on the Mini plant at Oxford's Cowley and cleared off. Rover continued for a time to produce. But the supposed 'general staff' of the Broonite economy, a finance-savvy management of the Geoffrey Robinson type, showed its form when Rover was sold to its 'rescuers', the Phoenix

Consortium, for £10 in 2000 (HBOS underwrote the purchase with an undisclosed sum). Phoenix got a dowry of £500 million from former owners BMW. John Towers, Peter Beale, Nick Stephenson and John Edwards, former Rover managers, then set up a £13 million fund for their own pensions, while the fund for the company's 6,500 workers had run up a deficit of £73 million by 2003.[25]

The rest of the story might have been written by J. B. Priestley in the inter-war years: this is the plot of *Angel Pavement* (1930), where an old-fashioned business is wrecked by speculators, but on a far larger scale. Rover could only survive with new models, and huge investment was needed for these. The Chinese found it cheaper and more effective to buy the intellectual property from Phoenix, who then allowed the works to go bust. The chancellor travelled to China in March 2005, and much was written about a likely 'Rover summit'. Nothing happened and Longbridge closed on 17 April the same year. The education minister Margaret Hodge, once a noisy figure of the far left, told the newly redundant workers to get jobs stacking shelves at Tesco. In 2006 her gloomy prognosis of the rise of the neo-Nazi British National Party in her Barking and Dagenham constituency was borne out in the local election results, and in June 2009 two BNP members would be returned to the European Parliament. When the official inquiry published its 850-page report on 5 July 2009, after spending £16 million, Lord Mandelson sent it to the Serious Fraud Office but no further action was taken. Government incompetence matched Phoenix's dishonesty. Rover was put to sleep.[26]

The City, international finance, Clintonomics and China proved too much for the industrial Brown of *Where There Is Greed*. Much of this pessimistic diagnosis was general amongst all anti-Blairites; from Ken Livingstone when he was Mayor of London in 1998 to Sir Bernard Crick, grandee of the moderate Left, now operating from Edinburgh and on speaking terms with the SNP. Both were for ditching the old shibboleths of nationalisation, but in the context of overall control provided by the European Union. In their pioneering critique of New Labour, *Safety First* (1998), Paul Anderson and Nyta Mann regarded Brown's initial post-Granita period as vaguely pro-European. Euroscepticism, though, appealed to the old Left in the party *and* to the City, since the 'liberation' of the Bank of England now allowed policy to be made up on the hoof. And by the millennium the flow into London of the investments, profit and expenditure of the well-off – whether West European, Middle Eastern, wild-capitalist Russian, American or Oriental – seemed to offer the chancellor the possibility of tapping this as a revenue stream to bankroll the welfare state. The crits were good. The 2009 *Oxford Handbook to British Politics* still applauded. But what of the revenue stream itself?

VI Funny Money

Brown's guidelines for joining the Eurozone initially looked like a timetable. Given the stumbling career of the new currency and the sustained hostility of the right-wing press, they became a barrier. In 2000, 48 per cent of UK manufacturing exports went to Europe, but manufacturing was dwindling and there was a counter-flow of European finance into London, attracted by the UK dot-com boom and its climax in 2001.[27] Such overall semi-detachment profited the City and injected dynamism into the housing market and retail nexus. Manufacture was sidelined. By January 2006 the celebrity fund-manager Nicola Horlick was praising Mrs Thatcher for destroying manufacture in the 1980s, thus allowing 'us' (that is, the City) to divert funds to the Far East, where rock-bottom wages, authoritarian communism and the threat of poverty or punishment could perform the work of Adam Smith's painstaking 'sympathy'. The problem was that in a world lacking 'sympathy', such a concentration of economic power would be difficult to control. Remember Mack and Kerner's *Crime Industry* (1975), which speculated on globalisation, tax havens and computers permanently blurring the legal/illegal boundary. By 2006 this was fact.

The ethos of the briefcase-and-bowler City used to be conveyed in the 1960s by solemn documentaries that explained the mysteries of stockbroking and stockjobbing and the Chinese walls between them, climaxing with Elgarian chords on the Square Mile's motto: 'My word is my bond.' David Kynaston's histories conveyed the boorish reality of the 'modern' form in a minor public school. After the Big Bang of 1986 cleverness came in, and with it the different spirit of 'caveat emptor'. Always indifferent to industry, hostile to Labour since the profits of privatisation had poured in via deals in discounted shares, the City had, through new PR outfits, sized up the new market of credit-worthy Sids and Sharons. Its attitudes were finessed as the Major government expired in disgrace and New Labour, anxious for cash, showed itself eager to please.

Issues about the functioning of finance and investment markets rarely get discussed in financial journalism until *after* things go wrong – and the dot-bomb slump in 2002 made the tone on Wall Street less reverential than inquisitorial. Matters were happier in London. By 2004, flexing the FSA's 'light touch' regulation, the City was on another roll. Its self-serving largesse – running at a record – was glaringly evident in the boardrooms of the FTSE 100 companies, whose directors regarded multi-million-pound bonuses as entitlements. The impact of this financial boom and its accompanying takeovers was, in terms of social capital, dysfunctional. A 'tipping point' had been reached where short-term gain distorted the whole political economy. But the music was playing and everyone, Whitehall included, was dancing.

Will Hutton, like Brown in 1989, regarded takeovers with hostility. Others saw them as a type of money laundering, in which dubious assets were sold on and the resulting returns regarded as pure. In the EU, upwards of 5 per cent of GDP was reckoned to be 'black' or pervaded by illegalism; Hans-Jürgen

Kerner thought that a level of 10 per cent became problematic, even more so when broken into regional components where the structure of civil society was suspect, such as South Italy or post-unification East Germany and points east.

By the time Brown became prime minister in June 2007, Britain was open country. We have met the megamalls turning home town into clone town. Financial services promotions came by letterbox or email; middle-aged carers finding parents fretting: 'But what should I do about this, dear? It looks official.' Age and computer-illiteracy were actually the best firewalls. Other doorstep pests, like high-pressure salesmen, got bonuses for making clients change their utility supplier.[28] Government favoured aggressive competition, but this showed the virus of illegalism mutating energetically and seemingly without limit.

Glossiest of all were credit offers from banks, building societies, supermarkets, charities and anyone else inclined to money-lending: seductive headline offers were usually qualified by pages of small print. In September 2005 the Office of Fair Trading found that a secret agreement between Mastercard and the high street banks to charge a 1.4 per cent 'processing fee' had cost 20 million British shoppers an extra £500 million over five years on annual purchases of about £43 billion. Offers of a year's free interest sounded like a good idea. But without an outright payment (by cheque) well ahead of the due date, high levels of annual percentage rate (APR) interest followed.

The rationale of financial sleight of hand, so quickly part of everyday British life, lay in the patterns of national regulation and control. In 2004 Professor Prem Sikka wrote in the *Guardian*:

There have been some puny fines for pension mis-selling, but no company executive has returned his or her financial rewards. No company has been prosecuted or closed for the biggest financial scandals.

Yet this is only a small part of the rottenness affecting the finance industry. Its fingerprints are clearly visible on the

Parmalat, Enron, WorldCom and other scandals. Many dubious transactions and schemes were designed by accountants,
lawyers, bankers and financiers with only one thing in mind:
their fees.

When executive pay packets are tied to financial results,
almost anything goes.[29]

Even those close to New Labour were questioning 'light touch'.
Despite his earlier enthusiasm for the chancellor, investigative
journalist Nick Kochan outlined how corruption related specifically to Britain's need to offset a trade balance going from a
£1.8 billion surplus in 1997 to a £50 billion deficit in 2006
by sell-offs to foreign capital and ineffective regulation. 'As the
UK feeds its addiction to finance and hot money, its regulators
bluster ever less convincingly about the security of its financial
system and its antipathy to money launderers.'[30]

VII 'The Economics of Arthur Daley'

'She adds the diplomacy of Alf Garnett to the economics of
Arthur Daley.' This was one of the many barbs of Denis Healey,
the lost Labour leader who in 1983 could probably have stopped
Thatcher in her tracks. Thatcher's response was to ask who
Daley was. The answer: he was a television Cockney of dubious
repute, played by the remarkable George Cole, who personified
the barrow-boy element in English commercial life. Not least
in the City of London: 'Your name Arthur Daley?' 'Depends.'
Tony Blair (whose father had travelled from the Music Hall
and the Red Clyde to Toryism) revelled in Daleyite company
– cronies included Lord Levy, Alastair Campbell and Derek
Draper. Gordon Brown apparently did not, even though the
cast list of entrepreneurs around government counselled caution.

After the 2002 slump there was an inflow of hard American
managers – refugees from the stern Sarbanes–Oxley Act –
demanding harder cash, the latest in a long stream of wealthy

incomers whom the City was desperate to recruit. They augmented the ranks of those who, fleeing disorder in their native lands, had established themselves in London or the various British tax havens. The very wealthy (who could, uniquely in Europe, claim a non-domiciled tax-free status) had expanded from imperial elites, South African diamond magnates and African or South American dictators to the 1970s Arab oil nouveaux riches, 1990s Russian oligarchs, Hong Kong Chinese, and the Mafiosi of the former Yugoslavia.[31]

About a dozen main types of financial malpractice could be detected, straddling Mack and Kerner's blurred border, and thriving under 'light touch'. These varied from fraud and scams based on 'letterbox' firms, 'boiler rooms', or hard selling to naïve clients, through firms from unstable territories using UK facilities and vice versa, to wealthy individuals and multinationals working through London to avoid tax and regulation. Add to these a penumbra of executives exploiting their own firms, City institutions promoting their objectives over the health of individual firms, and flaws in the regulatory mechanism.

Then there was financial instrument-selling based on deception: for instance the marketing of split-capital funds and precipice bonds; the underfunding of pensions, internal fraud and theft within firms; and bribery of supposedly impartial advisers and journalists. Megafraud worked through huge multinational firms exerting influence in London, and most menacing of all was corruption within the regulatory sector and police force.

Imagine this lot figuring in a holiday conversation at a Cape Cod resort between the chancellor and the ebullient Larry Summers, slightly his junior, who in 1999 repealed the Roosevelt-era Glass–Steagall Act. This was a post-Wall Street crash measure which prevented savings banks moving into the investment business. Ending it legitimised and boosted the 'universal bank'.[32] The problem before both men must have been the 'Arthur Daley' element. In countries with a written constitution the citizen would have a pre-emptive defence against his sort. Not so in Britain, where new business was integral to the wicked wealthy metropolis: Adam Smith's 'luxury and corruption' and the new, unpredictable cyber-current, to which he was no conceivable guide.

Here was where the dragons lurked in the early noughties, eight years into the 'Brown and Prudence' era: if one started with *old-fashioned scams, or their cyberversions*, then in Britain the snake-oil merchants seemed in rude health, and technically up to date. Mark Honigsbaum estimated their annual hit at a billion, which fell into seven main groups. The first three were 'too good to be true': telephone lotteries or TV quiz channels offering marvellous prizes, with a premium charge to pick them up and nothing more heard until the phone bill comes in. The *Guardian* valued the TV quiz racket alone at up to £150 million.[33] Was it a saviour of floundering terrestrial ITV, or an addiction as bad as drugs or gambling? Add on free gift or holiday offers, or 'opportunities in fine wines or timeshares': same result.

Exotic incomers were the Nigerian '419 fraudsters', named after the relevant article in the country's legal code, who sent ill-written emails asking mugs to help them access huge funds in Western banks. Or there were painfully handwritten letters from kids in East Africa, who turned out to be writing to order for local hoods. Account details required, and Bang! '419ers' actually enjoyed status in Nigeria for ripping off stupid, greedy whites: revenge for the scheming and bribing oil majors, whose operations made the kleptocrats rich and left the Nigerian masses poor.[34]

Pyramid selling was supposed to affect ingenous Albanians or Romanians, but see 'Women empowering Women', which originated in the Isle of Wight in the 1990s and cut a swathe through the suburbs. (The *über*-pyramid-seller, Bernie Madoff, twenty years a-scamming, was still above suspicion.) 'Matrix frauds' promised cheap hi-tech sweeteners for overpriced crap. Only a few buyers ever got them. Cheap credit offers, in return for a fee in advance? Pay it, and that's the last you will hear.

Add *Loan sharks*: See many of the adverts in the redtops, among the sex-contacts and ringtones. Many of these, once the small print was read, could involve rates of interest of 70 per cent and above, uncontrolled by any law (unlike in Europe). Some, like London Scottish, the 'Provident' people who circled the housing schemes as Farepak expired in 2006, were 'good investment opportunities' – but bust by 2009. There were newcomers, like the paralegal firms setting up Individual Voluntary Arrangements (IVAs) for chronic debtors to avoid *de iure* bankruptcy. Their operations were resented by the credit establishment, and they were in big trouble by autumn 2007.[35]

A few examples from the other categories had chilling implications:

Foreign racketeers: Only after the 2002 slumps did the big banks move in on the offshore 'shell banks' which laundered criminal cash. Credit Suisse admitted it 'hadn't a clue' about how many existed.[36] Were they successful in self-policing? See the career, *after* the 'clean-up', of the First Curaçao International Bank between 2004 and 2006. See also the EFT trust, based in London and Jersey, which had 'a stranglehold on power deals and dam-building projects in Bosnia, Serbia and Montenegro', largely because it was run by the Mafias of the region. Attempts to lessen its power by the UN Representative Paddy Ashdown were opposed by the intervention of the Foreign and Commonwealth Office and Robert Gelbart, a former Clinton aide.[37]

Wealthy immigrants weren't all tightwads: The Sultan of Brunei and his brother the scapegrace Prince Jefri kept such luxury concerns as Bond Street jewellers Aspreys and Rolls Royce going almost single-handed. The consequence of great wealth unaccompanied by much brain was a rip-off culture in the luxury goods/antiques area, carried to new heights by Sotheby's and Christie's.[38] But then, if wealthy nominal Londoners were under-taxed, who was going to make a fuss? Better to stay quiet and cash in somewhere else.

City fraudsters were a breed as ancient as their habitat, going back to Ben Jonson's day. During the 1999 European elections Labour's main broadcast consisted of Tony Blair, flanked by the pop singer Mick Hucknall, Sir Alex Ferguson of Manchester United, and Carl Cushnie. Cushnie was the chair of Versailles, a city finance company which made cash available to small businesses. It had gone public in 1996 and was then worth £690 million – one of the top 200 firms on the stock exchange. But it didn't do *anything*. Legitimate business was 20 per cent of its turnover; the rest was a series of transactions within the concern. By 2002 Cushnie was being chased by creditors; by 2004 he was in jail.[39]

Straightforward crooks like Cushnie found themselves alongside multinationals, even those that were controlled by high-minded nerds, like Bill Gates's Microsoft. Offenders persisted even though 'boardroom crime', not usually a jailing offence, could lead to fines of £100 million. Under pressure in their home states, they had to cope with EU interest in their monopolistic infringements, piling up fines at the level of £2.7 million a day. In late summer 2007 the European Court hit Gates for half a billion; not long afterwards the US Supreme Court did likewise to a secret price-fixing deal between British Airways and Richard Branson's Virgin Atlantic. Brown put Gates on his Council of Advisers. In April 2008 a four-year trawl by the OFT found British construction companies similarly compromised, usually colluding with 'competitors' to push up construction prices. The builders were eventually hit in September 2009, but even a £130 million fine was 'far less than they had expected'.[40]

Along with such corporate misbehaviour, regulators (given improbable levels of staff and cash) would have to cope with malfeasance against employees whose pensions funds were either being used for speculation or remained un-topped-up.

Like-on-like comparisons showed a loss of two-thirds of pensions capital since the 1980s, aggravated to the point of destruction by the chancellor's withdrawal of tax exemption in 1997.[41] One consequence of this was the aggressive marketing by reputable firms like Lloyds TSB of risky financial instruments such as split-capital funds and precipice bonds, both highly dependent on the upward movement of shares. In a declining market they would be catastrophic loss-makers. Between 1997 and 2001 some 250,000 people had been induced to invest in such speculative vehicles, knowing nothing of the market but assured that this was a reliable investment. The Financial Services Authority released its damning report on split-capital *on Christmas Eve 2004*, evidently hoping to 'bury bad news'. In fact the foregoing was, given subsequent evidence, a 'tip of the iceberg' situation.

In such operations, companies were quite prepared to hide the truth and bribe journalists, as with the rise and fall in 2004 of the precipice bond merchant David Aaron, who suborned journalists on *Bloomberg Money*. Because such investments were linked with powerful and well-connected firms such as Abbey National and Chase de Vere, the correct boxes had been ticked but the compliance didn't work; many lost three-quarters of their wealth. Journalists could be even worse, as shown by the trial of *Mirror* men in the 'city slickers' case for boosting stocks in which they had an interest.[42] In fact, as print journalism retreated from the online competition (by late 2006 it was possible to automate journalistic coverage of company reports), investigative reporting dwindled. PR colonised the City pages, as it had already done with the motoring, travel, fashion and book sections.

Small barrels, rotten apples? Not so. 'Go for it, hen!' applauded the *Herald* diarist in Glasgow, regarding a below-stairs fraudster as comic relief. This was Joyti de Laurey, the PA who embezzled a total of £4.4 million from two Goldman Sachs executives. Their pay and bonuses from the disreputable Vodafone takeover of Mannesmann in 2001 were so huge that they either didn't miss the cash for months or, more probably after the Karlsruhe verdict on Ackermann, kept schtum about earnings from a deal that they didn't want to draw attention to.

Steaming into all this like the Titanic were such outfits as Enron or WorldCom: effectively pyramid schemes in which first-comers took advantage of a market in which severe losses in the longer term were predictable, touting valueless shares at the highest level. Journalists surveying the wreckage were unlikely to reprint earlier, flattering treatments, but after March 2003 Bush and Blair had the Iraq invasion and 'our boys' to mollify them with.[43] NewsCorp and Downing Street familiar Dr Irwin Stelzer used to have 'adviser to Enron' on his strap line. How many more would follow?[44]

Finally there were the supposed guardians of the public interest. The Serious Fraud Office (SFO) was dubbed the Serious Farce Office, a Clouseau-like outfit forever panting in the wake of the hoods. In 2003 the Crown couldn't convict the property million-aire Nicholas van Hoogstraten of the murder of a business rival (the victim's wealthy family later revenged themselves in a civil action). In March 2005 the SFO had to take a jury through the huge Jubilee line fraud. This cost £60 million and failed. Defence counsel cost £14 million, paid for by the Crown under legal aid.

A lower profile case proved that investigators were often more screwed-up and corrupt than their quarries. The Butterfield Enquiry into malfeasances by Customs and Excise was fed inaccurate information by the very people it was supposed to prosecute. The most glaring example of this was one Alfred Allington, an informer who built up his own duty-free empire from the cash Customs paid him for informing. The entire trial collapsed, carrying the service's reputation with it. The SFO ended up a tragic victim. By mid-2007 it had disclosed a vast web of backhanders and corruption around the twenty-year-old Al Yamamah armament contract with Saudi Arabia, only for the case to be closed down by Blair and Brown on 11 December

2006 for 'reasons of state'. The High Court was unconvinced and condemned this as 'abject surrender' to a 'blatant threat'.

Interviewed in Tübingen, Professor Kerner argued that public investigators *inevitably* ran the risk of institutional corruption, as so much of their business involved running and protecting Allington types whom they needed as inside informants. The German criminologist Nicholas Leumann called this *Brauchbarillegalität* (useful illegality). The more 'open' the economy, the greater the risk. Hence – Larry Summers must have thought – the importance of having Chancellor Brown, a severe politician who exuded moral authority, rather than the eager, ingratiating Tony Blair, as its British figurehead. But if this catalogue of unorthodoxy, this metropolis microstate, could persist before Brown's eyes without severe punishment, the prospects for spectacular financial risk-taking were notably enhanced. About a decade before, Tom Nairn argued the same case inverted to regionalists and civic nationalists: the microstates, which he characterised as 'the Abbot of Unreason and the Lord of Misrule', were no part of the regional movement, but the ball-bearings on which global capitalism advanced, regardless of legal constraints.[45]

In what became a famous Mansion House address, on 21 June 2006 Chancellor Brown praised the City's 'innovative skills'. Nurtured through his light-touch regulation, London now handled 40 per cent of the world's trade in derivative financial instruments. He felt confirmed in his confidence.[46] But the information revolution had drowned the unwary in torrents of unsorted 'fact'; it had brought the criminal through the front door and down the ADSL line onto the family computer; it had skewed the morality of banks and the oversight of governments, making the telescreens of Orwell's *1984* look like Blue Peter. Against this the communications nerds, with their overspecialised shoptalk, had no defence.

4 Light Touch

If you owe the bank ten thousand bucks the bank owns you.
If you owe the bank ten million bucks, you own the bank.

Old Wall Street saying

We were suddenly dealing with crime and politics from
a part of the world that, to be honest, none of us in the
Metropolitan or Surrey police had ever heard of. We knew
nothing about the wars, about the crime and about the politics – we were frankly all at sea.

Metropolitan Police detective

I Wild Capitalism

When Gordon Brown addressed the Mansion House dinner in
June 2007, it was the last outing for his familiar bulky dark suit,
his equivalent to the black Geneva gowns of his Calvinist fore-
bears: a protest at the butterfly establishment. Another brooding
Scot, Thomas Carlyle, had philosophised about clothes in *Sartor
Resartus* (1834), though he would have seen dark suits in modern
Scotland as less straightforward: worn by MPs and MSPs, by
mourners at funerals, and by criminals to court appearances. Did
Brown, contemplating an unfamiliar, archaic rig-out, know his
game could be up? Or at least that his dinner jacketed audience
was up to something pretty weird?

For more than a year enterprises utterly remote from the City
as defined by Walter Bagehot or Lord Norman led the pack
in a culture of frenzied computer-driven trading. Little of this
risk was diffused; it was concentrated on property, real estate,

and shopping money borrowed on this collateral. Brown had let it happen. Blair would soon be leaving on the pinnace, like Bismarck in Tenniel's famous cartoon 'Dropping the Pilot'. For Brown it would be 'Women and children first!' Did this contribute to the gloomy foreboding that would characterise his government from the start? Had Brown realised that, far from markets offering 'invisible' or 'helping' hands, the one over which he presided offered a cocktail of deviance in international trade, financial instrumentation, and crime?

In November 2005 Tony Blair was asked, 'Is it possible to earn too much money?' He replied, 'Not really, no. Why does that matter?'[1] This wasn't the language of the chancellor, but it was he who presided over an economy pervaded by lax administration. 'Imaginative' finance was not deterred by thinly spread regulation. It simply changed its tactics, aware that most charges brought against it were unlikely to stick: moving in and out of different financial vehicles or financial centres; exerting political pressure through charity donations and niche financing of 'equipment' like think tanks; influencing newspapers by ownership, advertising or bulk purchases; and influencing the public directly by financing sport and the cult of celebrity. Britain under New Labour contributed to the basic conditions for local capitalist comfort: one of these was a public 'many of whom are on any realistic observation economically selfish, celebrity-obsessed, insular, prejudiced, overweight, drunken, xenophobic, etc. . . . .' – this from the model liberal Tim Garton Ash.[2] By European standards such folk had been surfeited in the iPod age; its masters were just skilful enough, notably in 'burying bad news', to enable the big fish to get clear.[3]

If the functions of finance are providing investment for infrastructure and industry, insuring of life and property, advancing cash towards homes, endowing pensions and (some distance after these) financing pleasurable consumption, then the British record was always patchy. In an orthodox capitalist society these functions are of national interest, with a greater or lesser involvement of the state. But the United Kingdom of London was anything but orthodox, not least because of the tax-avoiding flows it had to sustain: from Arab and other oil-owner wealth; from American speculators, from oligarchs fleeing from the Russia they had looted, and from the European wealthy who wanted free of the constraints of the social market.

Some of this was traditional. But the cost and the pace of the drama were changing. Self-regulation, the surge of post-Yom Kippur Arab wealth and the prospect of North Sea oil had pulled the City through the fringe banking crisis of 1973–4, when the fiddlers, tiddlers and crooks got hammered. Their replacements were the giant firms whose partners were looking for deals, usually hostile takeovers, in their own interests as consultants and arrangers. Their behaviour filtered sideways to the CEOs of non-financial FTSE 100 firms, who wanted security and bonus packages, regardless of the health of their firms.

By 2005 the UKL abounded in risky specialities. The highest profile of all was serving the influx of 'wild capitalists' from Russia, about whom countless stories circulated, concentrating on the cash which they would inject into the economy. Many were linked to Israel and in particular to the Israeli nationalist right, a grey area in which Blair already had considerable contacts through his aide Lord Levy.[4] When Tristram Hunt wrote agitatedly in the *Guardian* about Mayor Livingstone's attempts to induce more Russian oligarchs to settle in London, the paper got into trouble with Menatep's Boris Berezovsky. Livingstone protested to the *Guardian*, which deleted Hunt's piece from its website; sharper than Minitruth in *1984*. When the German weekly *Stern* tried to interview Roman Abramovich, owner of Chelsea FC and the wealthiest man in Britain, it failed to board his 5,000-ton yacht *Pelorus* at Kiel but ran into his political adviser, one Greg Barker – Tory MP for Lewes, shadow environment minister and confidant of the Conservative leader David Cameron. The Russian connection didn't feature on

Barker's Register of Interests; the tabloids were more interested in him leaving his wife for a male interior decorator.[5]

Meanwhile, Gulf wealth was building its own golden city/ financial tax haven in Dubai, initially financed by illegal trade out of Russia or India and the near-slave labour provided by a mainly Asian workforce of 800,000.[6] It was now buying into international transport utilities, with its 'sovereign wealth' Port Authority taking over Britain's last big ship owner P&O in early 2006, and was eager to rival London, filling the 'Swiss Levant' role long vacated by Beirut.[7] Such a challenge was unlikely to make the City more fastidious in its ethics.

Manufacturing? The City had never shown much interest in it – other than in arms dealing, or during the brief biotech and dot-com booms, or takeovers – when money could be got out of consultancy fees. The New Labour government was unlikely to react, or even to remind it of other priorities, as long as its taxation income – the City's report *A Capital Contribution* reckoned it at £87–93 billion gross, £12.7 billion net, in 2006–7 – came sloshing in. It was only in 2006 that the chancellor began to realise what it was mutating into, and how far he was from controlling it. At about the same time, Tom Burns, an Aberdeen academic specialising in finance law, wanted to find out what had been written and published about the law on securitisation and 'shadow banking', the current Big Thing, whose transactions were now into the trillions. The answer was alarming: nothing. Securitisation existed on, by and for computers. How could you control something that wasn't even down on paper? As Paul Mason, the economics editor of BBC 'Newsnight', wrote:

> In 2007 the GDP of the world was around $65 trillion . . . but the total value of derivative investments was $596 trillion, eight times the size of the real economy. The total amount of currency traded stood at $1,168 trillion, or seventeen times world GDP.[8]

But at some point in the game of pass the parcel, some poor sod would be liable for the virtual geld which sat in his lap. The scale of this paralysed the FSA and indeed the banks concerned, who didn't ask or own up until the music stopped in the summer of 2008.

This frenzy was partly propelled by the galloping growth of financial software capability, far outpacing orthodox juridical control, the precautions of which were geologically slow. The problem was not down, therefore, to the complete abrogation of responsibility by Brown and Blair. It wasn't just Sarbanes–Oxley refugees physically jetting into Heathrow. They didn't have to put a foot out of Manhattan if they didn't want to. The end of mutuality and the rise of private equity and hedge funds accelerated instant decision-making, and Cayman, Guernsey, Jersey, Liechtenstein, Monaco and London-domiciled investment banks provided a seamless financial web into which the torrent of composite initials denoting their 'products' would easily fit. The fact that they had been on the jump for a decade, alert to international intervention, made them even more aggressive bidders for business.[9] The FSA might just have had the chance of holding its own against the situation in 1998. But in 2005?

The 'policeman' FSA in the neoliberal economics to which New Labour had become fervently committed under Brown's guiding hand now looked like the men with ping-pong bats who once directed piston-engined Dakota airliners. They were now being used to control jumbo jets at Heathrow. We have seen the pattern of evolution: not something skewing a basically healthy organism but what Mack and Kerner foresaw: an industry driven not by one or two factors, but by a large number of dysfunctional elements which reached a tipping point. This made it plastic in the hands of the corporate rich – just where, in our metaphor, aircraft speed would go supersonic.

II Training and M'learned Friends

Orthodox economics still talked about 'the firm' but corporate identity had long left Goldman Sachs. The ill-paid, mainly Asian cleaners of its London HQ protested about their bosses' bonuses: £9 *billion* in July 2006 (enough to feed all 5 million Scots for a year). The more vocal opposition to this bonus culture (unsurprisingly coming from the less well-off professionals) had always boasted of Horatian rural virtue. Echoes of this hung around Brown: his life was modest, while the Blairs counted in millions. Yet such virtues thinned when one reached the old industrial provinces. (For a guide, compare the glossy mags on Virgin trains with Posy Simmonds's astringent *Tamara Drewe*). Newcastle, Bristol and their counterparts were public sector-driven, with flash stores and restaurants on their doorsteps, but ringed by a rampant booze-and-fast-food culture. This was New Labour in 'servitor capitalist' mode: enthralled by big business – in this case supermarkets, drinks companies, football clubs and 'iconic' multinationals (IKEA, H&M, Orange).

In late 2006 the Labour chair, Hazel Blears, said that her party's attempt to introduce a civilised continental drink culture had failed. Brits were congenital drinkers: violence was hardwired into their DNA. This was nonsense. The all-day drinking of the Victorians was curbed in World War I, and stayed that way for fifty years. Alcopops and 25p cans of lager from Tesco (cheaper than bottled water) weren't responses to spontaneous public demand. 'The quickest way out of Manchester' came directly from the new corporate culture and the collapse in morale associated with wholesale closures in manufacturing and the culture of training around it.[10] Cheap booze was a 'loss leader' to the supermarkets, and their remodelling of urban life was perhaps Brown and New Labour's master work.[11]

Surely Brown had solved unemployment? In 2006, yes; in 2007, no? Even that was optimistic. As early as 2001 the *Guardian* reported LSE professor David Webster's estimate that 'long-term sickness' in the UK accounted for 7 per cent of those out of work, compared with 2.1 per cent in Germany and 0.3 per cent in France. People moved off the dole and into incapacity benefit as Labour's New Deal made the terms of the former more rigorous. Allowing for such socio-medical factors as an addiction rate 300 per cent greater than the European level, teenage pregnancies and their consequences, and the connection between child poverty and ill health, 'real unemployment' was certainly greater than in much of Europe. Glasgow's nominal level was 12 per cent; add incapacity and it was over 30 per cent. Of Scotland's 2.3 million workers, moreover, over 25 per cent were part-time (15 per cent in Germany), so the decrease in actual poverty between 1997 and 2007 was barely discernible. Twenty-five per cent of Scottish teenagers left school at sixteen without qualifications; in Germany the figure was 9.1 per cent, with most going into some form of apprenticeship. The Scottish 'modern apprenticeships' were patchy, and *these* amounted to only 5 per cent of the age cohort, a tenth of the ratio in the 1970s. In their *Guide to the Scottish Economy* (1999, with a foreword by Gordon Brown) Bill Jamieson and Jeremy Peat largely attributed the problem to the lack of medium-sized enterprises (only 13 per cent of employees were in firms of between 50 and 249 employees, compared with about 25 per cent in Baden-Württemberg). Yet areas so afflicted, such as East Glasgow, were in their way dynamic, forming the centre of drug-based crime which diverted huge sums – computed at up to £40 billion in the UK and about a tenth of this in Scotland – to an international criminal oligarchy.[12]

Under Brown's chancellorship, Britain's industrial training, research and development, and enterprise initiatives became about the most ineffective in Europe. The basic problem was that good training required workplace instruction. Without it, outcomes varied from disappointing to scandalous. Despite the effectiveness of the Open University (where Brown had taught), the University for Industry attracted few takers and had to downsize drastically; Individual Learning Accounts (ILAs) were the scene of a heist on the public funds by various villains running bogus courses that cost £273 million.[13] Only a third of modern apprenticeships were completed. Once upon a time the trade unions had been not just a line of defence for the workers, with vivid leaders such as Lawrence Daly or Jack Jones to register dissent, but an opposition to capital which made employers act circumspectly. But with the decline of private-sector manufacture, union profiles had slumped even faster than their membership. Could anyone put a face to Bob Crow, Jack Dromey, Brendan Barber, or remember how Unison differed from Unite? TUC members now worked predominantly in the public sector so confrontations were more likely to hit passengers, consumers, health and welfare than bosses.

Education, meanwhile, occupied about 20 per cent of the population. About 50 per cent of eighteen to twenty-two-year-olds were at university, much higher than in Germany (36 per cent). But what sort of university were they in? Those of the Russell Group – Oxford, Cambridge, London, Edinburgh – eyeing the wealthy powerhouses of the USA's Ivy League? Or the civic redbricks and their Robbins-era successors? Or those (amounting to about half the capacity) which were former technical colleges, big but usually lacking in research facilities? The content of many of their courses was criticised. There were Aunt Sallies like media studies – which, if well done (and this was as demanding as learning Sanskrit), might deliver a mastery of the new media; its tools, languages, techniques and codes. But too often the culture it fed was the flim-flam coming through your letter-box, the scan-and-bin *Metros* on the buses, and the PAs and gofers of the spin business who were busy producing high-end glossies for public bodies instead of independent journals. Nose-diving numbers of students were studying modern languages, the majority labouring under the daft belief that 'everyone speaks English'. Most middle-class Europeans had a grasp of it at a tourist level, but the *Fachsprache* used in law, engineering, and medicine was still the native language.

'Rental occupations' like law had always been among Adam Smith's bugbears, but law boomed along with house purchases, divorces, 'marketisation' in society, disputes between what had once been integrated parts of firms, and the increase of illegalism. The faltering hands of the regulators caused spiralling increases in legal profits and the rise of megafirms like Linklaters and Freshfields. Even a capitalist roader like Dominic Hobson in *The National Wealth* was liberal with the word 'shyster', and we have observed the zero that was securitisation law. Accountants had once promoted terminal boredom but now acquired an Errol Flynn reputation, as predators swooped, swindlers fiddled, and public servants tried to regulate. David Leigh's book *Sleaze: the Corruption of Parliament* (1997) ended with an accountancy cliff-hanger, in which in 1995 a *Guardian* reporter rummaged through files in a derelict Swiss hotel in search of invoices to prove that the Tory minister Jonathan Aitken was lying. Faxed to London, this evidence would send Beaverbrook's grandson down for eighteen months. Copied to a Tuscan villa, it assured Labour's young leader that a crushing victory was in prospect.

This undoubtedly energetic industry was linked with the ever greater powers of the Big Four accountants (PwC, KPMG, Deloitte, and Ernst and Young), liberated by New Labour from the threat of unlimited liability. By 2005 there was growing fear that the involvement of any of these in corporate scandal, as in the fatal case of Arthur Andersen and Enron, would bring one of the Big Four down, with irremediable consequences.

What about the other end of the scene, the problem kids who seemed to be a national speciality? 'If a teenager in Walsall in the 1960s could read a technical drawing, and make a metal part from it, and vice-versa, he was on the road to skilled employment, with good pay.' The former metallurgist turned management theorist Noel Spare saw the end of this status relationship between apprentice and master as basic to a loss of social cohesion; its replacement by nerdiness on one side, and brawn, brands and bling on the other, was toxic. To the liberal Tory Ferdinand Mount the underclass reflected the New Labour patronage, which sapped the autonomous values that workers and their chapels, co-ops, friendly societies and allotments had once preserved, replacing them with the crass stereotypes of the soaps.[14] But the divergence went much deeper, tied to the disappearance of the work culture itself, felled by cheap imports and bereft of technological planning.

Survival in a non-manufacturing based world meant adopting different values. In the 1980s, observers in the Maze Prison noted that the IRA men read Marx and Fanon while the UDA's Prots did body-building: but a hefty body, even when packed with steroids, got a better job on the 'rest and recreation' scene. And at the local level of insecure or excluded Britain no well-organised gang in the burgeoning 'fourth sector' was without its tame solicitor and accountant, like the unfortunate Andrew Ramsay.

III PFI

Since New Labour had no real policy for industry, what was to be done with the vestigial manufacturing sector? The problem was similar to that of the 1970s: it had to be around to maintain and repair. Brown's solution was state intervention – not nationalisation but state subsidy to private contractors. The Private Finance Initiative (PFI) was not a Thatcherite invention. That other's privatisations had been car-boot sell-offs which, other than the sale of Britain's stake in North Sea oil (shrewdly disposed of at the top of the market in 1986), brought her far less than the continental practice of offloading portions in good market conditions. PFI privatisations, albeit informal, had from the outset largely been the work of Labour local authorities in the 1980s, selling off capital assets and then leasing them back: one reason why their accountancy had become labyrinthine by

1997. This was touted as a way of getting rid of underperform-
ing assets, but often the private purchasers got into unfamiliar
territory, with tears all round.

After 'Black Friday', 16 September 1992, the devaluation of
sterling and the exit from the ERM, Conservative chancellor
Kenneth Clarke used public–private partnerships as a means
of kick-starting delayed public works projects, but he had also
discovered their incidental benefit. They looked like state businesses and acted (most of the time) like state businesses – but as
the capital was coming from the private sector, they didn't figure
in the national accounts. It was as if a householder, instead of
buying a fridge on hire purchase, rented one. He or she would
pay out more, and have nothing in the end to show for it, but
the annual debt was, for the time being, reduced. 'Off-balance
sheet' transactions, which contributed enormously to the 'prof-
itability' of companies like Enron, made their appearance.

One of the earliest such projects proved anything but ideal:
the road bridge to the Isle of Skye cost £27 million to erect in
1989–95, brought its constructors the same amount in tolls of
nearly £6 a crossing, and in 2005 was bought by the Scottish
Executive for a further £27 million, an overrun of nearly 300
per cent. It aroused the wrath of a Scottish eccentric called
Robbie the Pict, who issued decrees against it from Pictland
and persevered when others gave up. By 2005 he was judged no
dafter than the idea itself.[15]

Gordon Brown, however, learned to love PFI because of the
selling abilities of Geoffrey Robinson, an associate of the first
and most sulphurous 'socialist millionaire', Robert Maxwell.
Robinson's own way up, exhaustively detailed by Tom Bower
in an unflattering biography, was as the financial adviser of a
wealthy Belgian widow, Isabel Bourgeois. This had enabled
him to rise to the top at Jaguar Cars, to survive the collapse
of Tony Benn's 'Triumph' motorcycle-manufacturing Meriden
Cooperative, which he chaired, and to continue through his
firm Transtec (until it went bust) to be a major supplier of parts

to the automotive industry. Robinson became Brown and Co.'s major link to the world of business and also the proprietor of the *New Statesman*, Brownite in persuasion but a long way from its oracular days under Kingsley Martin and Anthony Howard.[16]

Robinson's triumph came early in New Labour's first term in office, when he organised the 'windfall tax' on the excess profits of privatised utilities promised by Brown. He did this with the cooperation of Arthur Andersen, the international accounting firm, which schmoozed the incoming government as enthusiastically as it had Enron and WorldCom – although the £5.2 billion thus earned was only half what was originally hoped for.[17] Brown had come a little late to the cohabitation with the City that had characterised the Blair ménage, but with Robinson as his link-man, and later on the private equity boss Sir Ronald Cohen, he quickly made up for lost time.

According to Brown's figures, net investment by the state in 1999–2000 was supposed to be £6.4 billion (of which about £5.2 billion would be covered by the windfall tax) while a further £3.8 billion would come through the PFI.[18] By 2001 '150 projects worth over £12 billion, including 35 hospitals, 520 schools and 4 prisons' were in the pipeline. There were problems with these: the specifications were inflexible and over-sensitive to profit outcomes, and the participants were not always competent. Andersens in particular fouled up on a scheme for National Insurance Computers which went £45 million over budget. They got a slap-on-the-wrist fine of £4.1 million; their final nemesis came in 2001 with the fall of Enron.

The PFI schools and hospitals won few architectural awards. They tended to be dull, like the Union workhouses which had sprouted round the country after the Poor Law Amendment Act of 1834 and which often still did service as old folks' homes – though it was unlikely that the PFI build-ings would last 170 years. Thatcher's 'care in the community' had emptied many of the county asylums and special hospitals (the jury was still out on this one), many of which were then

made into chic flats for the well off. Only in 2006 did it dawn
on environmentalists that PFI 'newbuild' had undermined
the economics of much of Britain's urban Victorian landscape
of schools, hospitals and public offices. The demolisher's ball
and chain would soon be moving in on the elegant architecture of Alfred Waterhouse or George Brodrick, but the PFI
payments would go on for years.

So housing and retail were doing their bit, as elsewhere. But
as the saga of the Jarvis group (railway contractors so erratic
that when a train fell off the track railwaymen talked of it being
'jarvised') indicated, PFI had come to be a way of keeping
manufacturing and construction going, with the taxpayer foot-
ing the bill. It was a very rigid system, and in the long term a
very expensive one, as the studies of Professor Allyson Pollock
have shown: PFI meant that private companies could receive
public subsidy while still paying dividends to shareholders.[19]

Just how rigid was shown in the autumn of 2005, when the
TV chef Jamie Oliver attacked kids' snacks and school meals as
junk food. Blair instantly invited Oliver round to No. 10 and
promised initiatives, taskforces, kitchen tsars and so on, only to
be reminded by the chancellor that quality of meals was spelt
out in as many as 450 PFI contracts for up to twenty-five years.
A Turkey Twizzler was for life, not just for Christmas.

IV The Battle of Whitehall

Gordon Brown started his 'Britishness' speeches in 2004. They
weren't Dr Johnson's 'last refuge of a scoundrel'; indeed, he
presumably aimed at a contrast with Blair, who skittered across
such themes like a water boatman. As well as trying to generate
national solidarity at a time when multi-culturalism was being
tested by militant Islam in the aftermath of 9/11 and the invasion of Iraq, they were appropriate enough attempts to position
Brown as a future prime minister, yet they contained not a word
about war.

Presumably this reflected his work on Scottish Independent Labour, where Maxton's revulsion to war endured even when the enemy was Adolf Hitler. (This would change: by February he was calling for cadet forces in problem schools.) But Brown on Britain was a reaction to Blair's taste for drama: turning up for photo calls with 'our boys' in jeans and open-necked shirt (even snapped on one occasion mobile-to-ear and naked to the waist Mussolini-style) would always guarantee coverage in News Corp.'s papers and broadcasts. Brown, never photographed out of *that* suit, stayed well clear. However, 'Blair's wars' did expose a vulnerable Brownite flank. The more wars, the greater 'Tony's things' weighed in the Whitehall dyarchy: something which seemed truly menacing after the embarkation for Iraq. Despite mutual American enthusiasms, Blair cut Brown out of the war strategy circuit – although he still had to fund it. In late 2006 the cost of the British element of the Afghan and Iraq campaign had already reached over £7 billion, and even with a much reduced military presence (down from 50,000 to 5,000 troops) was running at over £80 million a month – a fraction of the US's $5 billion, but still piling up.

Moreover, war and defence in general had enveloped what was left of British heavy-industrial manufacturing. By 2005 the only substantial Scottish shipyards left were owned by the huge defence contractor BAe Systems, which was about to divest itself of its last civilian element: its stake in Europe's Airbus consortium. Much of the skilled labour in Brown's own constituency was employed at the privatised but still defence-dependent Rosyth naval dockyard. The joke used to be that if one followed the ethos of the Adam Smith Institute (which proved to be worryingly close to the chancellor and picked up £8 million in government contracts), the defence of the realm would go to the cheapest bidder – if that was the Red Army, fair enough.[20] Now something similar was happening in Whitehall, and the Treasury was only in fitful charge of it, as the prerogatives of 10 Downing Street increased: Blair hadn't forgotten how Thatcher had used the melodrama of the Falklands to pull herself out of the manure of 1982.

'All God's children got guns!' sang the Marx brothers and in 2007 the world spent $1.5 trillion on armaments. With a turnover of $29.9 billion, BAe was Europe's greatest arms producer, only a whisker behind Boeing, the world leader, at $30.5 million. In a vestige of Robin Cook's 'ethical dimension', its deals were supposed to be subject to government oversight – but only if the deals physically occurred on British soil. Its history showed a long tail of intrigue and backhanders. Such was the dominance of the arms trade in British manufacturing exports that in 2004 it was observed that 'Nearly half the work of the civil servants in the Export Credits Guarantee Department is related to arms exports'. This amounted to £180 million per year.[21] But these statistics notwithstanding, such exports were unprofitable. Support for arms sales (permissible under EU regulations) – dominated by deals with Saudi Arabia and increasingly the Pentagon – might cost government an extra £100 million; technology fee rebates ploughed in another £640 million. A sum of £125 million was recouped, leaving an £888 million net subsidy. Despite all this, BAe's pensions fund was £4.26 billion in deficit in February 2005.[22]

Half of BAe's business was with the Gulf and half of that with the Saudis, through the arms contract negotiated by Thatcher in 1986. (The UK got it as the Israel lobby wouldn't have sanctioned US involvement). Her son Mark 'received a large sum, perhaps as much as £12 million for helping with the Al Yamamah deal',[23] and the price of planes was inflated by 32 per cent to pay off the royals, notably Crown Prince Sultan's family, which, the British ambassador to Riyadh said, had 'a corrupt interest in all contracts'. Rumours abounded of huge illegal payments on the British side going back a quarter-century, and a lateral leakage of high-tech capability to the Wahabi fundamentalists of Al Qaeda. But the Serious Fraud Office had had been on BAe's trail, and revelations appeared imminent.

Such entanglements provoked only vague responses from the establishments involved, of whom 344 mandarins transferred to the private sector between 1997 and August 2004: still not enough for Brown and Blair. Blair opened the bottleneck with Sir Patrick Brown, who had privatised National Freight and the water industries for Thatcher, and Railtrack for John Major. Expertise was certainly needed. In the late 1990s the Ministry of Defence spent £250 million on eight Chinook helicopters that in 2009 had yet to fly because of missing software. In 2007 it sold off its research arm QinetiQ, bringing a huge profit to the civil servant concerned, Sir John Chisholm, and its American private equity partner the Carlyle Group, on whose board Major sat. When under attack, however, as in the Deepcut scandals (the suicide of young recruits which seemed attributable to a regime that was as perverted as it was brutal) the MoD proved a formidable adversary.

On 6 December 2006 the newly retired Commander-in-Chief Sir Mike Jackson claimed that the MoD was unfit to manage the welfare of his troops. An unprecedented outburst, it had plenty of successors. There was a whiff of South American *generalissimo* politics in the air. Hardly a week later came the news that Lord Goldsmith, the Attorney General, was calling off the SFO inquiry into BAe's slush-funds 'in the wider public interest, which had to be balanced against the rule of law.'

V Our Friends in the South

The other joker in Brown's pack was the growing instability of the City. When the economy crashed into recession in 1990, the electorate didn't punish Major. Did this affect Labour's strategy? 'It's *not necessarily* the economy, stupid.' The City bounced back by 1997 but would crash again in 2002. This did not indicate resilience. It was now dominated by under a dozen global concerns, with Goldman Sachs and Credit Suisse on one side, and PwC or KPMG on the other.[24] Slipping between them

were the specialist firms in which they bought and sold interests, and sharp young men rewarded for this and wont to 'make
markets' on their own account.

After 9/11 put all financial centres on the front line, and
the 2002 dot-bomb, most of the City's business moved into
the ever more exotic areas of private equity and hedge funds.
Figuring nowhere at all in Hobson, these instruments, with
their constantly-changing portfolios, and London as 'not New
York', hedged against bombs as much as slumps by shifting
investment in and out of commodities, specie, insurance and
property. In the tax year 2005–6 alone, hedge fund business in
the City and the Cayman Islands rose by 41 per cent. Brown
had called for financial stability in *Where There Is Greed*; now
he saw that the *instability* of hedge funds was their selling point:
'turn(ing) over their portfolio 20 or 30 times more than a long-
only fund'.[25] That the mushrooming of hedge funds went hand
in hand with the concomitant rise of spread betting was no
surprise; hedge funds *were* a gamble, without loyalty to any firm.
The Chinese wall between speculation and gambling crumbled,
which may account for the government's silence about both.
What rose steadily was government finance for London. If the
median level of government regional expenditure per capita was
£100, the Scots did pretty well at £115. But high-speed trains,
underground lines, airport connections, security, defence and
broadcasting outlays gave London £170.

What were the values of the City? Some customs – 'Into the
office by ten thirty, dead drunk by four' – had been superseded
by the American invasion after 'Big Bang' 1986, reinforced by
Thatcher jailing a symbolic Old Guard (mainly Jewish) after
the Guinness fracas. London settled down to be the third trading post (with New York and Tokyo) in the world time-zone
chain. But manufacturing investment didn't improve; about this,
Brown's thoughts were far less logical. Under Thatcher, deindustrialisation (outside specialised, cash-hungry offshore oil and
military engineering) gathered pace and was aggravated by the

export of capital, with West Germany, in particular the SMEs (small and medium-sized enterprises) of Baden-Württemberg, the leading beneficiary. This meant that the culture of innovation, adaptation and training was not adopted, crucially retarding the application of computer technology to mechanical engineering.[26]

London's advantage was being of but not in the Eurozone, using computers and real-time information but also survivals from earlier days: the closeness of the City to the geezers and the toffs; the immigrant adaptivity of the East End and the green baize tables of Almack's or White's: a culture which, unlike much of Europe, favoured gambling and pleasuring the rich. But if this was the goal the links to society would be attenuated and, if the prize was big enough, dropped.

Back in the 1970s the *Sunday Times*, then fairly radical, talked of a 'fish farm culture' in business life: a desire among business highflyers to grab a substantial personal fortune and spend the rest of their lives tending a fish farm in northern Scotland. The point was to find the optimal packet for long-term security through investment, and this seemed to be reflected in City and CEO patterns of short stays for big bucks: Chris Gent's four years at Vodafone–Mannesman against Arnold Weinstock's thirty-three (1963–96) at GEC. This was not necessarily selfishness, implied a German study of Gent; it could be trying to head off the threat of burn-out.[27] But what would happen if the price of such packets increased in line with that of the goodies on offer? More clients from Russia and the Gulf also meant more demand for scarce luxuries, so there must be either a price escalation or a decline in quality.

The consequence of such trade was that illegalism in the City snowballed as bonus culture increased and along with it the desire to avoid tax while heading for the 'ideal millionaire' savings account of £3.75 million. This, the *Sunday Times* calculated in 2000, would enable security, plus the equipment to speculate on one's own account and get in on the private equity escalator. Hence the big accountancy firms homed in tax and trust schemes to benefit their clients, ignoring such concerns as illegality, ethical conflicts with their auditing principles and regulatory threat. This deviance palliated straightforwardly crooked schemes, like pyramid selling or helping unsavoury clients to bank (or launder) their winnings in safety. Fines, KPMG discovered in a typical US case, would be $31,000 – against profits of $360,000. And in the UK, because of revenue overload, there wouldn't even be fines.[28]

In this winner–takes–all set-up, pressure on the captive domestic market was inevitable, as were the consequences: cutting pensions rights, screwing cardholders and poor credit risks who would have to borrow from unsecured sources. In a typical case, Glaxo's share value halved between 1999 and 2003, but its CEO Jean Paul Garnier's income – salary plus bonus and share options – went up from £1.2 to £5.9 million. In May 2006 Garnier became one of Brown's panel of prestigious economic advisers.

And no one in the financial media asked the further question: what was to prevent a group like Al Qaeda, whose origins were not in Wahabi Madrassas but in one of the world's oldest trading elites – the dhows of Jeddah plied the Red Sea and Gulf when Liverpool was a swamp – actually funding itself *through* the global market? Staging an outrage in a financial centre, buying shares cheap after the ensuing crash, and discreetly selling them on when the market recovered?

New statistics from the Bank of England, breaking at about the same time, made for remarkable reading. In 2002 Russians had £5.8 billion invested in the UK, which rose to £14.4 billion in 2004; by March 2006 the amount had rocketed to £49 billion. One-third of London's 'super-prime' properties were going to Russian buyers. The automatic response was to attribute this to the kleptocracy of post-Yeltsin Russia: the fortunes made by apparatchiks in the privatisation of the command economy while a Soviet-style public control and welfare system staggered on at a lower level. Tony Judt had already written that in

2004: 'Thirty-six Russian billionaires ("oligarchs") had corralled an estimated \$110 billion, one quarter of the country's entire domestic product. The distinction between privatisation, graft and simple theft all but disappeared: there was so much – oil, gas, minerals, precious metals, pipelines – to steal and no-one and nothing to prevent its theft.'[29]

Judt properly regarded the migration of about a fifth of Russian GDP as a crime, on a scale rarely acknowledged by the apologists for the transformation of 1989–91: the Lord Dahrendorfs and Tim Garton Ashes. But this was a crime that was wholly within the paradigms of Mack and Kerner's 'able criminal' in his chosen milieu. In the classic 'underconsumptionist' terms of J. A. Hobson, whose *Imperialism* (1901) influenced Lenin, the Russians oligarchs' coup was itself doomed if confined to Russia. Workers' living standards were so depressed that no large-scale consumer-based enterprise would flourish within Russia itself: the longer-term revival of the economy might be promising, because of oil and gas resources, but this was too far into the future. The UKL was different, far superior to any other European financial centre in the rapid availability of the investments and gratifications it offered. But how could such a place, with so many cultures, become in Adam Smith's terms *moral*?

The banks powered the market, but their money pool was increasing through inadequate supervision and two 'rogue' suppliers. As whistleblower the Financial Services Authority was weak, uncoordinated and thirled to the financial community. Though its annual budget of £323 million, about a third of which was spent on salaries, looked generous – the cost of the Scottish Parliament is £86.7 million –[30] it was up against an industry generating £150 billion, which it served as publicity bureau, lobby, regulator and anti-fraud office. In 2004 it became concerned about City risks, only to be censured by the Centre for Policy Studies, a right-wing think tank, which 'recommended that the FSA should be less accountable to the

Treasury and more to the industry it serves.'[31] Supervision was not improved by the long career of the chief inspector of state expenditure, Sir John Bourn, controller and auditor general from 1988 to 2007. His jollies would make absorbing reading in 2008,[32] and Parliament's weak Audit Committee allowed him to get away with it. Some of its members would later be compromised in the expenses scandal, which may have kept them quiet. John Tiner, late of the FSA, wrote in the 2008 review of Audit Office's governance: 'The NAO's senior management board is of limited value . . . in maintaining good standards of governance. There is no substantive discussion of major issues . . . making it very difficult to effectively challenge the executive and the C&AG.'

The FSA also flunked the real test: putting complex fraud cases before juries. This was down to foreign finance and the fourth (criminal) economy. The first of these was not subject to FSA oversight, which raised the risk 'of the kind of accounting fraud that afflicted Enron and WorldCom'.[33] The second pumped in its laundered gains, and found it increasingly easy to do so, what with split-second decisions (as with private equity and hedge funds). Its own rate of return through orthodox villainy was declining. East European oligarchs were now under pressure from authoritarian government, the criminals from the sharp fall in the cost of drugs like cocaine. There was competition on the Internet for 'adult' entertainment, aka pornography, through the pirate production of CDs and DVDs. The casual criminality among, say, file-swapping teenagers, was bad news for professional hoods.

Sir Callum McCarthy, hitherto a very quiet chair of the FSA, voiced alarm on 15 November 2005 about City mores: 'There is increasing evidence that organised criminal groups are placing their own people in financial services firms so that they can increase their knowledge of firms' systems and controls and thus learn to circumvent them to commit their frauds.' Patrick Hosking and Stewart Tendler, commenting on this in the *Times*, calculated that fraud in the UK cost £14 billion annually, and that £25 billion of the money processed in the city was 'dirty'. They added that McCarthy's FSA was actually withdrawing checks on 'tens of thousands' of City workers, in pursuit of the light-touch regulation Gordon Brown would exult in only seven months later at the Mansion House on 21 June 2006. By autumn 2007, with normality falling apart, this was being pitched by the Association of Certified Fraud Examiners at £72 billion.

This wasn't a question anyone important cared to ask, although this only became apparent quite late, Brown being a prolific spawner of committees and inquiries which kept awkward topics (such as the Al Yamamah investigation?) *sub judice*. Only in the spring and summer of 2006 did the details leak out of how New Labour had funded its 2005 campaign; nominal loans from very rich men in exchange for honours and peerages far outweighed union levies and members' subscriptions. This was 'Tony's stuff', but the chancellor's silence had to be explained – he either knew where the £18 million the party was shelling out was coming from, or he wasn't up to his job. This came as the economy, faced with a revived Europe, stuttered and slowed, and Labour losses to LibDems and the SNP at Westminster and council by-elections in Scotland served notice that North Sea oil, worth £13 billion a year with the $70 barrel, might be up for grabs.

2006 was the jubilee of John Osborne's *Look Back in Anger*, when the modern elbowed itself on to the London stage just as Anthony Eden and the Empire fell apart. The Royal Court theatre celebrated by reviving the play, only to find it a greeted as a quaint tirade. More credit went to the National Theatre when it staged Harley Granville-Barker's *The Voysey Inheritance* (1905), in which a young Edwardian lawyer discovers that his respected conservative family firm is in fact a 'long fraud' in which the clients' capital has vanished, while the dividends are paid by his family, doomed to live on the qui vive. Most reviews in Britain commented on the play's relevance, but an American critic dismissed a parallel revival in Los Angeles by David Mamet: 'Any theatregoer today who doesn't find the Voyseys reprehensible is living in a dream world in which a Martha Stewart–Enron approach to business ethics is acceptable. Granville-Barker may have been making news in 1905 but in 2005 we've heard it all.'

Nothing would be done about such a situation, just as no Westminster politician was likely to emulate the frustrated reformer Henry Trebell in Granville-Barker's other classic, *Waste* (1906), and shoot himself when the New Labour dream evaporated.

VI Social Capital: Transports of Decay?

Brown seems to have turned to Adam Smith in 2003, perhaps prompted by his move to Kirkcaldy. His awareness of Smith's writing on social capital – the necessary container of a market society – and 'police', whereby conspiracies of merchants as well as criminality were put under restraint, was timely if not consistent. Once a nation loses its manufacturing firms, and with them the development of high-value-added services such as design, power supply, training, marketing and specialised insurance, lasting recovery and the reconstruction of civil society are infinitely deferred.

The most visible failure on Brown's watch as chancellor was the transport sector. In late November 2006 the senior Treasury economist Sir Nicholas Stern, returning after secondment to the World Bank, logged a report on the economics of global warming. He stressed the need for congestion charging, which Alistair Darling had deferred for ten years or more, and increased taxation of air travel.

Transport had aggravated the country's post-war economic problem. Her manufacturing inferiority to Europe had been exaggerated: in the motor industry Britain had not been far behind Germany in plant efficiency, and in innovation probably ahead; Minis and Land Rovers outlasted Beetles. The problem was an infrastructure poorly equipped to deliver materials and products. In the 1950s railways were run down, motorways non-existent. Pro-motoring policies from both parties until the 1990s expanded the car market to a size that the native industry could not supply, even before the 'double whammy' of the 1973 fuel crisis and entry to the EEC. Thereafter North Sea oil diverted much of the cash for modernising industry.[34]

Nationalisation in 1975 at least reprieved British Leyland (though it didn't change equipment and work practices), and in 1971 saved Rolls Royce and Britain's aero-engine industry *tout court*. Privatised in 1987, it was the only high-tech leader left in the UK in 2007.

The continuum of policy after 1992 from the conservative Chancellor Kenneth Clarke to Brown produced economic growth but little social capital. Indeed, gambling and its convergence with City irresponsibility suggested the reverse. Sprawl induced a lifestyle that was less and less integrated with any notion of community. The shopping mall, the giant comprehensive school, the foreign beach-bound holiday, the airport: the stations of Mondeo Man's life were marked by atomised social behaviour even before Las Vegas started coming downline to the family PC. This, dignified as 'choice', reduced the citizen to a consumer. Against this, New Labour had neither a programme nor a philosophy. But with a record balance-of-payments deficit, the chancellor was grateful for every cash inflow, even if this meant that British public utilities and private companies – what Harold Macmillan called 'the family silver' – were sold off wholesale.

Transportation should provide an extensible net to hold together a society whose economics would otherwise fall apart. This according to Brown in *Where There Is Greed*. Matters were moving the government's way, if only slightly: free passes for senior citizens revived bus passenger numbers after long decline.

The national railway network survived beyond the UKL: the expense-account privileged in first class paid £200 for the Edinburgh–London single fare, while in standard young people and pensioners on railcards still forked out twice what Germans and three times what Spaniards were paying. At least some sort of system remained, unlike in the USA and South America. The worsening problems were the cost of congestion, the safety corners cut, and the impact of depersonalisation: something quantified by the late David Pearce in 1996. Commissioned by Chris Patten when Environment Secretary to Thatcher, he found that road freight covered only a third of its global costs. But trying to devise effective legislation was too much for New Labour, whose horizon went no further than schmoozing the voter qua consumer. Into the vacuum slipped the able criminal: overloaded trucks and overworked drivers made up 60 per cent of those examined at Dover and 30 per cent of those at Holyhead on 31 October 2006; unmarked lorries heading up the M1 to giant state-of-the-art warehouses at Daventry and Nuneaton.[35] The incredible adaptability of road haulage, which according to Adrian Lyons, chair of the Railway Forum, upgraded its technology every three years and was putting long-distance rail freight out of business – in 2007 less rail freight was going via the 'Chunnel' to Europe than in the train-ferry days – was in part dependent on the semi-slavery of East European drivers.[36]

Brown's transport minions could have prevented this but didn't. The practical consequences were made explicit by Labour's short-lived Strategic Rail Authority. Responding to Brown's restrictive finance, rail was to concentrate on where it could provide 'value for money': medium-distance inter-city services and south-eastern commuter trains. No electrification, no high speed, no German or Swiss strategy of using rail to decentralise investment to regional *Ballungsgebiete* (hubs and spokes). Urban investment was concentrated in the south-east of England; the remaining strategies were crudely electoral: car-owners voted; bus-users did not.

Devolved Scotland and Wales went their own way. By 2006 Brown had boxed himself into a situation where his Scottish ministers in Transport were prescribing drastic disinvestment for the English provinces, after the North-East rejected an Assembly in November 2004. With the Olympics looming in 2012, London fared no better. Bob Kiley, the New York transport boss hired by Ken Livingstone, tried fifty times to get Brown to a summit on London transport and did worse than Sir Alastair Morton. Brown wanted a PFI 'solution' for London's underground; Kiley's calls were not returned.[37]

VII Regulating the Regulators

'Light touch' operated long before Brown boasted about it. Turn to the *Civil Service Yearbook* in search of the 'enforcing' element of the Transport Ministry, and then of economic affairs in general, and you will be struck by minimalism coupled with profusion: lots of poorly funded bodies tripping over one another. Little 'itlers having run-ins with speeding motorists were a staple of the tabloids; but the problem was a lack of coherent and transparent power, with citizens' rights secured constitutionally.

In fact, the more you looked at the *CSYB* – and at the administrative chaos in other departments dealing with such things as tax credits and rural payments – the more worrying things seemed. Besides the police, there were about thirty quangos and agencies with financial investigation powers, many of whose responsibilities overlapped with those of other agencies. More than half had been set up in the last twenty years, over a third since 1997. Granted goodwill, this would still guarantee teething troubles galore, even before Whitehall's usually catastrophic adventures in cyberland. Brown's approach was to save on policing by making firms assess their own compliance with new and much tougher regulations, something pressed for by international bodies in the 1990s and accelerated after 9/11.

His touch was lighter than his continental or American counterparts when it came to Britain's remaining colonial possessions: the Cayman Islands, Bermuda, the Bahamas, St Kitts and Nevis, Gibraltar, and closer to home the Isle of Man, Jersey and Guernsey. Without their tax-avoidance business, effectively operating as outstations of City firms, these places would be a drag on the public revenues. In Whitehall their ministerial masters were all over the place. The Serious and Organised Crime Agency, for example, reported to the Home Secretary, but the Foreign and Commonwealth Office also had a Drugs and Crime Department, while the Serious Fraud Office and the Inland Revenue Crime Group reported to the Attorney General, who had a staff of only twenty-three. The Office of Fair Trading was under the DTI, which also had its own Legal Services Department, but the Financial Services Authority, 2,800 strong, reported to the chancellor.

Carve these bodies up between Blair's ministries (Home Office, Attorney General's Office) and Brown's ministries (Exchequer, DTI, Customs) and the scene got even more complex, provoking the suspicion that ministries and quangos were being developed to expand their masters' powers rather than to operate as an efficient and coordinated machine.[38] Given the sulphurous relations between 10 and 11 Downing Street described in Derek Scott's *Off Whitehall*, the worst could be feared.[39]

Added to this were two further factors. First, the agencies might be numerous, but did they have enough qualified staff? Revenue and Customs, for example, recruited around fifty graduates a year as trainee tax inspectors, with starting salaries of £25,000 rising to £47,000 after five years: adequate in professional terms but only a fraction of what a city accountant could earn. Assuming a career of forty years, this gave an establishment of around 2,000, presumably supplemented by non-graduate inspectors. Even so, when Brown diverted 1,600 staffers to combat the carousel frauds in summer 2006, this must have caused upheaval in a division already targeted for major job losses.

Second, the impression was that current civil service entrants would find detection and enforcement gruelling in comparison with, say, expanding their outfit's publicity network: always knowing that a sideways move would open up well-paid careers in the firms with which they dealt. The effect on public service morale could be imagined. Constitutional patriotism was a mug's game.

VIII Before the Crunch

Taxation could actually become a furtherer of fraud, in the VAT fraud crisis that enveloped Europe in 2006. There remains a mystery. The frauds were on a huge scale, but after spring 2007 they were pushed off the stage by the collapse of securitisation. Allegations of mortgage fraud were reckoned to be a defensive tactic from finance firms suffering from downgraded sub-prime mortgage debt, which their dealers had accepted gratefully before departing with volume-related bonuses. This suggests that much input may in fact have been the product of fraud, with properties being sold by criminally financed fleeting consortia to mortgagees incapable of sustaining the payments on them. Profits of around 50 per cent were banked, usually in tax havens. But the journalistic coverage, though often sophisticated, rarely surveyed the problem on a comprehensive, synoptic scale; this did not improve in the drama and panic of full-blown crisis.

How do these situations occur? Not through corruption on a huge scale. Hans-Jürgen Kerner emphasised the fact that the able criminal is always in favour of the rule of law. He has nothing to gain by seeing the system he milks falling apart. He values the links he has with authority, because these ensure that the game will have rules for him to avoid. It is much more plausible that there are several factors at work:

First, a low-level but substantial crime industry, such as the
drugs business and money laundering in the West Midlands or
Central Scotland, incubated in the lacunae of Brown's less than
successful industrial 'strategy' and operating through a fourth
sector of scrap merchants, pubs and clubs, minicabs, security
firms, tanning studios and so on. This provides both the 'entrepreneurs' and a lot of untraceable cash.

Second, a City focus on profit and investment-attraction,
without much concern about the origins of the cash. Cue the
Goldman Sachs high-roller versus the chancellor on under
£150,000, the uncharted extent of private equity, and the
prevalence of 'instruments' and 'conduits' whereby speculative
capital was based on 'assets' which were increasingly 'securi-
tised' but might be bogus. The problem was that telling the
two apart was almost impossible, even in the computer age. At
this stage the terms 'sub-prime' and 'credit crunch' were still
unknown to the press.

Third, the regulators. They might supervise the ticking of
the compliance boxes but following this up meant having to
cope with low pay, confused lines of command (local, regional,
national, European and international) and low morale, even
before they were faced with a huge investigative burden like
carousel fraud.

Fourth, a small, overextended and hyperactive political leadership, which is continually issuing targets, reformulating policy,
and burying bad news. Its responses involve 'restructuring' –
which generates redundancy, new recruitment, painful learning
processes and the illimitable expansion of PR – and thus the
institutional strengths of continuity and solidarity are lost.

Fifth, sudden systemic crises which cause political leadership,
however powerful, to crack. Pressure of work means priori-
tisation, and intractable longer-term issues get sidelined until
they reach a critical mass and blow up. Back in 1916 Lloyd
George's brilliance as a munitions organiser beat the kaiser with
millions of tons of high-explosive shell; his later ineptitude in

the micro-politics of Ireland meant he lost to a scratch guerrilla force to whom the capture of a machine-gun was a famous
victory.[40]

Occlusion – failing to string these factors together – means
a misreading of government competence. A British Academy
group of economists admitted this in a memo sent to the Queen,
who had asked why no one had taken pre-emptive action:

> Everybody seemed to be doing their job properly on its own
> merit. And according to standard measures of success they
> were often doing it well. The failure was to see how collec-
> tively this added up to a series of interconnected imbalances
> over which no single authority had jurisdiction.[41]

5 Annus Horribilis, 2006–7

Gordon Brown has been unstinting in his support for this anthology, and without his agreement to quote from his speeches, there would be no book.

Wilf Stevenson, May 2006

I have found a flaw. I don't know how significant or permanent it is. But I have been very distressed by that fact.

Alan Greenspan, September 2007

I 'Be Brave, and Don't Steal'

It would have been odd in May 2006 for the chancellor to stint his support of *Moving Britain Forward*, his selected speeches, endorsed by the great and good from Alan Greenspan to J. K. Rowling. Its publisher was the firm revitalised by Harry Potter, its royalties went to a medical research fund in memory of the Brown's firstborn child Jennifer. Its cover was abstracted from the windows of Norman Foster's Swiss Re Building, the phallic 'Gherkin' which was the most Freudian object in the City, a far cry from the Clyde shipbuilders on the cover of the *Red Paper*. By then, however, the bloom was off the year.

For Brown 2006 started well. Blair, bogged down in Iraq, faced mounting opposition to further market-driven reforms from his own backbenchers. He was defeated over home security and only got his way over education with Conservative support. Brown didn't directly challenge on those issues, but made speeches (often through his John Smith Foundation) which ventured far into Blair's territory: British identity, foreign aid and security. The handover seemed only a matter of time. Then, out of a more or less blue sky, the first disaster struck.

Brown had neglected his Kingdom. The next-door Dunfermline West Labour MP, Rachel Squire, who had suffered for years from cancer, died early in 2006. An 11,500 majority seemed unchallengeable, but there were no recent Scottish opinion polls and Scottish Labour was shrinking. The UK party was down 50 per cent from the 400,000 members of 1997, along with its local government and trade union partners. Its tabloid the *Daily Record* still monopolised Scottish government advertising (£4 million a year) but it had shed its political correspondent the previous autumn. Under the trusty Tom Brown (no relation), it was a functioning speaking-tube between No. 11 and the grass-roots: the Scottish Labour 'family' celebrated at the time of Granita, in Brown and James Naughtie's book *John Smith: the Life and Soul of the Party* (1994) had weakened.

Brown had squired Greenspan round Kirkcaldy and appointed him, along with Bill Gates and Thierry Gaultier, as his advisers. But the new Dunfermline West candidate, Caroline Stihler MEP, was hastily 'evolved', and – heavily pregnant – looked too much of a shoo-in. There was wrangling over factory closures (the China import factor) and the overloaded, deteriorating Forth Road Bridge. Promising a new bridge, Brown trod on the feet of the Scottish transport minister Tavish Scott, a Liberal. First Minister Jack McConnell came over to help the campaign and was ignored. The majority vanished and the Lib Dems won by nearly 2,000 votes. Brown's command of Scotland was exposed as an illusion at the worst possible time.

The real winner, as the later Moray by-election showed, was the Scottish National Party. Alex Salmond had resumed the leadership in October 2004, and by late 2006 some opinion polls on the Scottish Parliament elections, to be held on 3 May 2007, saw the SNP beating Labour in both constituency and list seats. After thirty years, the *Red Paper* situation was back, but where were the paperers? Premier Gordon Brown would rapidly detect them on Salmond's side. Instead of the clever James VI out to cement the regnal union of 1603, he found himself, like the old Austro-Hungarian Emperor Franz Josef, facing the break-up of his dual monarchy.

Old Vienna had figured strongly in Brown's political apprenticeship. A working knowledge of Robert Musil, Karl Kraus and Joseph Roth was demanded by Neal Ascherson and Tom Nairn. In 2006, the centrifugal problem affected both Scotland *and* the City of London: as cosmopolitan as Vienna, and even less loyal to its political master than the Imperial Diet whose classical façade fronted onto the Ringstrasse. In 1993 Salmond and I stood in this huge arena, deserted since October 1918, where Serbs and Germans, Slovaks, Magyars and Jews once contended before the gaze of the ancient Habsburg. Vienna was something London culture had previously coped with. It absorbed two of *England's* greatest dramatists: Michael Frayn (in his 1977 documentary *The Mask of Gold*) and John Osborne. The latter had the emperor ask of the double-agent Redl: 'The man calls himself a patriot. But is he a patriot for me?' Brown had rarely bothered to ask, and by 2006 none of the London literati would even raise the question.

Salmond, also a social democrat and as clever as Brown, was determined to put an end to the imperial order. In this he was like the Reichsrat Deputy Professor Tomas Masaryk of Bohemia, founder and leader of the Czech Realist Party, whose advice Ascherson commended to the SNP: 'Be brave, and don't steal.' In 1993, heading the SNP in the Commons, he was visiting the new EU member state, and the headquarters of OPEC, on whose policies the North Sea oil business depended. He did not warm to the 'wee pretendy parliament' in Edinburgh in 1999, and escaped back to Westminster in 2001, but in 2006 he reappeared as leader of the SNP. We shall hear more of him as first minister, but also much more – and he would rather matters were different – of his former employer, the Royal Bank of Scotland.

II Old Adam

As chancellor, Brown tried to make his version of Adam Smith the centre of his public value system. The synergy of Kirkcaldy and the City of London was to counteract the strains in the Union. Smith's failures were in many ways as decisive as his successes, but Brown took an almost Orwellian delight in rewriting the past. One of the achievements of his guru, the historian Linda Colley, in her book *Britons* (1992), an exploration of post-Union Britishness, had been to reverse the thrust of her original area of study, the *North Briton* Scotophobia of John Wilkes in the 1760s, and insist instead on the Protestant–imperial solidarity of Scots and English. But neither Brown nor indeed Smith had really explored what 'nation' meant in *The Wealth of Nations* (1776). Smith unfairly criticised his mercantilist rival, Sir James Steuart, over that issue, but Steuart's economic interventionism would be taken up by Hegel, Friedrich List and later Lincoln's Republican Party.[1] He asked whether any nation could create the technology that economic equilibrium (let alone expansion) required if it was continually disrupted by free-market competition. John Ruskin said this about short-term notions of value in *Unto this Last* (1861), influential notably on J. A. Hobson and Patrick Geddes. The idea had reasserted itself in ecological economics following E. F. Schumacher's *Small Is Beautiful* (1973), though not within earshot of the chancellor.[2]

By 2006 the flaws in Britain's social economy were showing up. On Brown's own welfare patch, complex tax credits caused unending crises over billions of pounds-worth of over or under-payments for low earners. While big money sloshed about in the state sector, big waste reduced real growth in welfare. When the social sums were added up, New Labour's net performance tended to slip behind comparable states in Europe. Some of this was Blair's fault: the Afghanistan and Iraq wars, endless tinkering with education and health, dishonest patronage, and a tacky public culture. It was enough to make poor old Ramsay MacDonald look a paragon, staggering on and on and up and up, but still aiming to liberate India. But true to the spirit of Granita, Blair's chancellor had dutifully rattled the taxation-by-stealth tin and raided the budget till to keep him going. By 2006 this was prompting doubts about the value of Brown's longevity in office. Mrs Thatcher used to claim that she had occupied Downing Street longer than anyone since Lord Liverpool (1812–27), the man whom Disraeli always referred to as the 'Arch-Mediocrity'. Likewise, Stanley Baldwin dominated politics from 1923 to 1937, even when not actually premier, only to be abruptly and rather disgracefully disremembered by his own party.

The Downing Street soap opera took up much of the media year. Even in happier times, it had always been in the background. Brown relied on the Labour rank and file, deploying Blair's own tactic of 'triangulation' – matching him with an unacceptable face to enhance his own position. Blair took increasing risks to protect himself. But at the turn of 2006 there was a new Conservative leader, David Cameron. Cameron was by descent a 'Taipan' from north-eastern Scotland, and was even a remote relative by marriage of Brown: a young toff at Oxford, going large on Thatcher's bounty, he then became an assistant to Norman Lamont, after which he spent seven years at the money-mill of Carlton Communications. Cameron, only twenty-three when Thatcher went in 1990, could project a new image; he repeated the cultivated spontaneity that had beaten David Davies in October 2005.

He attacked Blair. Remarkably, Blair hit back effectively and the two charming toffs went ahead of Brown in the polls. Thinking back to New Labour's own rise in the 1990s, was it only a matter of time – and a 40 per cent Tory share of the poll – before big business deserted a Blairless Labour or simply banked its bonuses, cleared off to the Caribbean, and left the switch to a new generation?

Brown's luck had always beaten his talent. 'Prudence' in 1997–2000 had meant raids on tax relief, mortgages and pensions. Through the 'windfall tax' on public utility profits, fat cats paid for job creation programmes, though he lost out on rail privatisation (1993–7). The dot-com boom enabled him counter-cyclically to inject investment into the public sector. He couldn't have done this within the eurozone and the austerities of the European Central Bank. But he couldn't invest in technology either. The research, development and infrastructure weren't there.

Coordinators, compliance and outreach officers and their ilk were swallowing much of the additional cash for the NHS. The Milk Development Council's school milk facilitators seemed a bureaucratic version of Marie Antoinette's Trianon dairymaids. Where large-scale investment was needed to innovate, notably in hospital equipment or industrial training, the story had gone sour.

Retailing encapsulated the Brown enigma: a mix of fashion, advertisement, marketing and persuasion; smoke and mirrors triumphing over rationality. In J. K. Galbraith's terms, a 'culture of contentment' could be put down to lower unit costs of motoring, food and consumer goods: the North Sea oil, supermarket and China factors. Otherwise, manufacturing investment fell. Sir Terry Leahy, the CEO of Britain's rampant supermarket chain Tesco, was typically New Labour in piling it high and selling it (in global terms) dear, while damaging both the ecology and the local economy that fostered entrepreneurial activity. Quangos such as Jack McConnell's £500-million-a-year Scottish Enterprise, begun as a socialistic development agency in 1975, coexisted with big consultancies, eager for their £600 plus per executive per day. Just after the Dunfermline by-election several SE schemes plunged into the red, and the organisation effectively went bust.

III Luxury and Corruption ride again!

Under New Labour there was no continuity with the mixed economy of Tony Crosland, or even with the somewhat Gaullist version that was Thatcherism. As some wag put it with plummy vowels: 'All power is *marvellous*. Absolute power is *absolutely marvellous*.' Broon had gone for the American business model, heedless of the warnings of a fellow Scot, the Oxford economist Professor John Kay: 'The countries where systems most resemble the prescriptions of the American Business Model – unbridled individualism under weak government – are Nigeria and Haiti, which are among the poorest on the planet.'[3] Robert Taylor noted that although Brown had ticked all the boxes of regulation what was in place only *looked* strong at a distance. The result seemed much stronger on spin and hyperbole than on fact . . . 'a delusion, a mirage and not a satisfactory answer to the country's labour-market and employment relations problems.'[4]

New Labour's press allies had spun against Conservatives who were divided and underfinanced, badly led by third-rate examples of the failing local capitalism which Leahy had stuffed. Even the right-wing press – the Murdoch papers, the *Mail* and for a time the *Express* – praised premier and chancellor for being anti-redistributive and anti-European. Tory self-regulation had been a farce, culminating in the Lloyds of London collapse of the late 1980s and early 1990s, where establishment insiders screwed the credulous rich by offloading high-risk underwriting on them. Yet after Brown's 1997 bank reform, overworked and underpaid regulators couldn't cope with immensely wealthy PR-minded corporations and unscrupulous incomers. Gillian Tett summed it up:

> The main concentration of Structured Investment Vehicles was found in London . . . In keeping with the light touch mantra that drove British regulatory policy the UK government saw little reason to monitor what these entities were

doing. They were rarely mentioned in any official reports of the Bank of England or Financial Services Authority . . . the financiers had created a vast 'shadow banking' system that was out of the sight of almost everybody outside the specialist credit world.[5]

Brownite regulation was worse than cartels. A cartel means a single head, to be carpeted by the political leadership, or chopped off. But corrupt officials – or those who simply gave up – survived. In financial services this paralysis, according to Nick Kochan, pervaded the 'offshore island' in a similar way to European road haulage manipulated by giant international firms such as Betz or Fixemer: adding corruptibility in Eastern Europe, well-funded lobbying in Brussels, systematic political pressure from legitimate companies and straightforward graft, backed up by the best legal brains money could buy.[6]

Such behaviour was tolerated by a management culture that was asocial and grasping. An interlinked growth of international PR and legal consultants warded off challenges by consumers, the press and media. New Labour had deliberately cut itself off from its former trade union associates, in what proved a vulnerable fortress. In summer 2006 Blair was helping Scotland Yard with its enquiries about 'cash for peerages' and illegal party funding.

Yet Britain was still a state, and states, in Adam Smith's view, had a 'great deal of ruin' in them: the origin of 'too big to fail' and its twin 'moral hazard'. Brown as chancellor seemed to have taken over the staying power of Old Industry in the shape of lords Bernstein (Granada TV), Weinstock (General Electric) and Hanson (building supplies), but at the cost of Cabinet and parliamentary control: an old system that had coordinated and promoted younger, independent-minded ministers or MPs who showed talent. With New Labour in charge, the more numerous and younger the ministers, the weaker they got in a Cabinet now expanded to twenty-six. This kept up the payroll vote of MPs dependent on government (Salmond in Scotland got by with six), but the result, though surrounded by a publicity machine three times its 1997 size, looked 'like sixth-formers doing a project' wrote the *Guardian*'s Simon Hoggart.

In 'rigid' Germany, a tough European departmental reformer, the Green Renate Kunast in the Schröder Cabinet, shifted her agriculture ministry from a fixer for farmers to a consumers' champion. Whereas the British Culture Minister Tessa Jowell had a husband, David Mills, who seemingly without her knowledge was bagman to Europe's most ruthless media tycoon, Silvio Berlusconi. Brown's longevity in fact masked the long run that Jeremy Bentham's 'sinister interests' needed to bed themselves in. His true forerunner, Henry Dundas 'Harry the Ninth', bought and sold Scotland for decades at the turn of the eighteenth and nineteenth centuries. He could use imperial, military and kirk patronage as collateral; Brown had to pay with the institutions of the state itself.

The British type of social market was celebrated fulsomely by the 'bard of Britishness' just as it seized up. Now with weakening of regulation came a collapse of civic virtue and worry among 'traditional' Labour cadres about the progress made by illegalism. Voting was down to around 60 per cent in general elections and 30 per cent in many local elections. There were flaws in registration on an American scale, and abuse of postal voting with no *British* reform in sight. Due to weak political education, the British public, and in particular youth, knew more about astrology than politics. In Wales political knowledge was roughly proportionate to the Plaid Cymru vote, and abysmal in all but English Wrecsam. Devolution had worked its leaven, but in November 2004 it was overwhelmingly rejected in North-East England. Wide powers remained at a publicly unaccountable regional level of authority, however, while a (foiled) attempt to rationalise ministerial prerogatives through the Public Regulations Bill of 2006 made this look near despotic.

Brown's Britain showed the limitations of 'growth' and 'employment' as indicators of social capital. See the 'positive' statistics of education in PISA One (2000) and their dubious provenance. Or the catastrophic decline of the study of 'hard' subjects, such as modern languages and technology, as the student population was over-expanded to cut the unemployment figures. Education, like the NHS, was manipulated by PFI deals which shifted it, at least pro tem, off the balance sheet.

Public-private hybridity meant faulty processes and statistics. The American pragmatic tradition showed that the sloppy use of targets would produce chronic confusion and breakdown. PFIs only postponed the evil day, while government responses were rhetorical: targets, tsars, task forces, reassurances, sudden spasms of activity; all undertaken – spun? bad news buried? – to gain media coverage, not strategic logic. Institutions were fissured and lines of responsibility confused by devolution and Europeanisation. Civic 'hollowing out' was masked by an absence of civic fora and dwindling chances of fulfilled and demanding lives. The rhetoric often sounded good – Timothy Garton Ash's *Free World* (2004), aimed at the wristband generation, felt warm and inclusive, and was more self-critical than the chancellor – until you saw the surrounding environment.

Housing-turned-speculation made UK growth and civil society suspect. Foreign travel by cheapo-jet subtracted from weekend commitments as basic as running football teams and scout groups. The winners were also abroad – from Dordogne to Dubai, cruising with Thatcher millionaires – enjoying a quality of life that was utterly remote from sink estates around Sheffield or Glasgow, market towns like Llangefni made hellish by drugs, or the desolate, gang-run Muirkirks and Drongans.

Such lifestyles were interconnected, though the 'matter of Britain' was blurring. Between 1860 and 1930 adaptive, frequently Celtic politicians created the powerful industrial civil society of 'West Britain', held it together, and linked it by parliamentarianism, civics, and culture to the London-centric imperial core. Constellations of civics and goodwill reinforced this and locally generated bodies like town councils, co-ops, port authorities, railway companies, trade associations, trades unions and nonconformist churches: not perfect, but they had resilience and a remarkable degree of national coverage.[7]

Could this informal federalism recreate itself? No. Or at least not in terms of the combination of metropolitan oligarchy and ineffective provinciality that Brown represented. Cameron represented at best a rerun of the fresh-faced Blair of 1994–7, with suspect backers and an even more negative European policy. Something seemed to stand ahead of Britain which could resemble the implosion of the Christian Democrat and Socialist parties in Italy in 1993. And after that?

IV Culture and Diarchy

Brown's chancellorship had misfired. Its good years were down to the foot soldiers of the Labour party in the provinces: what Ralf Dahrendorf called *Bildungsbürgertum*, or Coleridge's 'clerisy' if you like: teachers, social workers, academics and public sector trade unionists. Spurned by Blair, they had turned to Brown: 'Gordon will see us right.' But by late 2006 faith in this solution was ebbing with the economy.

The Tony-and-Gordon act worked quite well in controlling scarce resources until the Iraq War intensified the central conflict and undermined the resilience of civil society. Brown attempted to revive it with speeches, but without success: the progressive decoupling of Scots and Welsh politics; the 'supermarketisation' which both sapped any possible SME (Small and Medium-sized Enterprise) revival and increasingly bit into ordinary working-class security; and the flowing tide of illegalism. After early 2003 and the invasion of Iraq, Blair purchased a brief access of power through tabloid patriotism, a deception of the British political community that caused the former British commander in Bosnia, General Sir Michael Rose, to threaten him with impeachment.

Brown treated Europe with near-contempt. Europe coolly evaluated the British economy. Airports, electricity, insurance concerns and property trusts came under the hammer. Of the continent's eight greatest electric power concerns, not a single one was British. Electricité de France (EDF), still partly state owned, was worth €81 billion; Eon, its nearest German rival, €66 billion: this indicated a future more Napoleonic or Bismarckian than globalised. If Britain started building new nuclear plants, few could doubt who would build them, least of all EDF's Head of Corporate Affairs, Britain – Andrew Brown, brother of Gordon.

The Euroneurosis of the English press (as ever, owned by right-wingers, eccentrics and – see Lord Black of the *Telegraph* – crooks) was the result of an increasing realisation that beneath the trapeze of Brownite economics and the relentless takeover activity of the City, there was no safety net. Globalisation was touted by Brown and friends as institutionally American, yet by 2005, in post-Enron accountancy terms, the future was European. Marks and Spencer, no less, found that a loss in France could be written off against tax liabilities in the UK, costing Brown several-score million with the prospect of more to come.[8] The selling off of British assets left an ever narrower industrial base, so that when the housing and retailing current weakened its grip, an *Umwälzung* or 'enforced restructuring' became inevitable.

V The Dark Horizon

Brown's net achievement as chancellor was unreassuring. Manufacturing was down by a quarter, its control largely shifted abroad. The cyber networks of the rich knew an ill-regulated economy when they saw one. Still, it took some time to register that bonuses weren't what stuck to the City's shovels. They *were* the 'thing in itself'.

The chancellor had been the custodian of the intervention-ist tradition of Beveridge and Keynes, but fostered it though London's 'turbo-capitalism', no longer reckoned as really part of Britain. Its increasing wealth (with CEO incomes between three and ten times those of Cabinet ministers) had no philan-thropic element: at every boom or slump the wealthy wanted more commercial raiding, bigger bonuses and quick exits to the sybaritic, un-civic, sealed-off world of golf, villas and yachts. The effect of this on the building-blocks of British civil society – the firm, academia, and the 'culture industries' – weakened the once-clever ethos which tamed the 'creative chaos' of Schumpeter's entrepreneurial capitalism. 'Bestseller' and 'lifestyle' values doomed the Britishness that Brown strove to revive.

Political disasters often occur on terrain prepared by multi-detailed breakdowns in authority, making the whole apparatus unmanageable. This could be altered (or at least reprioritised) by personal dynamism, such as Lloyd George winning World War I, or in a negative sense Thatcher, who started breaking up Britain up in 1979–1990. Or there could be a grass-roots 'civic' movement of the sort generated by World War II.[9] A new chal-lenge existed, particularly over the environment. But Blair and Brown weren't up to the demands, and nor was a civic realm which stressed the voter as customer over the voter as citizen.

A sequence of moves loosened the Broonite monolith even before 'handover day'. First, *spatial*: the property speculators who went in for cosmetic urban reconstruction, backed up by PR and 'partnerships' with government, gave up after 6 July 2005 and turned back to Olympic London. Without powerful local authorities, they had already failed the 'submerged third' of the socially excluded. Now, with urban civility stuck in the malls, essential but expensive infrastructure – water supply, flood control, sewage disposal and recycling – was neglected. In 2006, in the vales of Trent and Severn, nature delivered its revenge: the literal submergence of Middle England.

Second, *egalitarian*: Chancellor Brown's credibility as a silent, stealthy social reformer dwindled with the eclipse of Blair and the exposure of statistical manipulation on the government's part. The poor were there as passive recipients, and illegalism on both sides was to neither's credit. Promising initiatives like 'Sure Start' gave way to box-ticking: privileging the rich led not to the 'trickling down' of wealth but to widespread social irresponsibility. This morphed into downright criminality, less among the poor (many of them elderly or unhealthy) but in a white-van-man culture that was parasitic both on the non-civic wealthy and on the excluded.

Thirdly, *diplomatic-economic*: the orientation of the UK towards the USA rather than towards Europe. Brown forgot the American radicalism, from Walt Whitman to J. K. Galbraith, which had once activated the UK West Coast in which both he and Blair had their origins. This echoed only rhetorically in their New Deal, and didn't engage with American structural failures. It depended on individual mobility at the cost of the environment. It simultaneously invoked Social Darwinism and a fundamentalist rejection of the scientific method. Above all, Brown's Cape Cod spectacles distorted America's paradoxes: a powerful statism which ran far beyond the military-indus-trial complex; the Europe-mindedness of the US's centre-left, Harrington and Galbraith, Putnam and Rifkin. Britain's consti-tutional flexibility had once seemed exactly what a rule-bound Europe needed, but deindustrialisation made her look either incompetent or a practical target for takeover.

Fourthly, Blair's *involvement in Iraq*: rejected everywhere in Europe except by Berlusconi, this isolated the UK. Brown didn't quarrel with it, took no pro-European initiatives, changed no policies even when in the 2006 boom the recovery of German manufacturing was described as 'stellar' by the head of the British Chambers of Commerce. The 'America or Europe' dilemma was miniaturised in Brown's own backyard. Devolution briefly boosted the London and Scottish elite: Brown and friends

intervened disproportionately in the South. But deindustri-
alisation and Labour movement indifference bred social decay
and illegalism, while a reviving Scottish National Party under
Salmond claimed North Sea oil as it rose towards $150 a barrel.
Could there have been new semi-federal policies to counter this?
No. Nothing was built on the 1998–9 settlement.

Granita had weakened the constitution; the UKL had made
premier and chancellor bit players in a game dominated by
people on ten times their salaries. This weakness wasn't debated
because post-industrial media society functioned for elites who
had an interest in keeping things as they were: notably Rupert
Murdoch, in charge – perhaps only just – of his own empire,
and weirdly spanning Wapping, Wall Street and China. Some of
New Labour's other backers persisted for the good reason that
other parties and other countries would have thrown them to
the magistrates. Businessmen knew that loose business controls,
PFIs, patronage and tax privileges kept them above water. Blair
was naïve, trusting or simply casual enough to count on this:
every man had his price. The chancellor was different: his vice
was hubris, particularly his confidence that public control was
a matter of regulation, not ownership, and that once regulation
was agreed on and the correct boxes ticked, things would run
fine. The mechanics of appropriate and detailed supervision –
'European' and so duplicitous in contrast to the well-broadcast
(in English) certainties of the United States – persisted.

VI The Islanders

Diluted into tabloid form, Brown's problems led him into the
debacle of the June 2006 World Cup. He risked unpopularity in Scotland by backing England, yet probably felt the echo
of 1978, when a hyped-up Scotland went down in Argentina,
wounding the devolution cause. In 1902, faced with the cock-
ups of the Boer War, Rudyard Kipling had fulminated in 'The
Islanders':

> Then ye returned to your trinkets,
> Then ye contented your souls,
> With the flannelled fools at the wickets
> And the muddied oafs at the goals.

Britain couldn't even manage the trinkets any more. Analogies were being made between football and economics. Would foreign backing mean the sale of the last remaining tranche of high-value-added firms? Before the crisis of 2007, key transactions and solutions still appeared fiscal. Either continental firms, backed up by the EU and elements of the City, would buy up this debt, or the government would summon private investors and offer them unprecedented privileges for bringing it under control and ensuring the future of such institutions as the NHS. The alternative would have to be the creation of a European financial overlord.

Were there still ways of playing for time? Could Brown retreat to his promises of the early 1990s and do a deal with the Lib Dems, gaining them as coalition partners in return for PR and the end of the two-party system? This was no longer possible. Through his repetitive anti-Europeanism and his pronuclear, pro-Trident declarations, he had burned too many of his boats.

Did Brown ever consider what could have happened in 1997 if instead of stopping Robin Cook becoming Scottish first minister he had gone for the job himself? He had the health that was denied Donald Dewar, the intellect denied Henry McLeish, and a political imagination remote from Jack McConnell. Had he built Scotland into a model provincial regime, with a lively and competitive mixed economy, this prototype could have been sold to the English regions, and used to inspire Northern Ireland. Drawing on Scottish political strengths, he could later have shifted back into British politics, just as in Germany Willy Brandt and later Helmut Kohl made the transition from being *Länderfürsten* into federal leadership. Something of the sort was

laid out in his then ally Henry Drucker's *Doctrine and Ethos* back
in 1978, recasting Labour in a pluralist society. Had Brown
chosen Scotland, he would have had a challenge because of the
semi-proportional electoral system, but he could have built on
the Lib Dem alliance to lay the foundations of such a compromise on the British level. There might have been the risk of a
Nationalist runaway, but even McConnell had been able to get
on top of this.

In 2006, Brown allowed the SNP to become a real and
present danger. Its policy was firming up, increasingly focused
on independence, which would give it control over Britain's
oil. This, managed along with the Norwegians, still with plenty
of oil and a per capita GDP twice that of the UK, could provide
the collateral for Scotland's technical reconstruction: to promote
renewable energy. Polls showed that this prospect was increasingly attractive north of the border. What was new was English
indifference. The more Brown touted the Union as essential to
Scots prosperity, the more Mondeo Man regarded himself as
Scots-ridden.

Polls done in December 2006 showed a majority of Scots
wanting independence – and most English prepared to
concede it. Three hundred years of the Parliamentary Union
of 1707 awakened not celebration but murmurings of divorce,
should the Scottish elections on 3 May 2007 hand the Scottish
Executive to an SNP-led government. Alex Salmond's prom-
ise of a referendum on Scots independence might blow up
in his face if he were confronted with a Labour government
in London: a 'Quebec situation' in which Scots, with their
Labour traditions, might not nerve themselves to make the
break. But if his Downing Street opponent was Cameron?
How could Scottish Labour survive in these circumstances?
Then another discord sounded, one which was to go on and
on.

VII Carousel

In terms of creating positive social capital, Chancellor Brown had his limits. But what about Adam Smith's 'policeman state'? It would shortly face an unprecedented challenge; and *that* was only for starters.

In August 2006 Tony Blair headed off to Sir Cliff Richard's villa in Barbados for his holiday. John Prescott kept house in Whitehall while the chancellor spent time with his young family at home in Fife. On 16 August the press ran photos of the youngsters and their smiling parents. But this was an inside-page story: the headlines had the public convulsed by terrorist threats to British airlines, aggravated by security disorganisation at the main UK airports run by the Spanish-owned British Airports Authority.

The happy snaps were not quite enough to obscure another fact: that the previous day five hundred police and revenue officers had descended on sixty addresses in the UK and arrested twenty-two people, fifteen of them (apparently Middle Eastern) in Glasgow, on charges to do with VAT fraud.

VAT fraud was a tsunami which had been building up for years. Criminals imported small hi-tech items – mobile phones or microchips – free of VAT. They were then sold with a VAT charge, both avoiding VAT payment – 'missing trader fraud' – and reclaiming fictive VAT payments from the tax authorities through forged invoices. By 2005 the business had become a 'virtual carousel', directed to a great extent from Dubai. The items themselves never moved but the deals were done on a greatly increased scale with specially constructed computer programmes.[10] In June 2004 at Bridge of Allan, near Stirling, a businessman called Michael Voudouri was imprisoned for four years for a fraud of £3 million. This paled into insignificance compared with two hoods sentenced in July 2006: Clive Saunders, an organiser of 'entertainment security executives' (bouncers) in Stoke-on-Trent, went down for £68 million, and 'Riviera Ray' Woolley, another bouncer-boss from Stoke, for £38 million – out of a probable turnover of £555 million. There were rumours of a far bigger fish who had got out intact with a clear billion.

In August 2006 Scottish Labour's *Daily Record* reported that carousel frauds were reaping organised crime syndicates massive rewards and were less risky than running Class A drugs: 'Law enforcement agencies have seen an alarming trend recently whereby gangs involved in narcotics are switching their attention to such frauds.'[11] The impact of these frauds was by then immense. According to KPMG's head of forensics in Scotland, Ken Milliken, 'It's getting so big now that it is beginning to affect the country's balance of payments. £50 to £60 million a time . . . makes our overseas trade figures seem higher than they are, because of the same goods going around and around.'

By mid-August Revenue and Customs estimated that up to 10 per cent of the UK's exports were related to carousel fraud: 'The most recent estimates are . . . £ 1.1 billion–£ 1.9 billion in fiscal year 2004–5. But since then activity has increased tenfold . . .'[12] If the EU guessed at total losses of €50 billion (£34 billion) a year, equal to the entire cost of the Common Agricultural Policy, the chancellor's 'policeman state' had turned out to be the centre of this megacrime.[13] And so clever were the crooks at fitting into nests of legitimate import-export firms that attacks by government or European agencies ended with *them* under attack by aggrieved traders. Glasgow, already awash with drug dealing, counterfeit sales, and money laundering,[14] was scarcely forty miles from Brown's own constituency. Fraud in Scotland had risen 370 per cent between 1995 and 2005, but KPMG's Milliken reckoned that the £18 million then surfacing in the courts might reach a billion.

By mid-September 2006 there were quasi-official statistics. The good news was that in July losses through carousel fraud had fallen to £1.6 billion, thanks to Brown's doubling of Revenue investigators to 1,000. The bad news was that they had been running at an average of £3 billion a month until then. The total 2006 hit wasn't the talked of £1.9 billion – it might be £23 billion.

The UK's addiction to hot money and light-touch regulation had exploded: even without the VAT business, the Revenue was already losing £1.17 billion in tax credit fraud,[15] suggesting a Scottish hit of £93 million. Mack and Kerner's 'able criminal' was loose in Mack's native city, doing damage that Mack – and Eric Ambler, for that matter – could never have dreamed about.

Ashley Seager cast light on one Scottish mystery: Andrew Ramsay, a Glasgow accountant who on 22 February 2006 was 'arrested' by two 'fraud squad detectives' and driven off in a black car. He never reappeared. On 30 July the *Sunday Mail* announced that Glasgow police, under Detective Inspector Willie Prendergast, had closed the case. But its reporter, Norman Silvester, wrote that Ramsay 'told friends he feared for his life . . . He had unwittingly become sucked into a worldwide carousel fraud involving mobile phones, with links to Al Qaeda'. From 2004 he worked for a Glasgow firm and was sent to Belgium and later Spain, Dubai, Holland and Saudi Arabia. In January 2006 he was quizzed by Customs officers and told he might be a witness in a future trial; Silvester reckoned another £40 million might be involved. Prendergast was almost certainly dissimulating to keep the villains in situ pending the 16 August raids. The sums were huge and it was obvious that the incompetence of the UK government was responsible. The *Sunday Telegraph* blamed the unravelling horror on the EU, where the chancellor's indifference to Brussels's concerns had long been notorious. Yet even this seemed buried under another piece of larceny in the shape of the iSoft scandal: directors were helping themselves to cash intended for NHS computerisation out of a runaway budget of maybe £6 billion. The carousel cash was stupendous, but where was it going? Was it inside the British financial system, part of the remarkable rise in bank profits? Or was it within the international networks of private equity? Or in the archipelago of microstates and tax havens? Surely Brown (who by now had 1,400 Revenue agents on the case) ought to know.

On 21 September Iain Cobain and Ashley Seager, writing in the *Guardian*, claimed that since May 2005 the Revenue had known that billions from the carousels were leaving the UK via the First Curaçao International Bank (FCIB), a 'shell bank' of the sort supposedly squashed after the 2002 slump. Its turnover rose from $60 million in 2004 to $6.5 *billion* when the UK government closed it in mid-September 2006. Until August it had received factored cash through respectable banks, including Barclays. The last was UBS, as the 2,500-odd 'carousel hoods' among its British customers were all silly enough to plump for the same money launderers. Even then, provincial villains still ran rings round the Treasury's finest.

Back in December 2003 in his pre-Budget statement, Brown had claimed that VAT fraud, then estimated at £2.75 billion, was 'in decline'. From then until the 2006 Budget, there followed only generalities about strengthening legislation. The chancellor told the IMF conference in Singapore, held on 15–16 September 2006, that the government was 'getting to grips with the problem', but Bill Keegan, the senior economics commentator present, wrote to me on 21 September:

All I can say is that at the World Bank/IMF annual meetings in Singapore last month, one needed several hands to count the number of people who were concerned about the possibility/probability of a great Regulatory Failure!

On 29 May 2007 a decomposed head fished up in the Clyde off Millport was identified as that of Andrew Ramsay, but there was no further word of those arrested in the summer of 2006.

By then Gordon Brown was within a month of 'climbing to the top of the greasy pole'. Sub-prime lending was ramifying and might, according to BBC's 'Panorama', prove worse than in the US situation. Around a million UK householders were poor credit risks, yet they had received mortgages from such firms as London and Scottish Finance and Home and County Mortgages of up to ten times their income. The FSA response to the latter's adventures was a fine of £50,000, the mildest of slaps on the wrist. By mid-2007 light-touch regulation would go very sour indeed, dimming the resonance of 'prime minister' and questioning Brown's whole achievement.

VIII Farepak for Christmas!

Within days, trouble came from a quite different direction. Two months before Christmas 2006 the Farepak Hamper/ Voucher Company collapsed. This hit at least 150,000 ordinary folk, robbing them of nine-tenths of their Christmas savings. *A Christmas Carol* in reverse, it seemed to show the UK's vice of hypocrisy in fine shape, with vintage performances from the neighbourhood of the Treasury. On 23 October, ten days after Farepak went into administration, Trade Minister Alistair Darling admitted that it was 'a matter of great concern' that families had lost millions – £40 million was computed – and announced a departmental inquiry. Since the affair was now *sub judice* he could remain quiet with a good conscience – and has done so, ever since.

He didn't have to explain that the writing had been on the wall for almost four months, since the beginning of July when the share price of Farepak's owner European Home Retail fell from 40p to 16.5p in a day – and *this* was down from almost 110p in December 2005.[16] EHR's shares were suspended on the stock exchange on 23 August: six weeks before the crisis broke. Why? Darling didn't bother to ask, since hamper schemes were savings and not credit ventures – and were therefore not regulated. EHR, however, was no obscure fly-by-night operation but the firm whose Kleeneze products had been a fixture of British homes for decades; good quality kitchen products sold by trusted local agents – often the same people who collected cash for Farepak. Its chairman was Sir Clive Thompson, formerly CEO of the Rentokil conglomerate, and in 2000 a notably combative chair of the Confederation of British Industry, 'the bosses' trade union', and close to its General Secretary Sir Digby Jones, scarcely a shrinking violet. His response to the collapse was to go on a luxury holiday to Argentina. Jones would become trade minister in Brown's first government in July 2007.

EHR was in funds in 2005, and Farepak, effectively a bank that didn't have to pay interest to depositors, was its cash–cow. EHR had used it to bail out some disastrous speculative acquisitions (notably a company called DMG, bought in 2000 for £35 million and sold in 2003 for £6 million), borrowing £17 million from Farepak. Why did it plunge? The question was one of accountants' sleight of hand, not straightforward crookedness, or of greed by EHR's bank Halifax Bank of Scotland (HBOS), which had just posted £5 billion in profits and seemed prosperous.[17] However, the bankruptcy in February of the gift voucher business that Farepak used, Choice Gift Vouchers, following the failure of another company, Family Hampers, broke the credit chain that had always governed such businesses. Vouchers would have to be bought up front and EHR hadn't the cash. Farepak was a belated casualty of the disastrous festive season of 2005, compounded by witless insensitivity at boardroom level.[18] Or so it seemed at first glance.

From July 2006 the government had had plenty of warnings and plenty of time in hand. There was certainly enough time for one Farepak director, William Rollason (earlier a colleague of David Cameron at Carlton Communications), to sell himself on, along with most of Kleeneze, to Findel plc of Bristol. He had earlier been responsible for withdrawing Farepak from the Direct Selling Association to avoid having to insure against the sort of disaster that actually occurred. And there was certainly time for HBOS to drive its own interests and get its money back from the receiver at the expense of the unfortunate Farepak savers, who were kept oblivious of their fate until the deal was done.[19] All this while, however, it was unclear that the government was doing anything at all, despite the chancellor's ultimate responsibility as regulator of businesses.

Farepak had a particularly strong presence in Scotland and Northern England, a relic of the benefit clubs which had preceded the trade union and co-op movements (which suffered in their time from a tendency of the treasurer to abscond with the cash: hence the Friendly Society and Trade Union Acts of the 1870s). Would Darling's inquiry find out what, in all this, the Treasury had been up to, because business regulation was one of 'Gordon's things'? A looming financial disaster for 150,000 householders could have immense electoral consequences – to put things at their crudest. But *sub judice* meant that comment was closed. Out of sight meant out of mind, and if one googled 'Farepak' after December 2006, the entries were few. Instead, the inquiry morphed into a general discussion of 'Financial Inclusion' carried out by the Office of Fair Trading. When the Treasury published it on 27 March 2007 it was ignored, though HBOS got publicity for its own 'hamper scheme'.[20]

Even the start of the credit crunch in September, with Northern Rock savers queuing round the block to get their cash back, didn't conjure up the name. By then Brown had reached the top of the greasy pole, Alistair Darling had succeeded him as chancellor, and the other respected and respectable polls were approving. The outlook, however, was grim: at best, a slowing-down of the house-price retail driver which had been pushing the British economy along. At worst? Did the high risk strategies of the government, and Brown in particular – in 2005 and 2006 he welcomed the vast sums that sloshed into the City in flight from post-Enron American prosecutors and from Russian Mafiosi – bear uncalculated risks? Did all of this not place an uncoordinated and overstretched regulatory system under unbearable strain, of which the Farepak folk were the first and most innocent victims?

The financial journalist Nick Kochan had written a sympathetic study of Brown's first year as chancellor, but in 2005, in his American-published study of money laundering *The Washing Machine*, the tone had changed:

> London increasingly looks like an offshore center serving many dubious financiers while at the same time claiming to have regulations which put it among the world's top onshore jurisdictions. . .
>
> But London's vulnerability lay not just in its laws but in their implementation. Government failed to invest in sufficient skilled law enforcement officers or regulators to curb its sprawling financial system. But this is no accident. The UK's economy cannot afford to curb its income from the 'invisible' financial sector while its industrial sector becomes anorexic. As the UK feeds its addiction to finance and hot money, its regulators bluster ever less convincingly about the security of its financial system and its antipathy to money launderers.[21]

In late summer 2006, while the Farepak crisis was quietly unravelling, the Treasury and Revenue had been obsessed with the 'carousel' frauds. The Serious Fraud Office was already reckoning with being overwhelmed in 2005. Such was the jam of cases that mistakes and aborted inquiries were inevitable: 'Anyone swindling less than £1 million will probably get away with it, and even those cheating a larger amount have the odds stacked in their favour.'[22]

Under Brown, there had been unending makeovers of a failing system, resulting in a chaos of competing quangos, with the Serious Fraud Office falling over the Financial Services Authority, Customs and Revenue, the Competition Commission and the Office of Fair Trading – to name but a few, and still omitting European Union bodies and the police. Unsurprisingly, a survey of fraud by two regulation barristers, Jonathan Fisher and Jeremy Summers argued that the system was completely dysfunctional, its personnel demoralised and in decline.[23] The number of fraud investigators had fallen from 869 to 600 between 1995 and 2003. 'The buck stops with Gordon Brown,' they concluded, with the carousels in mind, but this was only one fissure in an earthquake of financial collapse. Weirdly, Farepak anticipated sub-prime lending – but from poor people to a sub-prime company, an over-speculated bank, and their wealthy and well-connected owners. Were conclusions being drawn? We have accumulated enough evidence of serial industrial failure. Bad enough. But what of the chancellor as the policeman of the economy, a role he made much of in his encomia of Adam Smith? The old savant was continually leery of 'luxury and corruption' and 'conspiracies of merchants'. The chancellor was, in comparison, indulgent. As part of his savings strategy in Whitehall, Brown was cutting Revenue and Customs staff by over 12 per cent and closing a third of its offices.

Of particular concern was the situation at HBOS in 2004 where the Group Risk Regulator Paul Moore believed that risk assessment had broken down, and reported in these terms. In early December he was dismissed by Sir James Crosby, who had also been, since January, a non-executive director of the FSA, appointed by Gordon Brown.[24]

A detailed inquiry into HBOS's High Risk Department in Reading, 2005–7, found what could only be called large scale fraud by officials and consultants. Having lost £20 million on a company called Magenta, and £113 million on Corporate Jet Services, the manager Lynden Scourfield resigned in mid-2007. There was a culture of market-winning, but not of risk assessment; there had been no oversight of this by the board following the dismissal of Mr Moore. Vince Cable, the Lib Dem spokesman, commented on his own unsatisfactory dealings with HBOS: 'We do need to get to the bottom of this. Why there were failures of supervision. Why the directors didn't do their job.'[25] At this point, in the spring of 2007, there were the beginnings of City-wide suspicion that the HBOS banking strategy might not be cast iron. Head of Corporate Lending Peter Cummings was investing heavily in the private equity projects, particularly those matadors of property and retail: Sir Philip Green, Robert Tchenguiz, Sir Tom Hunter, Sir Frederick and Sir David Barclay, and Jon Asgeir Johanneson of Baugur. But in mid-September 2007, with Brown only eight weeks in power, all eyes were on Newcastle . . .

6 A Handful of Dust, 2007–9

I divide mankind into three categories. The first is us ordinary folk, who as children stole apples or stuck supermarket chocolate bars in our pockets, and that's about it. The second sort have minor criminal tendencies. The third are investment bankers, up to now more or less licensed evildoers.

Ex-Chancellor Helmut Schmidt, 21 May 2009

And I will show you fear in a handful of dust.

T. S. Eliot

I Charting the Disorder

Brown's Bible Class moralising about Britishness, Heroes, and Civic Courage in books and speeches wasn't rhetoric. In ocean liner terms, if Blair had been the charming captain parlaying the rich passengers in first class, Brown was the solid MacAndrew of the engine room. In 2007 he believed he had clambered from there to the bridge of the SS New World. Partly the result of Cape Cod and tutorials from Larry Summers; partly Churchillian: hadn't the half-American Winston admired Jimmy Maxton? Partly Judeo-Christian: the Rev. John Ebenezer Brown was a Zionist, a good introduction to Sir Ronald Cohen and the private equity entourage brought on board after January 2005.

For Brown the acceptable face of the City was the tax income he derived from financial services: in the Victorian radical-turned-imperialist (and American enthusiast) Joe Chamberlain's words, 'the ransom paid by great wealth'. This was linked to the ideology of Labour Australia: Charles Pearson's forecast of the Asiatic future of manufacturing, steered by welfare and service states. The 'White Australia' Labour movement, Scots-led, had been publicised by Keith Murdoch, father of Rupert, and President Theodore Roosevelt was another Pearson disciple; his ideas passed to his nephew Franklin. After 1945 Japan was incorporated into the USA's own co-prosperity sphere.

But now Brown looked out at the grey seas ahead and was less secure. He had let Scotland drift. Devolution had backfired on Scottish Labour; if the SNP vote *and* Southern taxpayer discontent rose, the Union was at risk. His Granita role had been too specialised. He hadn't Blair's skills – in dissimulation as well as diplomacy. In normal circumstances the transition would be difficult enough, but extraordinary things had happened.

The 1997 handover of Hong Kong was for the British an imperial terminus. But to the Communist Chinese it was part of a well-prepared industrial acceleration: they had sent thousands of students abroad and invested heavily in capital goods. In this they were further assisted by US fiscal policy, which drastically cut interest rates after the dot-bomb in 2001–2. Chinese profits were invested in US government bonds. 'Leninist capitalism', the property of the butchers of Tiananmen Square, whose repression in 1989 spurred East Europe into successful peaceable revolt, now underpinned the Western free market.

This was half the equation. The other was scarcely perceptible, even to the banking magnates who formally 'owned' it. In Anglo-Saxon capitalism property prices had been rising for two decades, buoyed by population and household expansion and finite private land. Adam Smith would have seen this as self-limiting and conservative: property would check consumption, or devour itself in investment bubbles. But the post-1989 situation provoked the search for 'more efficient markets' which would, thanks to efficient computers and their use to 'securitise' debt, mobilise latent property value. New investment vehicles converted illiquid assets, such as houses and their mortgages, into tradable commodities, a practice first worked out by bright youngsters working for J P Morgan in the mid-1990s. Computer programmes enabled them to calculate the proportion of 'super-senior' assets – denoted 'Triple-A' by the credit ratings agencies (CRAs) – needed to guarantee less realisable sub-prime mortgages, then to bundle the lot together to generate illimitable credit.[1] The problem was that the decline of the firm had weakened the networks of personal contact and trust founded on it, and replaced them by international real-time communication and constant transaction. This weakened the cohesion of firms, leading to loyalty by bonus and a reversion to pre-industrial tribalism.

What hit this strange coalition in 2007 and 2008 was more than financial crisis. It was the cyclical, speculative slump of 1929, sharpened by environmental, health, communications and juridical crises. The information, exchange and transportation revolutions made for economic shifts and worldwide effects as well as encouraging drug trafficking and pandemic infection. These provoked attempts to mediate or reverse change which were strongly regional in nature: notably religious revivalism and cults of charisma and celebrity. Brown's success in the UK became contingent on such unpredictability.

Markets were, however, challenged by new goals of regionalism and empowerment. Neoliberalism waned in the Euro-American region, with Chavez's 'Bolivarist' revolts in South America and ecological regionalism in Europe. The culture of the transnational company, once seen as a benign complement to regional self-government, now looked as flawed as any Central Committee: a conduit for oligarchic or third-world corruption. An Indian 'salaryman' for, say, the accountants KPMG was as far from his peasant cousin in terms of income as KPMG's London CEO was from his cleaning lady.

Terrorism grew out of religious revival, post-industrial political anomy, and the increasingly desperate attempt of industrial powers to insure themselves against Peak Oil. The West retaliated by reviving venerable geopolitics, not just Pearson but

Halford Mackinder's 'heartland' – centred on commanding Iraq and Afghanistan. International crime and religious fanaticism made use of the new technology. Defence-based nation states followed the Soviet empire and broke up as their minority peoples sought corporate self-government, and the rich fled from a turbulent civic life in another reversal to pre-industrial ordering. Eyeing their situation in conditions of extreme inequality, encouraged by rogue intelligentsias with the organisation if not the beliefs of the communists, the poor took their revenge in a terrorism that emphasised destruction and punishment. Orwell's Eastasia in *1984* had as ideology a death cult, probably his take on Japanese kamikaze pilots: 9/11 made the revenge of suicide bombers into a 'normal' risk.

The view from the bridge was both ominous and baffling. In fact confusion gripped nearly all the accounts of the financial disaster, not least because the usual containers of 'national' control were subverted by the flows of capital and, indeed, of orthodox manufacturing. Gillian Tett's *Fool's Gold* succeeded because she was an anthropologist, and used her expertise in 'pre-historical societies' to analyse a group – securitisation specialists – who, while at the cutting edge of financial innovation, acted as a tribe. Adam Smith appealed to Brown; his less idealistic friend Adam Ferguson of Raith, founder of social anthropology, of 'in-groups' and 'out-groups', might have been a better guide.

II Banking on Independence

So start with an election in a small European country. Not fanciful because Scotland was obviously central to Brown's Britain in an otherwise totally anomic maze. And the key to the place was arguably less Holyrood than the Scottish banks. They stood at the beginning of 'civilisation': a term coined in Smith and Ferguson's Scotland to describe communities governed by civil rather than criminal or feudal law. There was a conflict here, resembling party divisions but involving the banks that featured two models of Scotland's future.

The Bank of Scotland was founded in 1696 by William Paterson, after he had founded the Bank of England in 1695. It was intended partly to finance the Darien colony. The disastrous consequences of this imperial venture would underlie the economic drive to Union in 1707, which Paterson backed after financial concessions were made. But the Bank then fell into Jacobite hands, so in 1727 the Hanoverian Whig Party set up the Royal Bank of Scotland. Joint stock banking was thereafter strong in Scotland – and important in its industrialisation – where outside the Bank of England the practice was banned in the South after the excesses of the South Sea Bubble of 1722.

The Royal Bank was the great survivor, when the seven banks of 1914 had dwindled to three by the 1970s. In 1980 it, along with the entire Scottish establishment, resisted a takeover by Standard Chartered; under Conservative politician George Younger and Charles Winter (a no-nonsense Dundonian promoted from the ranks), it rose to respectability as a 'bankers' bank', handled much privatisation business, and expanded in Europe and China. One of Winter's protégés was Alex Salmond, the Royal's oil economist between 1980 and 1988, and under Sir George Mathewson (a notably explicit patriot), it became the 'nationalist' bank. In 1999 the 'Bank' (the affectionate term for the Bank of Scotland) merged with the Halifax, the biggest of the ex-building societies, to form HBOS. It was the 'unionist' bank, deeply involved in the housing–retail 'synergy'. Its Edinburgh-born chairman, Lord Stevenson, figured in the New Labour penumbra; its former general manager, Sir James Crosby of the Halifax, was another Brown friend.

At the cusp of 2006–7 Salmond was planning the Scottish general election, slated for 3 May. He challenged in the Liberal seat of Gordon (using Gladstone's 1879–80 Midlothian Campaign strategy of combining personal and national victory). His powerful propaganda campaign was backed by

prominent businessmen, notably Mathewson and Brian Souter
of Stagecoach, while still offering a social democrat agenda.
Edinburgh was Europe's second-largest financial centre, in terms
of financial services offered, and for such highly political reasons,
a place where Brown's light-touch regulation over banking was
in principle appropriate, though both he and Salmond would
stretch it to its limits.

The six-week campaign was hard-fought, with the SNP
spending most for the first time. In previous campaigns its propaganda had been amateurish; this time things were different. The
swing it achieved (from twenty-seven to forty-seven seats) was
considerable, and largely at the expense of the Scottish Socialists
and the Greens, who fell from thirteen to only two MSPs.
Labour held forty-six of its fifty-two seats but with the introduction of proportional representation it lost heavily in local
government, retaining majority control of only two authorities,
Glasgow and North Lanark, and most of its system of patronage and local power disappeared. The Liberals, losing two seats,
were demoralised. The Conservatives didn't budge.

Salmond's coup came on 16 May 2007. He formed a minority government, calculating that by seizing the machinery of
power while maintaining party unity, he could consolidate the
SNP advantage. Labour, which in Wales took Plaid Cymru as
a partner, obliged by sulking in London; Salmond's links with
Gordon Brown remained minimal, though they were good
with Dublin, Belfast and Cardiff. Coalition governments, for
example those in the 'cooperative federalism' of the German
Federal Republic, usually compromise on spending policies
– 'Of course *I* want to oblige you, but my partner won't let
me.' A minority government hasn't got that excuse; and in the
autumn Whitehall's Consolidated Spending Review was severe.
Salmond aimed to build up a populist momentum by freez-
ing local taxes, reprieving hospital departments, granting rates
rebates to small businesses, and ending tolls on road bridges. He
cut Scottish Enterprise and Highlands and Islands Enterprise,

probably inefficient and certainly pro-Labour. While Brown faced an inflation crisis, Salmond emphasised key areas of divergence with Westminster, first constitutional and then economic. On 14 August he published *Choosing Scotland's Future*, an independence white paper, beginning a 'National Conversation' which would continue until a referendum in 2010. A long shot, though oil rising past $100 a barrel made people realise that independence might disturb good relations with England and Europe less than the status quo, while federalism didn't count. London got on better with 'independent' Dublin than with Edinburgh or Cardiff.

Were the Conservatives to keep their *English* lead – and in 2007 this trend had lasted for several months (their Scots poll was rarely more than 15 per cent) – a confrontation with Scotland was programmed. An independence referendum, problematic against Labour, might succeed against a Cameron government. And what if the Scots business classes could be won for independence, by using the collateral of high oil prices to finance exploitation of Europe's main centre of tide and wave energy? A prestigious Council of Economic Advisers was set up on 29 June, including Oxford's John Kay and Frances Cairncross, and Ireland's Frances Ruane. Mathewson was in the chair. In Scandinavia, banks were the link between independence and economic manoeuvrability; in Finland, constrained by Russia up to 1989, they provided a shadow foreign service. No wonder they figured in Salmond's 'arc of opportunity': Ireland, Iceland, Norway, Finland.

III Riding Two Horses

Salmond and Brown had explicit intentions, but their constitutional instruments in Edinburgh and London had never been tested by political divergence. There was another model of political coordination. Connexity, the integration of social thought and political action, was made much of by Geoff Mulgan and

Charlie Leadbeater as the motor of post-industrial society, though it played down the problem of 'squaring interests': what politics was about. It fitted more snugly into the command politics of high finance, Chinese Communism/Leninist Capitalism or (*pace* Mack-Kerner) criminality than into the *Rechtsstaat* of social democracy, with its agreed and lengthy procedures. For Big Money in tax havens, things were simplified.[2]

What if Big Money thought taxes could be avoided full stop? In the light-touch order, would the rich throw in the towel, play the game, or call up their corporate lawyers? Surely a no-brainer: like the USA's Robber Barons of the 1890s, the likes of Lloyd Blankfein of Goldman Sachs argued that record profits validated them – 'Doing God's work!' – and that any serious assault would bring the structure down on everyone's ears. Such notions were closer to Ayn Rand than to Adam Smith, and as the money-mill ceased to grind, the appeal of cashing in grew. In retrospect the huge bonuses of 2005–6 did not signal success, but looming calamity.[3]

Samuel P. Huntington's 'clash of civilisations' thesis (1993) was useful here, stigmatising organisations competing with Western finance as inherently toxic. This showed the same logic uncovered by Richard Hofstadter in *The Paranoid Style in American Politics* (1964). Knowing itself to be perfect, a USA on George Dubya's drip feed of post-alcoholic religious primitivism, fortified by ex-Trotskyist New York Jewish realpolitik from Irving Kristol and friends, still fitted obliquely into Brown's Calvinist world view. He was the instrument who would police the wealthy and moralise them.

Yet Brown's London was already challenged by the astonishing Dubai, whose exotic real estate was keeping the London architectural giants in employment and ambitiously pumping cash into the London Stock Exchange and private and sovereign equity funds. Attempts were made in late 2007 by a committee under Sir David Walker to regularise this new wealth, with the growing sub-prime crisis in mind, but by then risks were turning into breakdowns. The moral issue posed by this new type of finance was dramatised by Hans-Jürgen Kerner: the car company which found one of its models was periodically lethal, but decided to let it go ahead on the grounds that the cost of lawsuits was less than the costs of production-line modification. This decision was not inherently different from the calculations of the intelligent criminal with a good attorney:

> Rational planning and preparation, the power of emotional detachment, the practical intelligence and management efficiency are attributes of professional crime in Germany and England; the descriptions of these operations are like those that fit legitimate business and remind us of the thin and often unclear line between legal and illegal enterprise.[4]

Once put 'reasons of state above the rule of law' – decisions that happened increasingly on Brown's watch as chancellor – and subsequent actions come easily. 'Moral hazard' had been christened. Strictly, it meant skewing 'market' decisions in the expectation that the state would bail you out; more generally it meant finance professionals undermining legal controls to profit by 'asymmetrical' (insider) information. Once political society had winked at such distortions, it became easy for the evil-doer to avoid its sanctions or threaten it with exposure. Dodgy expense claims, family favours and falsified accounts ultimately became chessboard pieces.

The London-centric compromise that appeared in the 1990s and was perfected by Team Brown incorporated two-thirds of Mack and Kerner's model: globalisation and computing. Worryingly, the UK was potentially rich in the third element: tax havens. Brown condemned the SNP in the 1970s for wanting a Scotland based on niche businesses – oil, whisky and tweeds – and finance. Team Brown updated this to combine the connexity of the think tanks with the dynamism of a benign, computer-enabled 'invisible hand', which was enthusiastically clasped. The naïveté came in believing that favours for the rich would bring reciprocity and breed Carnegies who would apply their great wealth, George Soros-like, to constructive social purposes. In the USA they did (or seemed to do: Bernard Madoff was a great giver), so why not here?

Charity started at home, funding the Labour Party. As premier, Brown could not alter Labour's dependence on great wealth. Henry Drucker's moderate fundraising schemes had been replaced by Lord Levy, who between 1996 and 2006 raised £40 million for Labour, most of it as undisclosed loans, against a total income of £5 million in 1995 and £6 million in 1996. In 2001 Labour spent £11 million on the election alone.[5] Brown's own economic strategy, beginning with the fancy finance of PFI and the New Deal, was directed by cheap credit and the housing-retail driver, and he assumed that power would come with growth. In 2000 this looked plausible. Manufacturing Germany was growing only slowly, as was France; manufacturing Japan wasn't growing at all. Britain's record, by the accepted (essentially American) standards looked good, and with the USA diverted into overcoming the 9/11 trauma, the UK had *Spielraum*.

But Britain didn't elevate or educate, cultivate or even socialise this. Post-modern irony didn't truly reinforce an elite that seemed to find it both profitable and fun to be technically backward, vulgar and intellectually lazy. This seeped into the highest-paid levels of the establishment, notably literature, journalism and the BBC. Such an establishment – from Laureate Sir Andrew Motion and the BBC's Mark Thompson to Jonathan Ross, Russell Brand or Jeremy Clarkson – didn't denote poise or security. But for nemesis to turn up, one big institution had to go off the rails.

IV From Mainwaring to Madoff

In 2006, the Swiss *Neue Zürcher Zeitung*, which made *The Wall Street Journal* look like a comic, reported on Scotland. It exposed

Glasgow's knife culture and blew cold on the SNP's desire for independence. The main feature was on the Royal Bank's ascent from high street to world leader. Banks had traditionally been restricted in their lending by the fact of being limited companies. Under Thatcherite privatisation they became leading innovators, funding the privatisation of British Telecom, British Gas, the electricity boards and the water companies, and providing mortgages for council tenants. The RBS was at their head.[6]

There was a lot of hot money around, and a chance to absorb and deploy it thanks to computing and tax havens. Until the mid-1990s the windfall profits of semi-monopoly private utilities were barely checked by regulators, but as competition increased, the big payoffs dwindled, and many companies were anyway controlled from abroad. Utility privatisation hadn't revived manufacturing, as Mrs Thatcher's enthusiasts had predicted. Training and research were instead ruthlessly reduced, and by the mid-1990s, orthodox options had narrowed down to defence and PFI-based construction, where protection yielded big returns – and real estate. The last was the real earner. A London house bought for £40,000 in 1984 was worth almost ten times that amount by 2005. In Germany the equivalent rise was only about 20 per cent.[7] Tapping this wealth, something not mentioned at all in *Where There Is Greed* (1989), became the main vehicle of government policy. This was in turn driven by the growing numbers of households in an increasingly fragile society. There were 1.9 million households in Scotland in 1990, 2.6 million in 2005. Marriages and families broke up, and the damage was limited in the middle classes through increased space and effectively a different sort of house (or, in many cases, houses).

In Euroland property had limited attractions; not so in the Anglo-Saxon world. By the 1990s it had become a panacea: the route to post-work affluence for all. The privatisation of housing created an interest in restricting supply in order to increase price. The wrinkly with his half-million flat in 2005 wouldn't ever be caught up by a young man starting out at the latter date. This wasn't something that dawned on 'the neoliberal luvvie' tendency like Ralf Dahrendorf and Tim Garton Ash, who might have been Germanists to trade but dissed Euroland whenever they could.

British banking was the animator. It had been personified up to the 1970s by Arthur Lowe's Captain Mainwaring in *Dad's Army*, a stuffy lower-middle-class branch manager. Later to be downgraded to 'debt counsellor', his function was a socialising one, dating from the inter-war years when retail banking was outdoor relief for the middle classes along with small town society's lawyers, clerics and bureaucrats. In the 1980s the façade remained (under Thatcher, neo-Georgian drove modernism from high street and housing estate) but its inner workings were revolutionary. Computers brought a new vocabulary of cost and profit centres, replacing the specialised functions of the old banks. Comprehensive digitalisation saved millions, and the new order of online accounts and call centres (the dividend from which was never passed on to the clients) caused profits to soar into the billions, ready for the further adventures of investment banking. In this, the Royal Bank led the field.

But study of banking practices post-Big Bang showed they hadn't improved, and Anthony Seldon's symposia on the Blair era scarcely mention them. Dominic Hobson's pro-market *The National Wealth: Who gets What in Britain* (1999) was long (1,350 pages) and partisan, yet gave the impression that (a) your money would be safer in a sock under the bed, because everything that would go wrong in 2007–9 had a precedent in the 1990s; and (b) that few of the big hitters named in 1999 would still be around in 2009. The *Guardian* found that time at the top had dropped to about five years for CEOs – the bigger the salaries and bonuses, the quicker they cleared off. Nor were accountants immune: Arthur Andersen exited in 2002 after it signed off the American megascam Enron's accounts.

Elsewhere in the City, beneath the elaborate 'instruments' and 'vehicles' with their global reach, things were visceral among the candidate rich: the analysts who surveyed the investment landscape, and the altogether more feral traders, who made the bids. The first were from the old universities; the second often from the East End. For both, scruples were optional and the late eighties had been year zero: read, though circumspectly, Geraint Anderson's *Cityboy* (2008)[8], adapted from his regular blog in Murdoch's *thelondonpaper* and so the cyberage equivalent of a Dickensian part work. Cocaine in industrial quantities transformed the *necessary* nerd and after £2.5 million he could continue the good life in Tuscany or the Caribbean. Why hang on? 'London's pernicious financial world reveals itself in all its ugliness' said the *Mail*; 'A necessary and valuable book', said the *Standard* – and they should know. Few women figure outside lap-dancing clubs, though trophy wives could cash several million by winning a strategic divorce settlement; the cash as aphrodisiac theme of the earlier New York *Sex and the City* (1998–2004). This was a different order from the policy wonks and munchkins who kept the Clintons and Blairs and Browns up to speed; but the latter had to be paid (however sparingly) so the City's credentials weren't rigorously queried.

Into the Square Mile and its outliers in Mayfair and Canary Wharf flowed looted wealth from all the continents, from African or South American dictators and drug barons, Russian or Chinese *nomenklatura* and the Mafiosi. These sidelined the careful organisation of pension funds by dull lawyers, sapped by Brown as chancellor in an act of uncreative destruction described by Peston in one of his best chapters.[9] Frequent conversions of mutual funds, hyped through member-into-shareholder gains through Initial Placing Offers (IPOs) on the stock exchange, typified supposedly 'reforming' governments whose voluntary supporters had long ago cleared off. They looked solid, but by 2009 not a single 'mortgage bank' survived independent.

This was the world of the *Weekend FT*'s 'How to Spend It' supplement, which cooed over hotels, yachts, watches, etc. London, more than anywhere else, was the centre of this, though the statistics were sketchy in the extreme, because so little was in fact paid in taxes. It was only connected to the political structure of the UK by its servitor the government, obsequious under Blair, boorish under Brown, incompetent and ineffective under both.[10] When the Financial Services Authority had tried to get its act together in 2003, fining Lloyds TSB over the losses suffered by investors in split-capital bonds, it was condemned by the Tories; the 2005 election result, which saw Labour losing twenty seats in the South-East, accounts for the chancellor's adoption of a similar rhetoric. There was no morality here, no sense of obligation, sympathy or duty. No sense even of statistical truth to be obeyed: streetwise conservative American political science in the Bush years was cleverly elevating 'stories' over 'statistics'. So when environmental issues constrained orthodox industrial expansion, and demography pressed on social welfare, the legitimate repertoire of gain narrowed.

British journalists loved 'scientism' – transforming analogy into an organising metaphor which looked like science. In the New Labour age, 1997–2009, the popularising of genetics and cybernetics created apparently new systems of comprehension, as well as dynamic sources of income. Computers could still be burdens rather than benefits, breaking down or wiping files. But once installed, they generated a need to be used. They provided a virtual market where information was apparently limitless and complex financial deals might be broken down and analysed in the same way as hits on Google, which after 2000 became a sort of global registry of accessibility and influence.

The joint-stock limited-liability bank had been constrained by its constitution from going universal. In a timely tract, *Frozen Desire* (1997), James Buchan (grandson of John, whose father was a victim of the City of Glasgow Bank in 1878) warned that the costs of universality were like pre-limited liability, in which shareholders were liable for their proportion of the bank's total debt. In a manufacturing society, profit was limited by the supply of credit. But if economic expansion rode on house-price increases, and loans enabled demand to be kept up, feeding growth by creating new house-buyers was a gain for (a) bankers, and (b) early entrants into the house-price stakes. The boom spread sideways into commercial property, retail and leisure, and created more banks – the demutualised building societies. The Brits made short-term killings on this and buy-to-let flats, in crisis in 2004 (too few tenants) but in recovery by 2006 (600,000 East European migrants). At every stage the winners banked extraordinary bonuses for fixing deals.[11] Hedge funds – essentially bets on the boom continuing – had reached £2.5 trillion in the summer of 2008, and 89 per cent of them were based in the remaining British colonies in the West Indies.

Just as Brown was about to enter No. 10 a new finance genre started to make waves, personified by a thirty-two-year-old black man from a Leicester housing estate. Damon Buffini probably became the public face of private equity because he was quite different from its usual performers – although similar to the USA's coming man, Barack Obama – and it was chasing the hedge funds as the cutting edge of new investment. This was a rerun on a far larger scale of a thirty-year-old phenomenon, dating from the 1972–4 boom and associated with Jim Slater and Peter Walker (later a very wet Tory minister), which used low interest rates to enable 'highly leveraged' (heavily debt-financed) takeovers. Groups like Buffini's Permira then 'rationalised' their captures, piled them with further debt and consultants' fees (like lawyers, but getting richer by taking even fewer risks), and set off on new conquests. Their streetwise manoeuvrability attracted further investment until by early 2007 private equity was behind every third takeover, with buyout funds up from $300 billion in 2005 to nearly $700 billion. Through Sir Ronald Cohen, Brown had a ringside seat of mutual value to private equity and New Labour's funds.[12] More exotic and when you thought about it, more worrying, were the youthful Icelanders who had used the 'carry trade' to borrow cheaply in low-interest Europe and invest in Icelandic banks where, because of the *weakness* of Iceland's tiny economy, the interest rate was 12 per cent. They then used this as collateral to raise cash for sweeping takeovers on the UK high street.[13]

On 27 June 2007 Brown announced a Council of Business Leaders to advise him (an idea borrowed from Salmond's Scottish Council of Economic Advisers). Buffini was among its eight members. The others were: Sir Stuart Rose, Marks and Spencer; Tony Heywood, BP; Sir Terry Leahy, Tesco; Arun Sarin, Vodafone; Stephen Green, HSBC; Sir John Rose, Rolls Royce; Mervyn Davies, Standard Chartered; and Jean-Paul Garnier, Glaxo. Anyone from the railways, renewable energy, or the SMEs (Small and Medium-Sized Enterprises)? Dream on . . .

And all this time, and for over thirty years before, Bernard Madoff of New York had been working his hedge fund through the oldest scam in the book – a 'Ponzi' based on attracting suckers (including Nicola Horlick, the RBS, Elie Wiesel and numerous funds for Holocaust victims) by paying them out of the capital subscribed by earlier suckers, and getting his books audited by a couple of old guys in a downtown block.

V Everything for Sale

The UK's trade deficits were countered by encouraging, or not preventing, FII ('foreign inward investment'): holding up the value of the pound by letting companies be sold to foreign concerns, either directly or via private equity. In 2005–8 these included most of the grand firms Jeremy Paxman had chronicled in 1992 in *Friends in High Places*: Pilkington Glass to the Japanese; Corus to the Indians; ICI to the Dutch; the great Hanson conglomerate to the Germans; BAA to the Spanish;

House of Fraser and various other high-street names (including, oddly enough, Iceland) to various Icelanders.

Inwards came the East Europeans, efficiently doing jobs Brits either wouldn't or (increasingly) couldn't do. At the other end of the scale, grand oligarchs brought in cash, few questions asked. In the UK and the USA career criminals moved fairly effortlessly into mortgage fraud, the goal of laundered 'safe' money often justifying losses. Besides increasing near-market drug production (cannabis and amphetamines) in empty properties, illegal cash was profitably rolled over and supplemented either by, or alongside, bankers wanting to inflate their bonuses, get out while the going was good, and live indolently ever after. The police were left far behind, as Joe Murphy, ACPO's specialist, told the *Economist*: organised crime 'has fallen somewhere between the demands of counter-terrorism and neighbourhood policing.'[14]

There is still a lot we don't know about bonus boys as well as hoods: how many exited successfully? Who were they? What did they buy with their loot? The answer lies in luxury house prices (something which made the ordinary householder complicit). The determined social historian would find the following of interest:

> the stately home Meaford Hall, a helicopter, yacht, two other properties and a number of prestige cars including an Aston Martin, Ferrari and two Bentleys. His Rolex watches and diamonds . . . are also subject to the confiscation proceedings.

These surfaced at the trial of Craig Johnson, carousel fraudster to the tune of £132 million and seemingly par for the lifestyle course. Add random goodies from cuisines, wines, racehorses, gardening, entertainment, tailoring, couture, and the arts . . . while remembering that this case took five years to complete, and that under £6 million was recovered. The bulk seems to have gone into 'property ventures' in London.

Philanthropy through donations was always a useful insurance. Sir Tom Hunter exited the *Sunday Times* 'Rich List' after
a £50 million profit in 2006–7 became a £190 million loss in
2007–8. In August 2009 he owed the banks £453 million on
advances made by Peter Cummings of HBOS to buy property
at the top of the market. He claimed that he wasn't actually worth
anything, and pledged to give his fortune away as a Carnegiean
philanthropist. He remained in Monaco but sold his house.

Brown himself fitted even less into London finance than he
had into the Scottish Left thirty years earlier. He seemed, George
Rosie found, to devolve City business to Ed Balls, content to
accept everything that the arbitrary tides of international transactions brought in, without developing any strategic 'police' other
than the Keystone Kops of Canary Wharf. He still kept Rupert
Murdoch on side, although the alliance of 1997, when the *Sun*
switched its Scottish support from the SNP to Labour practi-
cally in mid-sentence, was now fraying. Their Free Kirk was in
its element when confronted with the English hoi polloi. This
combined David Hume's 'sensualism' with Calvinism: ordinary
humanity gratified itself through private satisfactions, bought
through supermarket culture – food, fashion, sport, sex, mobility – which the tabloids expertly catered for. Its ethics were
quite different from the judgmental 'how we carry ourselves' of
Donald Dewar's patriotics as the Scottish Parliament opened in
1999: something that appealed to older identities.

The balance of payments deficit, domestic and trade,
increased throughout the New Labour years. The rise in oil
prices aided UK income, but this was sapped by the cost of
keeping troops in Afghanistan and Iraq – at least £20 billion
for both, 2003–13 – which Brown paid for without complaint.
Imports were cheapened by the 'China effect', giving at least the
illusion of affluence. If it was difficult to distinguish between the
genuine and counterfeit at the point of purchase, long life no
longer mattered. See the impact on the British high street and
note the effect of alcohol and drugs on the nimble entrepreneur.

Such Brits as were not on the property-retail driver (and for that reason often abroad on Ryanair or EasyJet trips, or going to second homes) grazed like aphids on cheap clothes and fast food. With 75 per cent of men and 56 per cent of women overweight, the Great Briton was becoming a distinctive breed.

Patriotism seemed to work in the smaller nations, so, buffered from reality by a sagging Labour organisation, Brown invoked Britishness energetically after 2000, although when combined with the 'London effect' of a self-obsessed media this aggravated problems elsewhere.[15] The UKL's financial power had huge conceptual voids, and a flood of commercialese made individuals flee from unverifiable information. In Brown's case, sales rather than analytical skill counted: Andrew Roberts, Niall Ferguson and Simon Schama being 'bestseller history' just as Jeffrey Archer was a bestselling novelist. Brown's puppets were no more convincing in UK terms.

But 'The Simpsons' were. The series was one of Murdoch's icons: the Abbot of Unreason in half-hour jolts, subverting the *Sun* because it was relentlessly funny and even radical. It was post-Wall, post-mall: sophisticated commentary, somewhere between Nathanael West's *A Cool Million* and Beckett's *Waiting for Godot*. Homer was ageless, brainless, working for C. Montgomery Burns, a seemingly indestructible robber baron, drinking Duff's witchpee, inhabiting a hicksville which periodically impinged on world politics and what claimed to be culture. In a weird way 'The Simpsons' validated Thatcher's 1988 claim. There *was* no society, only individuals (however mad) and families (however dysfunctional). Whether Homer prospered with figures around him like Krusty the Clown, Mr Burns, Sideshow Bob, Mayor Quimby or his owner Murdoch was another matter. But great financial concerns worldwide were only too eager to lend him all the money he fancied, Homer being sub-prime incarnate. He was also less dumb than the boards of RBS and HBOS, who hadn't a clue about the implications of their 'instruments'.

Homer's world was more secure than that of the Scottish Broons. On Hogmanay 2008 Brown and Salmond first-footed the *Sunday Post* brood at Glebe Street: not a hoodie among them, or a shell-suit in sight. Something of the sort actually happened – Brown took to cold-calling voters to ask about life, etc. – but this was British public life viewed by a press culture that was shrivelling because of online editions, blogs and the collapse of house prices. To post-industrial Scotland and its post-rational redtops, the vanishing of Madeleine McCann on 3 May 2007 mattered more than the new Salmond government. Still in print and portentous was Dr Charles MacKay's *Extraordinary Popular Delusions, and the Madness of Crowds*, which the editor of the *Illustrated London News* wrote in 1841 between the first and second railway manias. The Dutch tulip mania (which he largely invented) was there, and the South Sea bubble, and Galbraith dipped into it for *The Great Crash*. MacKay fathered Marie Corelli, godmother to British bestsellerdom. Its taste in fiction, from barking to zany, was still havering away as the UKL-registered *Titanic* steered towards the edge of the world.

But one UK advantage seemed to come to the rescue. While cash from real estate bankrolled shopping and Far Eastern manufacturing, the bonanza drove commodities trades from $70 billion in January 2006 to £235 billion in April 2008. Oil left its $10-a-barrel level of 1999 and soared. By mid-2008 it stood at nearly $150. Britain's North Sea oil income floated up and Salmond and Brown competed for it. Oil inflation, however, levelled a gun at overinflated, dubiously financed real estate.

The credit ambitious lenders like Britain's Northern Rock had been offering marginal borrowers, with loans of up to 120 per cent, depended on the extension of securitisation. In early 2007 the growing cost of energy caused the sub-prime clients to default, and investments unravelled. According to Gillian Tett: 'When this new breed of sub-prime borrowers walked away from their homes, they often left them in such a bad state that it was hard for lenders to realise any value from the repossessed properties.'[16] Mortgage fraud was often coupled with people trafficking or drug production, behind which lay organised crime. The Mafiosi were no longer hoodlums but 'into real estate'. Such hollowed-out assets, worth, say, 40 per cent of their book-value ('mark to market' became the voice of doom at this point) dragged down the 'super-seniors' as the housing boom evaporated. The Sarbanes–Oxley Act in 2002 made many dodgy operations migrate to London or the British tax havens, lured by light-touch regulation and the proven UK ineptness at doing it. They were aided by credit ratings agencies – Moodys, Standard and Poor – being overgenerous, if not worse: in 1994 the con-man hero of the erudite Professor Paul Erdman's *Zero Coupon* reckoned them fair game because they were unregulated. Erdman's books were almost instruction manuals on how to get away with it. On the basis of credit ratings, the gigantic monoline American International Group (AIG) had insured the lot.[17]

In 25 July 2007 Northern Rock's pre-tax profits were up 26.6 per cent to £346.6 million. But the CRAs had already spoken, turning gold into lead, or Triple-A ratings into junk bonds. Its shares started sliding on 13 September 2007. The Rock had played the securitisation game enthusiastically but now the loans had dried up, so queues of depositors tried to extract their savings – something not seen since the City of Glasgow Bank collapse in 1878. The Rock reassured customers by printing 'Rock Steady' on the jerseys of Newcastle United's players. But its mortgages were held in another Jersey, in a St Helier-based vehicle called Granite, and despite government assistance their value went over a cliff, falling from nearly £7 on 10 September to under £2 a fortnight later. By early November the rescue had cost Chancellor Darling £20 billion. Would the Royal Bank of Scotland, whose takeover of the Dutch ABN Amro made it fourth biggest in Europe, help out?

'We predict . . . more plaudits for Sir Fred as he again defies the odds. Scottish business is well-served by a banking sector that is ever more sophisticated and responsive,' *Scottish Business Insider* grovelled in December 2007, casting the runes for 2008. RBS had a remarkable board keeping Sir Fred Goodwin up to the mark: Peter Sutherland, ex-EU commissioner; Jim Currie, former head of Customs and Excise; and Sir Steve Robson, late of the Treasury. Despite the Rock, they felt that housing would stay stable. Their late-2007 due diligence on ABN was cursory, but it was further into securitisation than anyone else.[18] RBS rescued its ABN takeover with a £12 billion rights issue in spring 2008, though with a struggle. A £4 billion rights issue by HBOS in July failed, leaving it dependent on the wholesale market. Why had the government not intervened? Was Brown worried about Scots complaining of London intervention? Or was he considering it?

The truth took time to emerge. HBOS's finances were even worse than AMRO's. Its corporate investment arm under Peter Cummings didn't just lend to businesses in the now-plunging construction and retail sectors; it bought into them. Out of a loan book of £116 billion, £69 billion was reckoned to be risky.[19] Was this the reason for HBOS's reluctance to bale out the honest savers of Farepak two years earlier? European Home Retail had been one of its speculations, while the career of HBOS's 'High Risk' investment arm in Reading ended in a £500-million fraud.[20]

VII Dead Sea Fruits

Brown became prime minister on 27 June 2007. With characteristic insouciance Tony Blair rapidly became a Middle East mediator *and* a Catholic *and* a $30,000-a-night performer on the rubber-chicken circuit *and* a £5-million pensioner of the New York bankers Morgan Stanley. Ed Pearce's 'half-an-inch deep' man evaporated, or seemed to do so. Brown's initial gestures were conservative; including a photo shoot with Alzheimer's-stricken Margaret Thatcher at Downing Street. No one could work out why: a by-election in Glasgow impended, where Thatcher was loathed beyond the point of mania. Then on 30 June two would-be suicide bombers drove a van packed with explosives and petrol into Glasgow Airport. This might have been deadly, since airports float in kerosene gas, but baggage staff stopped them exploding it. Both Salmond and Brown rushed to praise the heroes.

Brown got the bonus because John Smeaton, the most media–friendly of the handlers, turned out to be an old-fashioned, Rangers-supporting Scottish Unionist. Conservatism had a role in the Brown scheme of things: his PhD had found that crises drove the working class right, not left. The first reverberations of financial eruption were, however, audible. Moody's downgrading of structured funds to junk-bond level meant that banks had become increasingly averse to lending, and savers realised that their deposits in things like money-market accounts were only guaranteed to the first £10,000. The Rock's troubles – no one wanted to buy it – would drag on until 18 February 2008, when Brown and Chancellor Darling had to nationalise it.

The Brown government had been enjoying record support in the polls; but what had seemed a shoo-in general election was halted in October by David Cameron's rhetorical rally at the Tory Party conference. This was the second time (the first was when he was unexpectedly made leader) the young millionaire had used a device otherwise found in rather sentimental Jimmy Cagney gangster movies: 'I'm just a liddle guy, an' I'm doing dis for all the udder liddle guys.' And so on, to great effect. Tory support shot up, and on 5 October a rattled and awkward Brown 'bottled out'. Labour's poll ratings fell, and by early 2008 had hit a twenty-five-year low.

In 1998 Brown failed to augment state pensions and voters were indulgent; on 14 May 2008 he abolished the low 10 per cent tax rate and they were not. House prices were starting to fall and inflation was increasing steadily, a dangerous mix in a debt-dependent economy. This led on 1 May to the resilient

Ken Livingstone being defeated in the London Mayoral election by Boris Johnson, ex-editor of the *Spectator* and a colourful Tory toff of the Cameron totem. In Wales, once a Labour fiefdom, revolts cut the party down to only a couple of local authorities and in Scotland there was a minor revolt by Brown's usually obedient ally, Labour's new Scottish leader Wendy Alexander: her démarche – 'Bring it on!' – favoured Alex Salmond's scheme to hold a referendum on Scots independence. Her own party harried her on expenses for her election campaign and on 29 June she resigned. How bad things could get had already been shown on 22 May when, after the death of the Old Labour institution Gwyneth Dunwoody MP lost her safe Labour Crewe and Nantwich seat. With Brown's approval ratings at 15 per cent, the party hit a sixty-five-year low on 1 August.

But the Tories had yet to rival Blair's 61 per cent poll rating in 1997 (their 2009 Europarliament results only registered an increase of one point to 27 per cent) or assemble a war-chest on Labour's pre-1997 scale. This was probably because City winners didn't bother with politics except as a flutter. Cameron's shadow Cabinet was valued at £42.8 million. Party paymasters were the spread-betting oligarch Michael Ashcroft, valued at £1 billion, whose empire was located in the tax haven of Belize; and Michael Spencer (£250 million), whose currency trading companies were supported by complex loans. Stanley Fink, joint treasurer and now partner of Tony Blair's benefactor Lord Levy in ISAM, had grown the hedge fund Man until it was worth £118 million, but its value fell by over a fifth in 2008–9.[21] Had an elaborate superstructure had been erected on something resembling thin air? This fate had already struck the Liberal Democrat Party, which was backed in the 2005 election to the tune of £2.6 million by Michael Brown. The supposed bond dealer based his fortune on a £36-million fraud, and cleverly skedaddled before his trial in spring 2009.

Among the few *prominente* who kept the faith in Scotland were Brown's two literary neighbours, the crime writer Ian

Rankin and *Über*-novelist J. K. Rowling. As Lehman and HBOS collapsed and millionaires left Labour in droves, and the brothers from the trade unions turned up with invoices for their support, on 19 September 2008 Rowling presented Labour with a £1 million donation: Harry Potter and the Great Clunking Fist. Yet, like Thatcher fighting off Kinnock in 1985, Brown had hit a 'known unknown': bottom. When the full horror impacted, only days later, his fortunes had only one direction in which to go, and that was up.

VIII Falling Apart Again

The roots of the problem which presented global finance with its greatest ever disaster have already been detailed, along with the 'occlusion' that made them appear like F. A. Schumpeter's 'creative chaos', and not the financial world breaking loose from its moorings. After the dot-com bust in 2001–2 and the Enron and WorldCom trials, the magnates were being challenged. The Mr Hyde market-rigging element in Bill Gates's Microsoft or Intel was being pursued through the courts by, among others, the EU, for $100 million. In the City a small number of 'activist' investors, analysts and dealers were moving, as political scientists would put it, from 'voice' to 'exit' before the roof fell in. A classic case was the aggressive London estate agent Foxtons, sold by Jon Hall to Bank of America in July 2007 for £370 million. Within months its actual asset value was perhaps £20 million.

Post-Thatcher capitalism looked like J. K. Galbraith's 'culture of contentment' in 1950s America, replicated in the focus groups of New Labour. But something – the *ci-devant* revolutionism of many New Labourites – carried on the dynamism of Marxism, if nothing else. Capital, once liberated, knew no bounds and destroyed all relationships. Nowhere was it more visible in its sheer naked power than in London. Given their audience, the likes of Robert Peston had to impute usefulness to what had been going on: it was better, they said, than the institutional paralysis of the 1970s. This clashed with the Richard Layard/ Andrew Oswald view that the values of society had relatively little to do with affluence and much more to do with culture and trust. Little of either was visible in or around Downing Street.

In early 2006 reports started to emerge in the USA and the UK of defaults on 'sub-prime' loans, which had been marketed to rent-paying suckers by 'mortgage consultants' paid in proportion to their success in selling the things. On closer inspection, these were often means of recycling criminal activity; as Nick Kochan had forecast, the giant Citibank Group was cited as a leading activist. Wall Street and the City regarded 'toxic' loans as: (1) a small drop in an ocean of healthy finance; and (2) adequately guaranteed by the 'securitisation revolution', the fruit of a couple of decades of Chicago-schooled, Nobel prize-crowned research on markets. Now people began to talk about the 'absence of transparency'; far from the good cash outweighing the bad debt, the latter devalued the lot. This was a game of 'pass the parcel' on a global scale.

By 2007 high-leveraged hedge funds were quitting property and switching to commodities. Citibank was in trouble because of the bigger and more ruthless Goldman Sachs, which didn't care for property; instead it was clever at 'shorting' suspect finance firms (i.e. 'borrowing' shares and offering them cut-price to force company value down, buying low and cleaning up when it rose again). The crisis was given a particular bite in the UK by a failing military financial complex, bogged down in Iraq and Afghanistan, where Blair's 'blood price' of conquest turned out to have been the easy bit. Rudyard Kipling, who knew the place, once wrote:

> When you're wounded and left on Afghanistan's plains,
> And the women come out to cut up what remains,
> Jest roll to your rifle and blow out your brains
> An' go to your Gawd like a soldier.

There was a hellish symmetry here. The squaddies were in Helmand to crush those responsible for 9/11. But heroin from Afghanistan continued to flow westwards to render still more wretched the post-industrial areas they came from.

In early 2008 the disruption increased, with a Presidential contest in the USA in which the Iraq-inflicted implosion of the Republicans was matched by 'the audacity of hope' of the Obama Democrats. On Wall Street, Monday 17 March saw the Bear Stearns investment bank (worth $170 a share in 2007) taken over at fire-sale prices ($2 a share, later upped to $10) by J P Morgan. In London on 15 April Brown called in the banking CEOs and pumped out £50 billion to ease loans, and shares sorted themselves out a little, but the pressure on investment houses on both sides of the Atlantic was now unrelenting, and it rose to crisis point in September. Britbloke knew AIG only as the logo on Wayne Rooney's red jersey; its insurance strategies (which had backed the 'securitisation' bubble: all these triple-A credit ratings) were now being reassessed by the agencies and the Securities and Exchange Commission.[22]

Why had people acquiesced in what would be seen as 'robbery by bonus'? At the end of 2008, Manchester City, owned by a former Thai premier, was set to pay €110 million to InterMilan for 'Brazilian superstar Kaká'. On the assumption that their activities were 'earnin' fuckin' millions for England', City boys were placed on a similar pedestal, helped by expressing obsessive interest in football, supermodels, and fast cars: a commonwealth of bling.[23] The assumption was made that this was all necessary to the national cause, and when – as with Farepak – this wasn't the case, the press moved on.

To the UK's trade deficit, however, was added inflation – overtaking economic growth – and the problem of the Union, which came back on stage in May. The Crewe defeat was the prelude to another Scottish crisis: on 24 July Labour's second-most secure Westminster seat, Glasgow East, would vote. 'This could be the most important by-election ever', wrote part-Scots

Martin Kettle in the *Guardian* on 4 July. In the 1920s the seat had been held by Maxton's colleague John Wheatley, the father of the dull but reliable 'council schemes' which housed 52 per cent of Scottish households by 1982. In 2005, this had fallen to 15 per cent, with a further 12 per cent renting from housing associations. This implied Blairite modernisation, and indeed parts of the constituency were cheery and hopeful. But Calton Ward was an anthology of despair: fast food and short lives; endemic crime; drugs; and the counterfeiters' paradise of the Barras, said to turn over £2 billion in fakes each year. David Marshall MP had treated the place as private property and cleared off. His local party was catatonic. The SNP, running a local Baptist lay preacher John Mason, though quartered in a snazzy car dealer's catering for Celtic players – 'If ye want the toilets, they're on the left at the Lamborghini' – were well organised, well fed and expectant. On 24 July they won on a 22.5 per cent swing (enough to give them a majority of Westminster Scots MPs). Alex Salmond was triumphant but contrary to Kettle's expectations, Brown survived, only to face another by-election at Glenrothes in the Kingdom of Fife.

Perhaps Brown's own channels told him that elsewhere in Scotland things were getting rocky for the Nats and their 'arc of opportunity'. RBS's Citizens' Bank subsidiary in the USA was leaking cash: it posted an $8 billion loss in April. HBOS had a sharp young CEO, Andy Hornby, who had come from Harvard Business School via Asda's clothing chain George and believed supermarkets and banks were interchangeable – remember Howard the singing bank teller, if not the Farepak failure? The Royal had only just pulled off its rights issue in May, but after the Bear Stearns imbroglio in the USA, and with house prices slithering, HBOS's attempt could only cover 15 per cent of its needs. It had to go to the wholesale bankers, and run the risk of being shorted. 'Banks have tightened lending standards in the repurchase market, where cash is borrowed against hedge funds and others', the *FT* had observed in the spring.[24] This meant a summer in which the securitisation balloon steadily deflated and share values fell. On 15 September the grand American investment bank Lehman Brothers, under such a hybrid attack, exhausted the patience of the Department of Commerce, which had made saving AIG its priority. Hank Paulson let it go bankrupt. Only hours later speculators, tasting the blood in the water, turned on HBOS.

Things accelerated very rapidly and Downing Street moved in. Lending between banks had already become difficult, as sound banks feared cash flowing into hopeless cases and becoming irrecoverable. Interest rates had fallen to below inflation, but effective 'interbank' or 'libor' rates of interest went high and stayed there, despite central rate cuts. Further shorting drove Hornby into talks with Eric Daniels, the Chinese-German-American CEO of the smaller Lloyds TSB group, whose low profile (but much higher salary) concealed a long stint with Citibank, schlepping cash out of Chile and Argentina in the days of (and for) the dictator Pinochet. On Thursday 16 September the pair announced a planned fusion, and within hours it became known that Brown had been in on the negotiations through his City allies Sir Victor Blank and Lord Dennis Stevenson since the beginning of the week.[25]

This didn't help either bank. The disappearance of HBOS provoked hostility from Salmond and Holyrood and the Edinburgh financiers, led by Mathewson and Sir Peter Burt, HBOS's former general manager. The *Financial Times* approved their stand until the charnel house of HBOS's loan book was revealed. But the housing market closed down, with experts forecasting falls in property values of up to 30 per cent, and the knock-on effect on car purchases and shopping kicked in. In the USA General Motors would follow Citibank on to Skid Row. Far from Darling's rescue of Northern Rock closing the issue, nationalisation became one of the few weapons Bush or Brown had to hand. On 28 September Hank Paulson put a $700 billion bailout to the US Congress, literally on his knees before the dissenters: Democrat left and Republican right. The House of Representatives threw it out on 30 September, and the damage could not be repaired before 2 October. The consequences became tangible: for investors in bank shares (often charities and churches); for back offices, builders, small businesses and road hauliers. Private equity bids would collapse from $700 to $200 billion in 2008 and were under $20 billion in the first half of 2009. In 2008 hedge funds registered their worst year ever, with a capital decline of 17 per cent.[26] The bears had descended on the Goldilocks economy, snacked on her, and were off to find their main course.

It became apparent just how flawed were the ramifying skeins of indebtedness, particularly the CDS – credit default swaps – which supposedly underpinned the 'financial engineering' and 'more perfect markets'. The stability of RBS was by then crumbling as fast as that of HBOS (its valuation fell from £75 billion in July 2007 to £6.2 billion in late January 2009). With the lack of understanding of the products it had been buying, the ABN Amro takeover had been suicidal.[27]

By 13 October RBS was in state hands and Sir Fred Goodwin had left with the most controversial pension deal in British economic history. The Irish chat show host Terry Wogan observed that none of the main actors had trained as bankers. He had: Goodwin was an accountant who had won his spurs at Touche Ross investigating the bankruptcy of the Bank of Credit and Commerce International – *the* scam of the 1990s at $20 billion – between 1992 and 1995. Had this acquaintance with villainy bred a misplaced confidence that he knew the ropes in this complex rigging?

On 11 December Bernard Madoff would surrender himself to the New York authorities, admitting liabilities of $65 billion (over $500 million of it from Goodwin's RBS) and saying, 'There is no innocent explanation.'

X On and Off the Summit

> And how can man die better
> Than facing fearful odds,
> For the ashes of his fathers,
> And the temples of his Gods?

Thomas Babington Macaulay's 'Horatius' would still be recited in St Bryce's Manse. It is a great democratic poem. The Grand Whig was, after all, a Lewisman by descent, like Alistair Darling, and probably related to Sarah Macaulay, the future Mrs Brown. With the worst poll ratings in memory, facing the key by-election on 4 November at Glenrothes, Brown galvanised himself with greater determination than any other Western leader. On 23 September, having backed a new generation of nuclear power generators, he sold British Energy to the state-owned Electricité de France, and on the 28th he took over the threatened Bradford and Bingley Bank (a smaller version of Northern Rock). He was condemned as a sucker by Cameron, but managed to get savers' deposits guaranteed at up to £50,000 and threatened Iceland to get cash back for British investors.

The Paulson bailout was too messy to be convincing; at the end of the first week of October the City was within forty-eight hours of meltdown.[28] On 8 October, Chancellor Darling threw a £50 billion package at the high street banks, effectively taking over RBS *and* HBOS. A further £250 billion went to stabilise the loan books run up by the likes of Cummings and Goodwin and £200 billion to take over risky mortgages, the whole lot coming to £500 billion – or more than a third of the annual value of the British economy. This was getting close to the US rescue package, for a much smaller economy. Darling managed as usual to be boring about this, but Brown told a Downing Street press conference: 'This is not a time for conventional thinking or outdated dogma but for the fresh and innovative intervention that gets to the heart of the problem.' David Cameron was nervously neutral but on the 3rd he had said to Andrew Marr: 'What you won't hear from me this week is sort of easy, cheap lines beating up the market system, bashing financiers.' On the floor of the House Brown flung this back at Cameron, who floundered in what even the *Telegraph* called 'one of his worst performances.' Brown came out a temporary hero, 'The man who saved our savings', and instructed the rest of the West to follow him, which it did. Accounts and responsibilities would have to be audited later.[29] Had the UK not managed to take the initiative and impose order on its ramshackle financial estate, the overall transatlantic reprieve would have failed.

Things got worse for Cameron as a story came in from the Greek island of Corfu; another vintage Disraeli novel intrigue. Cameron's economics spokesman, the Hon. George Osborne, holidaying at the Rothschild family's villa in August and September, had sailed out to the £81-million yacht of Oleg Deripaska, top oligarch and owner of RUSAL aluminium (though at the time he was in some financial trouble), to ask for £50,000 for Tory Party funds: an absurdly small sum, but still illegal, even by London standards. He had, it seemed, been shopped by one of his fellow holidaymakers, either by EU commissioner Peter Mandelson or by the Hon. Nathaniel Rothschild, his host.

But by then Brown had made up with his long-time enemy. Lord Mandelson took the ermine as business minister on 16 October. Brown again swatted a David Cameron rendered silent and apparently effete on the 22nd. The result was a comeback in the polls, although inflation was fast increasing and economic growth had come to a halt. Paul Krugman, Nobel Laureate, praised his alacrity in the *New York Times*: 'The Brown government has shown itself willing to think clearly about the financial crisis, and act quickly on its conclusions.'[30]

As for Glenrothes, Sarah Brown drove along from North Queensferry every day and charmed a docile elderly electorate. On 4 November, to everyone's surprise, Glenrothes voters chose Brown's all but apolitical candidate Lindsay Roy, head-master of his old school, Kirkcaldy High. He beat the SNP's Peter Grant by 6,000 votes. Grant had the misfortune to be Council convener. A defeat would have finished Brown. But although the swing showed Fife Labour voters continuing to go Nationalist, Roy won through tactical pro-Union voting by Liberals and Tories, whose numbers disintegrated. The Kingdom had bailed its son out, but hardly anyone noticed because a day later Barack Obama was elected against John McCain.

Reflecting on this period almost a year later, the BBC's Robert Peston wondered why Brown had dropped out of world economics after 8 October, when the US power vacuum gave him a potential star role. Glenrothes, and the threat to the Union, was the answer. Failure in Fife would have finished him, but victory was evanescent. However hard he subsequently worked, and work he did, the light would now be on the White House.

The Union was saved. Next on the agenda was a G20 meet-ing on 15 November in Washington. Brown flew off to this and got a commitment to a London economic summit, slated for May 2009 but later brought forward to April 1 and 2. Obama had Scottish connections. Canongate Publishers, the small but lively Edinburgh firm which had risen in the aftermath of the *Red Paper*, had bought the UK rights to his books *Dreams of My Father* and *The Audacity of Hope*. They prospered, because this some-what cloudy idealism was what the British wanted. The blend of shocking corruption and awesome incompetence of the Dubya years was at an end, and little extenuation could be granted to the Blair–Brown government for acquiescing in a degradation comparable to the Harding–Coolidge 1920s, the prelude to the Crash of 1929. The acceleration forward into the Obama presi-dency had a spirit reminiscent of Kennedy in 1960, but the strings were false. In 1929 the West had been swarming with new tech-nologies: talkies, civil aviation, telephony, household electrics, cheap fashion and mass-motoring – what Gramsci called Fordism.

In 2008 the ecological outcomes of all of these were negative, and the cumulative impact of three decades of neoliberalism had eroded civil society's ability to cope with them.

On 20 January 2009 Obama was inaugurated. It was almost exactly a century since Buchan had written of John Laputa dancing on Kirkcaldy shore. Not only was Obama in the White House; in Canada Michelle Jean – a Haitian, francophone, female Governor General – occupied Buchan's Rideau Hall in Ottawa. But was there not a British parallel to the gloomier side of American politics? Scots occupied the power points in Whitehall because the London financial elite were off to richer pastures, just as in the wake of Martin Luther King, black mayors in the 1970s had to confront the inner-city decay left behind after the white exodus to the suburbs: the forerunner of the same autistic capitalistic impulse that would inaugurate the real estate boom and bust.

The decision for a London economic summit had been formalised on 26 November. There were two preliminary meetings: at Berlin (under Angela Merkel) on 22 February and at Horsham, Surrey (between finance ministers) on 14 March. Meanwhile Brown jetted across the globe, evangelising and trying to reconcile the main parties: the 'old Europeans' who wanted tighter regulation and controls on expenditure, and the Anglo-Americans, who saw their overinflated consumer economies in immediate danger, and wanted debt diminished by 'quantitative easing', aka devaluation. The demand was for investment 'innovation' such as hedge funds and private equity to be put under restraint, along with 'leverage' (borrowing), bonuses and tax havens. The authority and cash resources of the IMF had to be increased. The divisions were not simply technical: putting assets in a 'bad' or 'zombie' bank was a form of state confiscation, while getting the banks to dispose of them was subsidy. The bonus earners kept a low profile; in return the press (which had once praised them to the skies) changed the subject: it was now up to the politicos.

What then ensued was grandiloquent and/or absurd, depending on your position. G20 London was an inversion of light-touch regulation though it also turned out 'something the Brits did well': perhaps best summed up when at the Downing Street bash that preceded the official dinner at Buckingham Palace, the Russian President Dmitry Medvedev shyly went up to J. K. Rowling and asked her to autograph the latest Harry Potter book for his kids. The meeting and ritual feeding of the press corps with information and – well – food (from Jamie Oliver) took place not in Whitehall but at a hangar called the ExCeL Centre in London's Docklands. Everyone won and everyone got prizes.

There was a $1.1 trillion boost for the world economy. There was a strengthening of the IMF, and the doubling of its finances (its resources had been at the start rather less than the debt spun out by the Royal Bank of Scotland). There was greater oversight of tax havens, private equity debt and hedge funds. Brown as honest broker kept the potentially fractious Merkel and Sarkozy in line, bluntly reminding them that if the grasshoppers (Obama and himself) went bust, the ants would lack customers. The young, well-briefed and charming Obama couple (more community activists than Camelot, just as the ultimately cooperative Brown and Merkel were children of the manse) overcame tensions between the French and Chinese. From beginning to end the banker culprits stayed away. Nor was anything heard from the fractious nations of the British Isles, who could have brought the whole thing to a halt at Glenrothes. 'After a successful summit, Gordon Brown's standing among world leaders has never been higher', proclaimed the *Telegraph* on 3 April. Its poll a day later showed the Tory lead cut to seven points (from 42 per cent to 34 per cent). Things could then advance smoothly to Darling's Budget on 22 April.

No, they couldn't. At a confrontation with demonstrators in the City a truncheon-bearing, body-armoured Metropolitan policeman had lashed out at a forty-nine-year-old newspaper-seller called Ian Tomlinson. A former alcoholic from the sort of milieu TV viewers would be familiar enough with from *Shameless*, but who had struggled out of it, he had been caught up in the crowd. A banker with a video camera recorded the blows. Tomlinson died. This meant a return to the de Menezes case and the murky internal politics of the Met.

'When troubles come, they come not in single spies, but in battalions,' Macbeth, another power-Scot, had remarked. Scarcely had the barriers and catering waste been cleared away than a sheaf of emails surfaced on 11 April showing dirty tricks rampant in Brown's private office. Damien McBride, his press fixer, was conspiring with the equally devious Derek Draper to sink the Tories through a blogging campaign of salacious stories, of doubtful provenance or sheer fabrication. McBride went, leaving Brown looking like Richard Nixon transfixed by Watergate. The obsessive control freakery of New Labour was devouring itself, so that even the party's adoption of a 50 per cent rate of income tax on high incomes in Darling's 22 April Budget was cast into shadow. That wasn't all.

Newspaper owners we have already met, along with the pornographers, tax avoiders, fraudsters and outright jailbirds among them, but in early May their crimes were as nothing to those of MPs making a slick buck out of expenses. The mayfly attention span of the redtop journalists forgot all about City bonuses. (Shortly afterwards they nearly forgot all about MPs' expenses too, as Jordan, a surgically enhanced glamour model, split noisily from her husband.) Back in the 1990s John Lloyd of the *FT* had cited a *Sun* picture of the Page 3 girl Samantha Fox (clothed), dancing with an OAP, as an acceptable image of British populist democracy; now it was as if one of Shakespeare's tragedies had got crossed with a Jonsonian city comedy about graft and lowlife. Palace conspiracies alternated with the crudest sort of burlesque show; great would-be world-changing gestures were followed by Westminster pratfalls. Beneath the political theatre, the people were urged to panic about swine flu in a repetition of the bird flu coverage that had produced the Cellardyke swan back in 2006.

There was no vast enthusiasm for the Conservatives. They still didn't reach 50 per cent, and Cameron's charm had to work hard to excuse expense scandals and unsavoury far-right European associates. But in the YouGov May 2009 poll – thirty years after Thatcher's election – it looked as if they (41 per cent) would thrash Brown, if as expected Labour (22 per cent) lost badly in the 4 June European Parliament elections. But 19 per cent were down to vote Liberal and 18 per cent chose none of the main parties. On the other hand, the whole tenor of life in Britain had by this time partaken of farce – which, as Bernard Shaw once wrote, was only a syllable or gesture away from tragedy.

A. J. P. Taylor wrote that Bismarck's genius was in extricating himself from problems of his own creation. At a point of self-inflicted crisis, when financial technology collided with a ramshackle, corrupted society, Brown had bought time at a critical moment and at immense cost; particularly in Scotland, where the Edinburgh financial centre was maimed. What had happened was not another Dunkirk but a trauma more complex, the same sort of shock that hit Denmark in 1863 when she was defeated by Prussia, or Spain in 1898 when Cuba was lost; perhaps more positively the shock that hit the Genevan Henri Dunant on the battlefield of Solferino in 1859, and drove him to found the Red Cross in 1863. There was no longer the expectation that a conventional change of power – 'the rascals thrown out' – would produce realistic reforms within a deflating great power. The UK's citizens – if they stopped being subjects – had still to come to terms with living in a damaged, second-class European economy.

7 Walking with the Others

There are no easy answers. But there are no difficult answers either.

James Callaghan, 1978

I At the End of His Rope

On 20 August 2009 Gordon Brown delivered the eulogy at the memorial for Lawrence Daly at Dunfermline Abbey. He was confident, warm, and witty, alert to the loyalties of the retired miners and their families in the pews. Daly correcting E. P. Thompson's proofs down Cowdenbeath pit; Daly rallying the General Council of the NUM against Edward Heath in 1973 on Euston Station platform, after a whisky or two, by reciting the whole of *Julius Caesar,* Act I Scene 2 – where Cassius wins Brutus to the conspiracy – and doing all the voices. Brown had only nine months to rally Labour before the UK voted in May 2010.

Outside Fife the omens were not good. For months, Labour had been stuck in the polls at around 25 per cent. Brown had nationalised the East Coast Railway (National Express, who had the franchise, were going bust) and received the report on the collapse of MG Rover in 2005 (long delayed because of insufficient inspectors). The latter went to the Serious Fraud Office, but despite the greed and culpability of the 'Phoenix Four' it went no further. The standing of the Tories was admittedly stuck on a low 40–45 per cent (at this stage in Major's decline Blair was polling over 60 per cent), and systemic failure seemed still to unite both parties in discredit. Bankers, spared from and even benefiting by the consequences of ruining their savers and customers, were out for bonuses again, and the electorate naturally blamed the government, not the opposition. A win for Labour in the Glasgow North-East by-election on 11 November diminished the constitutional threat, but was the lowest poll ever recorded in Scotland convincing?

Despite the public money thrown at the banks, the renascent bonus culture emphasised the perilous fragility of the October 2008 settlement. Brown's former tutor Larry Summers was now advising Obama, and lunched austerely with the *Financial Times* in a White House canteen: 'I don't think the worst is over. It's very likely that more jobs will be lost. It would not be surprising if GDP had not yet reached its low.'[1] The collapse in trade and shares and the failure of the banks to lend, despite a bank rate of half a percent, was knocking over factories and chain stores, investors and charities, throwing former employees onto public funds. Unemployment grew from a stable 5 per cent in early 2008 to 8 per cent by summer 2009. It would rise further when public expenditure cuts sanctioned by both parties took effect.

The downfall of General Motors in the USA showed that oil-based industries like road and air transport could not, as after 1929, renew the economy. But the overarching impression was less of disaster than first of confusion, and then of injustice. This was in itself unusual. In his Britishness lectures, Brown had stressed an innate concern with fairness, what E. P. Thompson had earlier called the 'common possession' of the law. Was this still the case?

We were back to Walter Bagehot's architecture of British power. Its two pillars, Lombard Street and Downing Street, had depended on their psychological acceptability: powerful architectural impressions of solidity encouraged by lazy public tolerance. Not much of this remained by mid-2009. Through ruthless and deceitful speculation, the City had forced the FSA's 'light touch' to become, in its own words, 'credible deterrence'; yet there were new assaults *by those responsible for the crash* on the

economically marginal. Even in the good years, the *FT* found
that brokerages systematically oversold dubious bonds, and the
closer bank–broker relations were, the worse things got. Now,
in payback time, instances of malpractice mounted – theft of
computer data, pensions and insurance scams, price- and fare-
fixing: only to be expected in a slump. It could be taken for
granted that anything incriminating had been shredded or
wiped. Along with Securitisation Redux and the bonus boys'
demands, mortgage interest rates increased, with nationalised
Northern Rock leading the way.[2] It and Lloyds, dependent for
survival on the taxpayer, were recorded in Guernsey offering
undercover BBC reporters a safe haven for up to £4 million
pounds, tax free and no questions asked.[3]

At Downing Street the MPs' expenses scandal refused to
blow over. An attempt by Parliament to publish individual
details, nearly all blacked out, further degraded its reputation.
The protracted *Telegraph* campaign was revealed as a protest by
military men against the ill-equipped venture in Afghanistan,
and not even the fact that Tory misdeeds seemed to outdo Labour
– two of Cameron's closest associates, Alan Duncan and Andrew
Mackay, were involved – could halt the obloquy. Since 1911
the MP salary had been an upper-professional average, currently
£65,000: expenses had been used to cope with London as the
world's fourteenth most expensive city. A real Middle English
fear grew of losing jobs, houses and savings, as the banks set out
to recover their cash at the cost of their customers. It was cari-
catured as UKIP chauvinism (its 13 MEPs equalled Labour's) or
loutish racism among the white underclass after two neo-Nazi
BNP candidates were elected to Strasbourg on 5 June.

Did the Conservatives gain? Cameron's own expenses
were substantial, despite a personal fortune of £3.5 million.
He demoted Duncan and Mackay announced his withdrawal.
His anti-federal line in Europe isolated him from Sarkozy and
Merkel – even from Berlusconi – and landed him amongst the
grotesque rightists in Poland and the Czech Republic. Closer

inspection of 'the Tories most likely to succeed' found they weren't Cameron 'A-listers' but unreconstructed Thatcherites and wannabe lobbyists. Matthew D'Ancona of the *Spectator* might compare Brown to Michael Jackson in Neverland, but he found Cameron backed by private equity barons and spread-betters from Caribbean tax havens, headed by the questionably British Lord Ashcroft, spending heavily in the marginals with the government of Belize on his tail.[4]

Brown rediscovered manufacturing, suddenly announced the railway electrification programme he had opposed for a decade, and even hinted on 10 June at constitutional reform and proportional representation, going back to Henry Drucker's pluralist socialism in *Doctrine and Ethos*. But the 'quantitative easing' that his bailout of the City implied – absorbing bank losses by depreciating the currency – loomed over everything. Annual bond purchases rose from £80 billion in August 2008 to a 2009–10 figure of £220 billion. The willingness of both front benches to sanction spending up to £100 billion on a new Trident nuclear submarine and missile programme, and the two giant aircraft carriers at £5 billion and counting, made things no better. 'Is Britain bust?' James Buchan asked in *Prospect*, before reassuring himself that 'muddling through' might work. But in saving profligate capitalism, Labour was dying of intellectual perversity as much as unpopularity.[5]

This was where Brown's metropolitan unease showed up: the immersion in reading, the closed cabals, the crashing gear changes. The reflective, discursive element was thin. He didn't admit mistakes, while the older generation who had mentored him lived more easily. But John Smith, Donald Dewar and John Mackintosh were dead. Mrs Thatcher memorably said of her amiable and wettish adviser William Whitelaw, 'no Prime Minister should be without a Willie', but the Granita pair didn't do frankness, or, for that matter, Cabinet government. After Blair's departure, Brown had unprecedentedly appointed outside the party. But his new 'government of all the talents'

ministers – cheekily acronymed as 'GOAT' – spread the conta-
gion of patronage from failing party to failing establishment, and
were gone within two years. Diarchy was back in the shape of
Lord Mandelson as effective deputy premier. Government was
now *dependent* on a member of the unelected Upper House.
To find an equivalent, you would have to go back to 1916
when Lloyd George's War Cabinet had two of its five-man
team there: Viscount Milner and Marquess Curzon. But Milner
had governed South Africa, Curzon India; among the nineteen
members of Brown's Cabinet, hardly anyone could connect a
name with a face.

Robin Cook, had he lived, might have made a difference.
Victorian in style, he had acquired something of the integrity
of that period; his Edinburgh gravestone read, optimistically: 'I
may not have succeeded in halting the war, but I did secure the
right of Parliament to decide on war.' He knew the pragmatic
morality of the political novel better than John Major, who had
cluelessly presented Trollope's *The Way We Live Now* (1876)
to Bill Clinton in 1996: the book describes a City of London
bound for hell. Tony Blair had shown no interest in literature
or philosophy, which had come naturally to the likes of Dennis
Healey or Ian Gilmour. His 'going over' to Rome, with its
capacity for policy grandstanding, would have given Disraeli the
plot for a novel: two nations, creepy *monsignori*, caricature and
pathos. In October 2009 he was – incredibly – back, with a
chance of becoming first European president, and Brown was
backing him.

This was almost out of Disraeli's last, *Endymion* (1880), where
his babes in the wood end up as prime minister of Britain and
empress of France, but the Old Jew's grand pantomime didn't
reprise. It couldn't survive in the world of soundbite TV, and
of large and youthful elements of the populace who no longer
bothered. Scots teenagers knew far more about 'Rockstar' and
the Hobbesian brutality of 'Grand Theft Auto' (50 million hits)
than its Edinburgh neighbour the Scottish Parliament (2 million

hits). Brown's Britishness discourse had its literary roots, through his friends Bill Campbell in publishing and Alastair Moffat at the Edinburgh Fringe. He tried to invoke his wide, rather random reading to remedy the galloping alienation of political life. But this only emphasised the amoral fog in which electors could simultaneously oppose and endorse the Afghan war; condemn errant MPs yet deliver a by-election slap to Brown out of sympathy for Ian Gibson, ejected from his Norwich seat and regarded as hard done by. 'Aw a muddle', as Charles Dickens, no enthusiast for Westminster, would have put it.

There had to be some sense of community, yet Brown's generation were professional politicos, who studied rather than lived the business from university on. This sort of background didn't necessarily lead to the 'hands in the till' of the *Telegraph* investigations. MPs as villains were rank amateurs. For the real thing, see Senate and House in Washington, on £120,000 salaries but marinated in corporate bribery by lobbies innocent of any notion of financial morality.[6] Westminster was a part of the British problem: like the BBC (under the control of Norf London teenagers on six-figure salaries); rail companies where unending logo relaunches went with duff technology and chaotic organisation; BAe bribing its difficulties away; accountancy and law ringing their cash tills; police done up like Transformer toys; and everywhere the black domes and swivelling cameras of Europe's most monitored society.

Brown seemed complicit in part of this: obsession, ill temper and rows with Blair took their toll. At Dunfermline, amid the old banners flapping in the August rain – 'Brother Lawrence Daly, Brother Keir Hardie' – he could show a continuity between family, region and politics, which made the 'new politics' mantra incanted by Cameron's Tories at each by-election seem even further from Smith's 'local or provincial society'. 'This place is like Doctor Who's Tardis in reverse,' a Scottish BBC producer had whispered outside the fabulous pinnacles of Westminster, back in 1987. 'Once you get inside, it's *smaller.*'

II 'Human Nature and Politics'

In an equally symbolic building across central London stood
the statue of Sir John Betjeman. Out of the Auden–Orwell age,
a symbol of Englishness, he surveyed the Eurostar expresses
swishing into and out of St Pancras Station. A poet of region
and class, a mimic and satirist, he was crankily perceptive:

> For us of the steam and the gaslight, the lost generation,
> The new white cliffs of the City are built in vain.

In the 1960s Betjeman saved Gilbert Scott's Gothic
fantasy from demolition. At Euston, where he failed to save
Hardwicke's Greek portico, the 1960s terminal was unspeak-
able. The 'parlour pink' and fragile Christian (troubled by
credibility, dominant father, sex and so on) made the human
condition constructive and enjoyable through churches, trains
and 'home towns'. If England was interesting and fun, it was
Betjeman's England. St Pancras was the quickest way out of
it, its only high-speed railway, and Brown was selling it to the
French.

Brand Betjeman, anyone? Who, offshore, could have decoded
him? The Irish, perhaps. President De Valera had been an
enthusiast. Brand Freud, though, was international. Psychiatry
had surveyed British politics with little hope from the time of
Graham Wallas's *Human Nature in Politics* (1912). Behaviourism
and its doppelgänger the British homogeneity thesis – typified
by David Butler's general election studies – was orthodoxy in
Brown's Edinburgh days: 'the nation broken down by age and
sex' was the gag. The nation *unified* by age, sex, class – not region,
history, ideas. The Freud family, if not the full Sigmund himself,
had featured widely in the Blair–Brown years. There they were:
Lucien painting Kate Moss (fetchingly nude and pregnant) as
muse to the retail colossus Philip Green; Matthew marrying
Elizabeth Murdoch; David advising Gordon on social welfare

and then ditching him for the Tories. Rather than personality or religion, the Freuds demonstrated the quick transition from intellect to market in Blair–Brown London. But over much of Britain, particularly the Celtic periphery, political behaviourism was long defunct.

Analysing Brown in the context of cultural and religious frameworks within the islands, not to speak of 'the condition of England', invoked archetypes: back to another son of the Calvinist manse – Carl Gustav Jung, like John Buchan born in 1875. The preoccupied, clumsy premier had changed from the potent enigma of, say, 2001, when Posy Simmonds found his campaign presence 'magnificent, like a Roman Emperor or prize bull'. His literary allusions to his role – Emily Brontë's Heathcliff, Joseph Conrad's Captain MacWhirr – were misfires: hadn't MacWhirr steered incompetently *towards* the typhoon in Conrad's tale?

Interrogate the story through the old exam tactic: remove the actor and test whether outcomes might have been different. The milieu had altered since 1979. It was then frowsty but collegiate; it had saved things in 1975. Had Brown carried the Scottish Assembly then, Labour would have survived to take the bounty of oil privatisation. Instead there was Thatcher. This provokes a question never asked in Britain: how did she compare with Helmut Kohl? A no-brainer. Kohl left Germany unified, with its industry intact, more gender-equal, and environmentally active in a more integrated Europe. Thatcher dismembered Britain, enthroned inequality, privatisation, and commercial hocus-pocus. Blair–Brown's New Labour 'rebranding', its claim to inherit from her, marked a surrender to markets and market-makers that were far wider than the nation. You could not have profit-driven culture industries – New Labour's 'Cool Britannia' – and *retain* culture as critique. That question was answered in 2008.

III No Continuing City

The core of all this was the City, ironically given its crucial role through the invention of another Kirkcaldy boy. Sir Sandford Fleming, chief engineer of the Canadian Pacific Railway in 1881, wanted reliable checks on the line's progress, and divided North America into recognised time zones in the early 1880s. Business centres subsequently communicated on this basis, the framework for the torrent of dealing that would set in after the 1990s. Add to this the isolation of subject specialists, networking globally. 'Sympathy' was supposed to arise from lived community, where calculation was domesticated by civic obligation. What replaced it, as Gillian Tett of the *FT* found, was a reversion to a tribal identity not too remote from that, say, of the Mafia or 'Ndrangheta. Hence the attraction of connexity, of swift appraisal and decision, and the role in this of the 'in-group and out-group' – a concept that had been around in Scotland since Adam Ferguson's *History of Civil Society* in 1767. The City's exotic clients – Russians, Arabs, Indians and Chinese – stretched the in-group's reach, but also made it even smaller, more compacted, more hermetic.

This was what confronted Brown in the late 1990s, when – after the Americans had effectively taken control of the banks – the UK's oil revenue, at its point of maximum production, was slumping to $10 a barrel. London, with an important, if not wholly friendly, outstation in Edinburgh, rapidly became the centre of a constellation of financial satellites, which the UK government had nodded into existence in the 1970s as a means of bankrolling micro–colonies which were otherwise a burden.[7] Under the John Betjeman/Ian Fleming surface of garden parties and ostrich plumes was light-touch regulation in its purest form, and the Blackberry-type micro-computer made it possible for the minute Cayman Islands to become the fifth-biggest banking site in the world by 2005. In a 1996 essay Tom Nairn (along with Anthony Barnett and Neal Ascherson, he was an originator of Charter 88, then a Brown–friendly constitutional pressure group) had sketched an alternative to 'bourgeois regionalism': namely the microstate as 'The Abbot of Unreason and the Lord of Misrule' – gutsy medieval versions of Luxury and Corruption which nevertheless made the wheels of international commerce whirl round.

What ended in the slump of 2008–9 was a decade of increasingly frenzied profit-taking in a metropolitan financial sector run out of control. The Conservative political elite had migrated to it as dealers, executives and corporate lawyers, and no longer supported the elite plus middle-class 'public servant' consensus Schumpeter had praised in *Capitalism, Socialism and Democracy* (1942). It could expand the numbers involved, square its own interests, and exit into relative security.

Mastering the system involved privileging the already privileged, as the Farepak episode showed, confirming its inegalitarianism and long-term untenability. In 2008 as much as during the stagflation of 1975 the financial oligarchs were hated, and Chancellor Darling would get some praise from the old Left for trying to make them pay. But rescue forces were no longer apparent in British politics, where Brown's party was morally discredited. Financial concentration continued, skulking from the anomic forces of militarisation and ethnic hatred which appealed to the dispossessed.

In this moribund establishment, the London political and economic system operated remote from reality, without reference to democratic sanction, similar to Vienna in the last days of the Habsburg Empire, or the bourse in France during the post-Napoleonic Restoration in which Stendhal set *Scarlet and Black* (1830). This was increasingly reflected in its academic and intellectual back-up: hyper-individualism in the 'bestseller' world, near-autistic greed in commerce, aggravated by toxic quangos and the micro-intellects produced by MBA factories.[8]

Britain-wide constitutional reform had flourished briefly as a cause in the late 1980s but it depended on consent, and this reckoning was postponed by New Labour's rebranding; bringing in new personnel, new stories. These sometimes represented – or claimed to represent – desperate challenges, such as the environment crisis or the technology deficit, but they were constrained and ultimately throttled by the means of projection available: slick and shallow, moulded to the low attention span of texting or twittering; ultimately swamped by the sheer volume of transactions the technology now enabled.

The irony was that a specific 2008–9 crisis within the Anglo-Saxon world was caused by 'the audacity of hope': political inclusion coinciding with the end of market dogma. In the November 2008 election American electors threw out (or thought they threw out) rule by giant corporations and corrupt politics, but could they install a new order? By late 2009 it was evident that the public endorsement of the 'united state' didn't suffice. But for a vital half-year eyes had been diverted from the British crisis, and in the UK there was no such presidential endorsement. Brown's original socialist politics could scarcely be revived by an individual at the end of his rope, regarded as alien by much of the country. The political business seemed deprived of any real character through the ideological fusion of economics with the media and PR. The merger of history writing and literary capitalism – the reduction of Simon Schama and Niall Ferguson to the level of Dan Brown – compromised the instruments of criticism and control. The massive frauds of Enron and WorldCom in the USA in 2002 should have inspired intervention; instead they reinforced British complacency enough for it to promote Wall Street migration to London, where corporate semi-criminal ingenuity ran rings round poorly budgeted regulation. 'Special financial instruments' had been a means to Enron's rapacious end; thereafter they expanded to become ends in themselves, and hit the UK hard because of the laxity of Brown's controls. As with Fred Goodwin and BICC, expertise in dissecting London's high-end frauds had ended by convincing the players of the infinite elasticity of the rules.[9]

Scottish banks contributed a further disruptive factor, which impressed itself on Brown when the May 2007 election revived the independence threat. The failure of the political conventions had put the controlling power of London in jeopardy in Scotland, with Alex Salmond considering RBS as an informal foreign office. But the semi-independence of banking had also become another way in for Tom Nairn's international 'Lords of Misrule', in search of 'more perfect markets' and the riskiest of deals. It was well into 2009 before the full story of RBS and HBOS became apparent, as the Scottish Parliament's Economy Committee sifted through the wreckage.

IV James Gordon Brown

'Enrichez-vous, messieurs!' Brown seemed for a moment in 2004 to resemble Daumier's cartoon of François Guizot, Protestant premier of Louis-Philippe's France in 1847, scattering cash on the speculators. By summer 2009, like Guizot in February 1848, he was bust. This couldn't be said of the City boys. 'How to Spend It' in the *Weekend FT* was still looking horridly healthy. They had cashed in and cleared off, or had bought viable interests in slumping banks at fire-sale prices and could now sell them on, winning cash which seemed to equal the savings that both front benches said would come from shrinking the public sector. Prices of London properties worth over a million were booming. Otherwise, no one pursuing legitimate commerce appeared to be thriving.

For the SNP its Atlantic 'arc of opportunity' of fast-growing economies from Norway to Spain seemed to dissolve. Iceland had been looted by its New Vikings. Ireland had pushed from sharply steered growth into a disastrous property boom. Salmond's alternative to PFI, the Scottish Futures Trust, had yet to leave the garage. The Farepak case had predicted the limits of Darling's rapport with depositors, and his ability to kick financial misdoings into very long grass for a very long time, but the overstretched credit of HBOS – a staggering £250 billion – had ultimately to be reckoned with.

I visited Guernsey in mid-June for a Commonwealth Parliamentary Association conference. It bustled with banks, builders and presumably bonuses: rather like Watford with a governor. Its bailiff, the newly knighted Geoffrey Rowland, was insistent that the banking scene had been purged. This raised the supposition that EU-imposed reforms *and* the securitisation boom had elbowed fringe banks and 'Sark larks' (the exploitation of the minute feudal territory as a letterbox-company metropolis) aside. But tax havens were under general pressure, and unheard-of possibilities, like access to details of Swiss bank accounts, were now under debate.

Were many of the bonus barons likely to turn over a new leaf and start contributing to regional development or education? Would they respond to appeals to become a Carnegie or a Soros? This was optimistic: no way could they be numbered among Max Weber's 'ascetic capitalists', when they had long been experts in avoiding taxation, penal or otherwise. And among wealthy patrons facing the need to shift their tax domicile as old havens ran into trouble, they would have a dependable clientele.[10]

By autumn 2009 Lloyds Group was sinking with the HBOS burden as the expenses scandal drove government and Parliament down to unprecedented unpopularity. Did this verify Mack and Kerner's thesis: that the representatives of legality were too compromised to control the Lords of Misrule created by light-touch regulation? MPs were now moral lepers, less trusted than journalists, and the spotlight was off the bankers, although when totted up Westminster expense-fiddling might not equal what *one* CEO trousered in his £15 million bonus and pensions endowment. EU reservations about the size of operations like Lloyds–HBOS – 'too big to fail: too dumb to live', as John Kay put it in the *FT* – might ultimately be decisive.

Sorting this out clashed with Brown, and at base with the *conviction* of the man. He had not gone passively with the economic flow, seeking to divert it to worthy causes – he wanted to take the initiative in driving it on. World finance capital London would be his bequest to Britishness. But he didn't anticipate the velocity of transactions and of innovations in the computing world; nor did he imagine the effect on London business of quite new economic players such as China and India, of erratic authoritarians like the Russians, of an EU waking up to its responsibilities in governing multinationals. If such forces worked synergistically – and this had been one of the City's strengths – this might have balanced the need to regulate. But control decentralised within *Britain*, perched in offshore havens from Belize to Switzerland (whose elites were bound to guard their privileges furiously) and at the lower end morphing into outright crime – not just among gangsters but seemingly reputable businessmen like Bernard Madoff and Sir Allen Stanford – wasn't just problematic. Comparatively small failures could ruin everything.

There may even have been a touch of personal defiance about this: Brown deliberately distancing himself from the moralistic economics of inter-war socialism. Attacks on 'bankers' ramps' were legion in papers like *Forward* in the 1930s, when some of Maxton and the Scottish Left's ideas came close to Social Credit, hostile to finance and even anti-semitic. With the smoke billowing from the Twin Towers in the far distance of his vision, Brown's ambition was a great city-state founded on efficient trade, which it would use to ameliorate international divisions. Neither the prospect of a decentralised Britain or a federal Europe appealed to him or his entourage.

What he didn't calculate on was the constant need to intervene in the many-headed politics of the islands: with the likes of Gerry Adams (imaginative operator, blowing up banks and buying them . . .) or George Mathewson at the other end of the line. The threat was the wearying, demoralising paralysis that would result; the chance was to ride the course, risks and all, to whatever advantage there was.

'A deep and smooth river' was Walter Scott's image of the Union in *Waverley* (1814), but anyone looking at the latter days of capitalism from the Fife coast would have Ibsen in mind, in particular that sequence of plays which went from young tormented Pastor Brand to old tormented *John Gabriel Borkman* in his penultimate work of 1896. The dying Borkman, a banker jailed for fraud, struggles from his house up to a belvedere where he imagines his 'Kingdom': his steamers, his factories, and the gold he has animated to build them:

> That blast is the breath of life to me. That blast comes to me like a greeting from subject spirits. I seem to touch them, the prisoned millions; I can see the veins of metal stretch out their winding, branching, luring arms to me . . . You begged to be liberated and I tried to free you. But my strength failed me; and the treasure sank back into the deep again.

To stockholders in the Royal Bank of Scotland, in Lloyds TSB, in HBOS, who had seen their shares crash by as much as 80 per cent, Brown, as much as the boardrooms, was as guilty as Borkman. On 25 March 2009 someone shied a brick at Sir Frederick Goodwin's front window in Edinburgh; this was 'Mob Rule!' to the press, even though he was by then in a villa on the Mediterranean. The most Brown had to suffer was smut and spittle from Jeremy Clarkson. Disraeli's denouement in *Sybil* (1845) was by contrast on the John Martin scale. In his 'Condition of England', if you weren't a One Nation Tory you were dead.

V 'Fifty Days to Save the World!'

Brown was accused of escaping from mounting problems into big generalities: 'Fifty days to save the world!' screamed the papers on 20 October, which was the PM trailer for the Copenhagen climate conference. Cry wolf? Where *was* Britain at the end of 2009? Different and despairing, in comparison with 1997: a discredited government, a suspect opposition, and beneath both a political and economic system in disgrace. MPs were not regarded as representatives of people and resolvers of their grievances, but were still a visible group on which revenge could be taken. Bankers could not be trusted with money: they would stash it away in tax havens, seemingly immune from the punishments dished out in America and in continental Europe; or the threat of the bullet in the back of the head that kept China's Leninist capitalists in order. Lawyers likewise: the Right accused them of enforcing transnational jurisdictions such as the EU, whose enactments infringed British liberties; the Left saw domestic 'sinister interests' complicating ordinary business like buying and selling houses or getting compensation for injuries or malpractices elsewhere, and feathering their own nests. 'Public servants'? Would that term even be used? Social work bosses allowed non-intervention to endanger the vulnerable. Doctors could pull in huge bonuses for unremarkable service. Unless incompetence could be proved *and publicised*, the result wouldn't be more than a slap on the wrist.

Administrators at central and local level seemed a privileged caste, able to secure for themselves early retirement with golden handshakes: 'the perks of office'. Only nine days after Brown's climate alarm, an enquiry into the crash of an ageing Nimrod reconnaissance plane in Afghanistan with heavy loss of life found against the Ministry of Defence, BAe and QuinetiQ. The conduct of all three was summed up by its verdict on BAe:

> It has failed to implement an adequate or effective culture, committed to safety or ethical conduct. The responsibility for this must lie with the leadership of the company . . . BAe systems has been a company in denial.[11]

The counter-claim had traditionally been that the British system was at root sound: inadequacies were 'a muddle, not a fiddle'. Yet the coiner of that phrase, Gordon Brown's Fife ally Henry MacLeish, was sitting on a pension of £34,000 and a 'handshake' of £24,000 for under a year's service as Scottish first minister. Did the swollen numbers of the Brown administration (thirty-one Cabinet-rank ministers) not mean a rush for such payoffs? Many of the mandarins responsible for the maladministration and complacency that had led to financial catastrophe were defended by professional associations and compensation schemes. Such solidarity, well organised within immigrant elites (particularly in the metropolis) served to integrate a minority while leaving other 'New Britons', particularly from failed states, in highly marginal situations.

It would have been unusual for this not to have produced a reaction but by late 2009 this was coming from a far Right claiming to represent the 'white British working class'. By 2009 the British National Party was biting into the solidarity that the Conservatives had never been able to disrupt, in inner London boroughs and northern England. Unpleasant and violent, it was still able to exploit concerns – voiced prominently by Liberals – stemming from environmental and international crises which were all but intractable.

Climate deterioration was a fact, expressed in continuous drought in North Africa: the results were Muslim–Christian conflict over ever scarcer resources, failed states and migration into Southern Europe. As we have seen, conflict in Afghanistan and heavy commitments of western troops only increased that failed state's heroin economy, which attacked the weak civil societies of Western Europe, thus contributing to the illegalism which had helped propel the banking crisis.

VI Advice to the New Nations

This sense of world interdependence was more apparent to the Parliament of semi-autonomous Scotland – as it had been to Adam Smith, Burns and Carlyle in the eighteenth and nineteenth centuries – than it was to Brown, hemmed in both by his Free Kirk parochialism and a London dominated by international institutions that he couldn't control. In October 2008 he *had* to secure Scotland – defeat at Glenrothes would have been fatal – and in so doing took his eye off the world economic crisis. But the constitution could still kill him.

On 15 June 2009 the Calman Commission on devolution and Scottish government set up by Wendy Alexander MSP reported. Its prescription was radical as to finance, aiming to transfer half of assigned revenues to a Scottish Treasury, with the existing block grant from Whitehall cut proportionately. Would federalism result from this? In 1982 I wrote Fabian Tract No. 484, *Against Metropolis*, proposing 'home rule all round' on German lines, with PR, eight English regions and a federal parliament. Little interest was initially aroused, though it became the basis of 'Grasping the Thistle', which I made for BBC-TV Scotland in March 1987, in a series called 'Scotland 2000' which started the movement for a Scottish Convention. Calman specifically excluded federalism. There was an alternative patent to anyone in Scotland: the rearrangement of Britain into somewhere like Iberia or Scandinavia, a confederation of sovereign states. This was probably becoming inevitable because of economic crisis and the sell-offs. If electricity, gas and nuclear power, railways, factories and phones were all coming under European control, why not follow them? The European Central Bank beckoned, along with effective economic coordination: almost certainly more effective than light touch and the FSA.

Reconstructing 'Britishness' was attempted by the Right under Major. (Thatcher, though Welsh by origin, had no feel for it at all.) The net outcome was the oafish disaster of rail privatisation, through which Britain fell fifteen years behind Europe, where all the larger states had high-speed links by 2005.

Marseilles was three hours from Paris, 750 km away; Edinburgh, 632 km away, was four and a half hours from London. Brown took the Britain issue seriously but got the story wrong even before he was undermined by London: his unconvincing, strained attempts, founded on the misunderstandings of Linda Colley, were added to vague ideas about good behaviour which the historian Kenneth Morgan regarded as the simple stock-in-trade of any democracy, and more likely to be found in Adam Smith's 'local and provincial governments' than at the centre.[12] Brown's exhortations merely restated the dilemma: could you have Smithian sympathy when all human relations had been made subject to profit and loss calculations, often by people far from the UK?

If you didn't have a sovereign UK, how would you run the island? Rather better than in recent years, according to the nationalist parties who ruled or at least shared power in Scotland, Wales and Northern Ireland. For everyone but fulminating anti-Europeans (a noisy rather than populous race, often sundowning in tax havens), it would be painless to empower the existing nations, subject to ad hoc institutions which provided for common services. England might have its eight regions, with a federal council replacing the Lords, or large city-regions with their surrounding territory. Should the islands become confederal, their collective voting weight in Europarliament and Council would be greater than that of France or Germany.

Scotland's future governors would have to reverse Brown's deindustrialisation, resurrect manufacturing industry, master renewable energy and carbon capture. Brown's infrastructural neglect would mean overseas partners concentrated on public transport, particularly high-speed rail and dedicated freight routes. A Scottish government would have to prepare an alternative finance and enterprise package, and get it under way. The price of oil would probably sink during the slump, but could then only rise, maybe as high as $400 a barrel by 2030. Such long-term collateral could make Scotland attractive to public and private investors through its energy output as European centre of renewable power, and as a reservoir for as much as 150 billion tons of 'captured' CO_2.

What if this were interdicted by a British government intent on cutbacks? Investment was possible from Arab sovereign wealth funds, or from the Chinese. The Norwegian Pensions Fund and German *Laender* like Baden-Württemberg were already into financing renewable technologies. Hit by the export slump, they could be recruited to organise a technical and financial programme. This would weld together West European hi-tech industrial centres, combining regional banking (with assets comparable to those of the Royal Bank pre-ABN Amro) with a revived Scottish mutual sector. With this organised on a local level, by reviving the Trustee Savings Banks, there could be a Scottish State Bank linked to the European nations with an interest in carbon-free power. Surely this was a better prospect than the residue of RBS being run from the City by Stephen Hester, a financial Bourbon with no interest whatever in Scotland?

What would be lost? The monarchy? Probably not, although whether the next generation would manage better than the Queen was doubtful. Sport, already damaged by the pay-TV collapse? But what, other than phoney hysteria whipped up by the tabloids for couch potatoes, did that consist of? The dismantling of the redtop press would be pure gain; the death of urban freebies like *thelondonpaper* was a start. A rational regional media, printed and online, coupled with TV channels, was the only option for a civically and technologically competent public.

John Lloyd of the *Financial Times*, who had reported on the brief democracy of Russia, tried and failed to get Brown to read Lampedusa's *The Leopard*. The Prince of Salina saw the Sicily of 1860 as a centenarian in a wheelchair being propelled around the Crystal Palace:

understanding nothing and caring about nothing, whether it's the steel factories of Sheffield or the cotton spinneries of Manchester, and thinking of nothing but drowsing off again on beslobbered pillows with a pot under the bed.[13]

In 2009, fifty years after the book's publication, post-imperial Britain was murmuring its historical memories, with white van man as bouncer on the door. Or did something with greater potential exist, an antibody generated within the United Kingdom of London, whose *Bildungsburgertum* could change its life chances? Could this life chance outride the simple propositions of Great Power status?

In April 2009 David Cameron briefly appeared to suggest that a Tory government might walk away from the 'Great Power' delusion, abandoning Trident and Brown's giant aircraft carriers: 'Airstrip Two' and 'Airstrip Three' in Orwell's Newspeak. Might the future of an England the size of Spain or Italy recover under a Disraelian 'Young England' class prepared to get its hands dirty? The Scottish Tories had actually taken such a line, and survived only through devolution's PR system. No. Within hours all was as before. Westminster's elite, slithering into 'West Wing' fantasies, had nothing in their immigration policies to offer multiculturalism, let alone Scotland or Wales. Their attitude to Europe would be toxic. The Scots could look beyond England, beyond the Anglophone world. Their function as satellites, destined to prop up British Labour, was over. But prospects for a Nationalist government deprived of real autonomy remained grim.

There remained the Carlylean tragedy surrounding Brown's attempt: revisiting the 'Condition of England' and making it worse. Hugh MacDiarmid wrote in the 1930s of the *Marxisant* generation around Auden: 'You cannot strike a match on a crumbling wall.' And their talent was vast, compared to the literati around the Blair–Brown governments. Brown's Britishness might have been an attempt to strike out, but it failed so completely that it sank with him. The challenge of international respect wasn't compatible with the commitment to UKL as a haven for the rich. When he praised 'The Union Jack as a symbol of democracy' he didn't mean drums and bigotry; but in Ulster it would be taken this way.

Ireland's relation to England became productive because Tony Blair had actually managed to get an alternative 'con-social' form of Ulster government operating under the Good Friday agreement. The entries from 7–15 April 1998 are the one point in Alastair Campbell's diaries where the capability of the man comes alive.[14] The agreement at least suppressed sectarian conflict and had the potential to recreate the 'Atlantic arc' and set it against the London-centred core of cash, which was what mattered. If anything retained the 'positive' international legacy of the United Kingdom, it was 'the west', its potential power resources and its talented, effervescent people. Extended to Scotland and Wales, it promised a Europe revived by cooperation and convention. This chance momentarily appeared to Brown at the April Summit, but not when shackled to Tridents, giant aircraft carriers, and BAe's merchants of death. In early July it offered itself again, in an Institute of Public Policy Research (IPPR) report condemning rearmament, which was backed by generals and even Lord George Robertson.

'Hinterland [the 'back-self'] is important', wrote John Buchan. Had Brown's PhD been centred on John Wheatley – socialist businessman, Catholic Marxist and Irish Nationalist – rather than the ineffectual Maxton, this imagination might have developed in a way that engaged the radicalism of the islands. 'The Red Flag', still sung as Labour's remnants rallied, was written by an old Fenian, Jim Connor. Of all the socialist verse of the 1930s, that of Louis MacNeice – a dialogue with his own country as well as with the people – still wears well, and can carry us along the common road:

None of our hearts are pure, we always have mixed motives,
Are self-deceivers, but the worst of all Deceits is to murmur
'Lord, I am not worthy'
And, lying easy, turn your face to the wall.
But may I cure that habit, look up and outwards
And may my feet follow my wider glance
First no doubt to stumble, then to walk with the others
And in the end—with time and luck – to dance.

Notes

1 Through the Whole Island

1 Gordon Brown, *The Red Paper on Scotland*, Edinburgh: EUSPB, 1975, 14.
2 John Rentoul, *Independent*, 18 March 2004.
3 Christopher Harvie, *The Centre of Things: the Political Novel from Disraeli to the Present*, London: Unwin Hyman, 1991, Ch. 7.
4 Robert Peston, *Who Runs Britain?*, London: Hodder & Stoughton, 2008, 32.
5 Peston admitted to the Economy Committee in Edinburgh that this was an autumn 2007 guess, but the £13-billion estimate remained in his paperback edition, summer 2009.
6 Dave Osler, *Labour Party PLC: New Labour as a Party of Business*, Edinburgh: Mainstream Publishing, 2002, 223.
7 Hank Paulson, his American counterpart as Treasury Secretary, had indeed come from Goldman Sachs, where his 2005 income was $37 million, or £20 million, over a hundred times Brown's.
8 The use of 'Broon' – as Gordon is known, not wholly affectionately, in Scottish political circles – may puzzle, unless you're a regular reader of the *Sunday Post*, Scotland's folksy weekly, once condemned by the likes of moi, but now recognised as far superior to the redtops. 'The Broons', founded in 1935 by the immortal Dudley D. Watkins, creator of Lord Snooty and Desperate Dan, were a classic Scottish artisan family of c. 1910, consisting of Paw, Maw and *eight* children: Hen, Joe, Maggie, Daphne, Horace, the twins and the bairn. Gordon is Horace, who wears glasses and is an intellectual.
9 Cf. Michael Wolff, *Independent*, 4 October 2009.
10 Jonathan Raban, *Coasting*, London: Picador, 1987, 166.
11 Peston, *Who Runs Britain?*, 8–11; Polly Toynbee and David Walker, *Unjust Rewards: Exposing Greed and Inequality in Britain Today*, London: Granta Books, 2008, Ch. 1.
12 John Ruskin, *The Stones of Venice*, London: Smith Elder, 1851, Introduction to Vol. I.

13 Christopher Harvie, *Travelling Scot: Essays on the History, Politics and Future of the Scots*, Glendaruel: Argyll Publishing, 1999, 163–73.

14 The *Ausgleich* of 1867 maintained the unity of the Habsburg Empire by allocating permanent privileges to the two major political players, the Austro-Germans and Hungarians. It lasted for fifty-one years.

15 See Brown's interview with George Rosie in 2008 for further details.

16 Alexander Coyle, et al., eds, *New Wealth for Old Nations:Scotland's Economic Prospects*, Princeton: Princeton University Press, 2005.

17 Paul Mason, *Meltdown: The End of the Age of Greed*, London: Verso, 2009, 119–21.

18 I first encountered her in 1966, through a distant relative, David Aikman, who was later an academic associated with the Christian right in the USA. My piece on possible Rand–Brown links in the Glasgow *Herald* (2000) brought a civil editorial letter agreeing with my points: this from a paper pretty closely linked with Brown.

19 Christian Tenbrock, *Die Zeit*, 26 July 2007.

20 Christopher Harvie, *Mending Scotland*, Glendaruel: Argyll Publishing, 2004, 68–74.

21 Will Hutton, *The Observer*.

22 Nina Bawden, *Dear Austen*, London: Virago Press, 2005.

23 *Financial Times*, 13 November 2008.

24 Nick Davies, *Flat Earth News*, London: Chatto & Windus, 2008, Ch. 1.

25 Joanna Blythman, *Shopped: The Shocking Power of British Supermarkets*, London: Fourth Estate, 2004.

26 Christopher Harvie, *Fool's Gold*, London: Hamish Hamilton, 1994, 8.

27 Charles Grant's *Delors: Inside the House that Jacques Built*, London: Nicholas Brealey, 1994, is a rare example of compelling readability. See also Stanley Johnson, *The Commissioner*, London: Century, 1987, a sprightly and usefully educational thriller by the father of the more famous Boris.

28 Edward Luttwak, *Turbo-Capitalism: Winners and Losers in the Global Economy*, London: Weidenfeld & Nicolson, 1998.

29 Gillian Tett, *Fool's Gold: How Unrestrained Greed Corrupted a Dream, Shattered Global Markets and Unleashed a Catastrophe*, London: Little, Brown, 2009, 289ff.

30 In Scots, 'the policies' means the estate around a country house, but the word shares the same root as *police* and *politics*, implying husbandry, management and control.

31 Anuj Gahangar, *Financial Times*, 16 April 2008.

32 Since 1991 I have run the Freudenstadt Symposium on regionalism with Paddy Bort of Edinburgh University for the Friedrich
Ebert Stiftung, the education and research arm of Germany's Social
Democrat party. We have conferred with Neal Ascherson, Herta
Daubler-Gmelin, Ron Davies, Tom Nairn, Dai Smith, Allan
Massie, Joe Lee, John Osmond, David Walker, Nuala O'Faolain
and many others, reporting on and discussing regional issues from
across Europe. In July 1999 we hosted the first visit to Europe of
a Scottish Cabinet member, Sarah Boyack, minister of transport.

33 I am deeply indebted to Noel Spare of Offenburg Technical
University and Scotland's technology minister Jim Mather for
introducing me to this discipline, as well as to Shewhart and
Deming.

34 Christopher Harvie, *Fool's Gold*, 84–8.

35 Adam Taylor, *Guardian*, 10 January 2007.

36 Louis MacNeice, *Collected Poems*, London: Faber & Faber, 1966.

2 Gordon's Kingdom, 1295–2009

1 Adam Smith, *An Inquiry into the Nature and Causes of the Wealth of
Nations*, London: W. Strahan and T. Cadell, 1776, Bk 1, Ch. 10,
Pt. 2.

2 Cuthbert Hill, *Edwardian Scotland*, Edinburgh: Scottish Academic
Press Ltd, 1976, 68.

3 So named after Gothenburg in Sweden, which pioneered cooperative or local authority-owned pubs, selling ale and foreswearing
spirits.

4 *About Property*, 31 December 2007.

5 Marcus Binney, *The Times*, 30 January 2009.

3 Where There Was Industry, 2005–6

1 Gordon Brown, *Where There Is Greed*, London: Mainstream
Books, 1989, 26; Gordon Brown, *Moving Britain Forward,* London:
Bloomsbury, 2006, 84–136.

2 Christopher Harvie, *Fool's Gold*, London: Hamish Hamilton,
1994, 294–5.

3 Sir Geoffrey Owen, *Financial Times Business Magazine*, 1 January
2000; Richard Lambert, *Guardian*, 20 August 2006.

4 Pat Kane, *The Play Ethic: A Manifesto for a Different Way of Living*,
London: Macmillan, 2004, 69–73.

5 Douglas Hurd, *New Statesman*, 27 April 1988; CAF press release, 13 October 2004; Lucy Ward, *Guardian*, 30 November 2005.

6 The National Council for Voluntary Organisations put the total spend on charity at £8.2 billion or £3.50 per household per week, 0.9 per cent of GDP – the USA managed 2.0 per cent – but this also included corporate giving. Cf. www.ncvo-vol.org.uk/press/br/ind.

7 Polly Toynbee and David Walker, *Better or Worse? Has Labour Delivered*, London: Bloomsbury, 2005, 304–5.

8 *Statistisches Jahrbuch Deutschlands*, 2005.

9 Other studies, adding in the publicly owned Totto-Lotto, which funded much cultural expenditure, put the overall spend at a more realistic £24 billion or £305 per capita.

10 Adam Jones, *Financial Times*, 20–21 September 2003; Peter Jones, *The Scotsman*, 12 September 2006.

11 Christopher Harvie, *Fool's Gold*, 70.

12 Robert Peston, *Who Runs Britain?*, London: Hodder & Stoughton, 2008, Ch. 7.

13 Ibid., 255.

14 David Smith, *Sunday Times*, 22 January; Conal Walsh, *Observer*, 24 January 2006.

15 Robert Winnett and Holly Watt, *The Sunday Times*, 3 December 2006.

16 COI, *Britain 2001*, 379.

17 Brown's close associates had stayed with him for years, but in 2007 his small Treasury team – Stephen Timms, 2006; John Healey 2005; Ed Balls, 2006 – was remarkably untried in parliament. Only Dawn Primarolo dated back, to 1999 when she had succeeded Geoffrey Robinson.

18 Michael Wolff, *Independent*, 11 October 2009.

19 Gordon Brown, *Where There Is Greed*, 61.

20 Will Hutton, *The State We're In*, London: Jonathan Cape, 1995; *The State to Come*, London: Vintage, 1997.

21 *Manufacturing News*, 9 May 2009.

22 Robert Peston, *Who Runs Britain?*, 117.

23 Christian Sylt, interview with Bernie Ecclestone, *Voyager*, April 2009, 28–30: *The Times*, 4 July 2009.

24 Larry Elliott, *Guardian*, 4 October 2006.

25 David Gow, *Guardian*, 20 November 2003.

26 Tim Webb and Iain Griffiths, *Guardian*, 11 September 2009.

27 Polly Toynbee and David Walker, *Did Things Get Better? An Audit of Labour's Successes and Failures*, London: Penguin, 2001, 146.

28 BBC 'Watchdog', 20 December 2005.

29 Prem Sikka, *Guardian*, 6 February 2004.
30 Nick Kochan, *The Washing Machine: How Money Laundering and Terrorist Finance Soils Us*, New York: Texere Publishing, 2005, 353.
31 Nils Pratley, *Guardian*, 29 September 2003; Conal Walsh, *Guardian*, 24 January 2006.
32 Paul Mason, *Meltdown: The End of the Age of Greed*, London: Verso, 2009, 56.
33 Mark Honigsbaum, *Guardian*, 3 February 2005.
34 Karin Brulliard, *Washington Post*, 7 August 2009.
35 Pat Collinson, *Guardian*, 12 February 2005.
36 Jill Treanor, *Guardian*, 6 November 2002.
37 David Leigh and Rob Evans, *Guardian*, 15 February 2005.
38 Jon Ashworth, *The Times*, 7 February 2005; Peter Watson, *The Times*, February 1997, *passim*; Van der Weyer, *Lords and Liars*, 2005, *passim*.
39 Simon Bowers, *Guardian*, 26 and 31 May 2004.
40 Graham Wearden and Tim Webb, *Guardian*, 22 September 2009.
41 Cf. Robert Peston, *Who Runs Britain?*, Ch. 7: this is the best and most damning part of his book.
42 *Private Eye*, *passim*.
43 Paul Mason, *Meltdown*, 74.
44 Bethany McLean and Peter Elkind, *The Smartest Guys in the Room: The Amazing Rise and Scandalous Fall of Enron*, New York: Viking, 2003.
45 Tom Nairn, *Faces of Nationalism: Janus Revisited*, London: Verso, 1997.
46 Keith Marsden, *Wall Street Journal Europe*, 15 June 2009.

4 Light Touch

1 Jonathan Freedland, *Guardian,* 23 November 2005.
2 Tim Garton Ash, *Guardian*, 15 December 2005.
3 Ferdinand Mount, *Mind The Gap: Class in Britain Now*, London: Short Books, 2004, 235ff.
4 Nick Kochan, *The Washing Machine: How Money Laundering and Terrorist Finance Soils Us*, New York: Texere Publishing, 2005, 12–15; Glenny, *McMafia: A Journey Through the Global Criminal Underworld*, New York: Alfred A. Knopf , 2008, 130ff.
5 *Stern*, 7 June 2006; House of Commons Register of Members' Interests, 2006.
6 Misha Glenny, *McMafia: A Journey Through the Global Criminal Underworld*, 177–80.

7 Nick Kochan, *The Washing Machine*, 222–4; *Guardian*, 2 January 2007.

8 Paul Mason, *Meltdown: The End of the Age of Greed*, London: Verso, 2009, 66.

9 George Graham and Robert Wright, *Financial Times*, 24–5 January 1998.

10 Paul Mason, *Meltdown*, 45–6.

11 Alex Brummer, *Jewish Chronicle*, 21 May 2009.

12 Tanya Thomson, *Scotsman*, 10 March 2008.

13 National Audit Office Press Release, 25 October 2002; Donald MacLeod, *Guardian*, 10 December, 2004; Tom Bower, *Gordon Brown*, London: HarperCollins, 2004.

14 Ferdinand Mount, *Mind The Gap*, 2004.

15 George Monbiot, *Guardian*, 28 June, 2005.

16 Tom Bower, *The Paymaster: Geoffrey Robinson, Maxwell and New Labour*, London: Simon & Schuster, 2001, 31–8.

17 Andrew Rawnsley, *Servants of the People: The Inside Story of New Labour*, London: Hamish Hamilton, 2002, 43.

18 Polly Toynbee and David Walker, *Did Things Get Better? An Audit of Labour's Successes and Failures*, London: Penguin, 2001, 104–5.

19 Allyson Pollock, *Guardian*, 11 April 2007.

20 Will Hutton, *The World We're In*, London: Little, Brown, 2002, 261.

21 Andrew Wood and Ian Pritchard, *Guardian*, 16 August 2004.

22 Michael Harrison, *Independent*, 25 February 2005.

23 Tim Kelsey and Peter Koenig, *Independent*, 10 October 1994.

24 Studies of New Labour and the Northern Ireland Peace Process are silent about the relation between the IRA's ability to cause billions of pounds worth of damage with few casualties, and the attitudes and actions of influential financial interests vis-à-vis a threat which could have finished London as a trading centre in weeks. Another Good Friday theme, the relationship between the State Department, the curbing of the IRA's American income and the post-truce availability of thousands of UK troops for foreign duties (from Bosnia and Kosovo to Afghanistan and Iraq), deserves further research.

25 Elizabeth Rigby, *Financial Times*, 22 July 2004.

26 Cargill, 1987, Ch. 1.

27 Reiner Luyken, *Die Zeit*, 2 November 2000.

28 Andy Beckett, *Guardian*, 29 September 1999; Prem Sikka, *Guardian*, 8 February 2004.

29 Tony Judt, *Postwar: A History of Europe Since 1945*, London: William Heinemann Ltd, 2005, 689.

30 Alex Brummer, *The Crunch*, London: Random House Business Books, 2009, Ch. 6.
31 Jill Treanor, *Guardian*, 4 March 2005.
32 David Hencke, *Guardian*, 11 November 2007; *Private Eye*, 5–18 September, 2008.
33 Conal Walsh, *Observer*, 24 January 2006.
34 Christopher Harvie, *Fool's Gold*, London: Hamish Hamilton, 2004, 358.
35 Ann Brown, 'Today', BBC Radio Four, 1 November 2006.
36 Interview with Adrian Lyons, Stuttgart, 21 October 2005.
37 'Dispatches', Channel Four, 21 August 2006.
38 *CSYB* 2005, 53, 261, 256–8, 267.
39 Derek Scott, *Off Whitehall*, London: I.B. Tauris, 2004, Ch. 1.
40 Christopher Harvie, *A Floating Commonwealth: Politics, Culture, and Technology on Britain's Atlantic Coast, 1860–1930*, Oxford: Oxford University Press, 2008, Ch. 3.
41 Heather Stewart, *Observer*, 26 July 2009.

5 Annus Horribilis, 2006–7

1 Christopher Harvie, *A Floating Commonwealth: Politics, Culture, and Technology on Britain's Atlantic Coast, 1860–1930*, Oxford: Oxford University Press, 2008, Ch. 6.
2 See the Ruskin Foundation's glorious *How to be Rich, 2005*: *Unto this Last* put over in the style of the *Beano*.
3 John Kay, *The Truth about Markets*, London: Allen Lane, 2003.
4 Taylor in Seldon, 2005, 186; Gillian Tett, 2009, 100ff.
5 Ibid., 116.
6 Nick Kochan, *The Washing Machine: How Money Laundering and Terrorist Finance Soils Us*, New York: Texere Publishing, 2005, 353; Christopher Harvie, *Deep Fried Hillman Imp: Scotland's Transport*, Glendaruel: Argyll Publishing, 2001, 57–60.
7 Christopher Harvie, *A Floating Commonwealth*, Ch. 8.
8 Laura Smith, *Guardian*, 15 December 2005.
9 Calder, 1969.
10 BBC1, 'Panorama', 16 July 2006.
11 Richard Elias, *Daily Record*, 16 August 2006.
12 Ashley Seager, *Guardian*, 16 August 2006.
13 In comparison, the Eurostat scandal, which helped bring about the fall of the Santer Commission in 1999, and thrilled the Eurosceptic media, seems to have involved a maximum of £3 million over several years (Anthony Browne, *Times*, 26 September 2003).

14 Christopher Harvie, *Mending Scotland*, Glendaruel: Argyll Publishing, 2004, 68–74.
15 Phillip Inman, *Guardian*, 24 October 2006.
16 *Digital Look*, 10 November 2006.
17 David Robertson, *The Times*, 15 November 2006.
18 James Hall and Louisa Gault, *Telegraph*, 29 October 2006.
19 *Edinburgh Evening News*, 7 November 2006.
20 *Scotsman*, 28 March 2007.
21 Nick Kochan, *The Washing Machine*, 353.
22 *Guardian*, 3 May 2005.
23 Jonathan Fisher and Jeremy Summers, *The Times*, 13 June 2006.
24 [Cf. http://ftalphaville.ft.com/blog/2009/02/11/52320/hbos-the-moore-memo/>].
25 BBC, 'File on Four', 26 May 2009.

6 A Handful of Dust, 2007–9

1 Gillian Tett, *Fool's Gold: How Unrestrained Greed Corrupted a Dream, Shattered Global Markets and Unleashed a Catastrophe*, London: Little, Brown, 2009.
2 Philip Inman, *Guardian*, 8 April 2006; Misha Glenny, *McMafia: A Journey Through the Global Criminal Underworld*, New York: Alfred A. Knopf, 2008, 170ff.
3 Paul Mason, *Meltdown: The End of the Age of Greed*, London: Verso, 2009, 119–23
4 John A. Mack and Hans-Jürgen Kerner, *The Crime Industry*, Glasgow: Saxon House, 1975, vii; Hans-Jürgen Kerner, 2006.
5 Paul Vallely, *Independent*, 18 March 2006; Ros Wynne-Jones, *Independent*, 17 March 1996; Marie Wolf, *Independent*, 18 December 2001.
6 *NZZ Folio*, 8 August 2006.
7 British houses struggled to reach the EU's grade C – most German houses were Grade B; in May 2009 attempts to offload unsellable newbuild houses onto housing associations foundered because their quality wasn't high enough. (BBC, 'Today', 16 May 2009.
8 To give him his full title, the Hon. Geraint; his father was the anti-devolution Donald Anderson, Labour MP, later Lord Anderson of Swansea, chair of the Foreign Affairs Select Committee in his Commons days.
9 Robert Peston, *Who Runs Britain?*, London: Hodder & Stoughton, 2008, Ch. 7.

10 Emma Rees, *City AM*, 8 February 2008; George Monbiot, *Guardian*, 16 December, 2008.
11 BBC, 'Panorama', 22 August 2006.
12 Peston, *Who Runs Britain?*, Chs 2 and 8; Martin Arnold, *Financial Times*, 27 June 2009.
13 Andrew Pierce, *Telegraph*, 6 October 2008.
14 *Economist*, 16 July 2009.
15 Nick Davies, *Flat Earth News*, 287–328.
16 Gillian Tett, *Financial Times*, 9–10 May 2009.
17 Paul Mason, *Meltdown*, 9–14.
18 Gillian Tett, *Fool's Gold*, 105.
19 Cf. www.ianfraser.org/,13 July 2009.
20 BBC, 'File on Four', Radio 4, 26 May 2009.
21 Man Annual Report, 2008–9.
22 Paul Mason, *Meltdown*, 2009, 6–14.
23 Mike McGuire, *Goalcom*, 15 January 2009.
24 Michael Mackenzie and Saskia Scholtes, *Financial Times*, 8 March 2008.
25 Banking Crisis Timeline, *Guardian*, 30 October 2008.
26 Martin Arnold, *Financial Times*, 27 June 2009; LBS, *Bizresearch*, 18 February 2009.
27 Informal interviews, October 2008.
28 Jeremy Peat's evidence, 11 November 2009.
29 *The Telegraph*, 8 October 2008.
30 Paul Krugman, *New York Times*, 13 October 2008.

7 Walking with the Others

1 Chrystia Freeland, *Financial Times*, 11–12 July 2009.
2 Brooke Masters, Paul Betts and Michael Skapinker, *Financial Times*, 7 July 2009.
3 'Panorama', BBC, 21 September 2009.
4 Nick Cohen, *Observer*, 27 September 2009; Andy McSmith, *Independent*, 31 October 2009.
5 James Buchan, *Prospect*, August 2009, 28–33.
6 Christopher Caldwell, *Financial Times*, 15 July 2006.
7 Nick Kochan, *The Washing Machine: How Money Laundering and Terrorist Finance Soils Us*, New York: Texere Publishing, 2005.
8 Polly Toynbee and David Walker, *Unjust Rewards: Exposing Greed and Inequality in Britain Today*, London: Granta Books, 2008, Ch. 5.
9 Keith Marsden, *Wall Street Journal Europe*, 19 June 2009.

10 BBC, 'Panorama', 21 September 2009.
11 Richard Norton-Taylor, *Guardian*, 28 October 2009.
12 Kenneth Morgan, 2009, 621.
13 Giuseppe Tomasi de Lampedusa, *The Leopard*, Rome: Feltrinelli, 1958, 144.
14 Alastair Campbell, *The Blair Years*, London: Random House, 2006, 287–98.